Quantifying Language

Multilingual Matters

Please contact us for the latest book information:
Multilingual Matters Ltd,
Frankfurt Lodge, Clevedon Hall, Victoria Road,
Clevedon, Avon BS21 7SJ, England.

Quantifying Language

A Researcher's and Teacher's Guide
to Gathering Language Data and
Reducing it to Figures

Phil Scholfield

MULTILINGUAL MATTERS LTD
Clevedon • Philadelphia • Adelaide

Library of Congress Cataloging in Publication Data

Scholfield, Phil, 1945-
Quantifying Language: A Researcher's and Teacher's Guide to Gathering
Language Data and Reducing it to Figures/Phil Scholfield
Includes bibliographical references and index
1. Formalization (Linguistics). 2. Mathematical linguistics. I. Title.
P128.F67S36   1994
401'.51–dc20   94-30330

British Library Cataloguing in Publication Data

A CIP catalogue record for this book is available from the British Library.

ISBN 1-85359-254-4 (hbk)
ISBN 1-85359-253-6 (pbk)

Multilingual Matters Ltd

UK: Frankfurt Lodge, Clevedon Hall, Victoria Road, Clevedon, Avon BS21 7SJ.
USA: 1900 Frost Road, Suite 101, Bristol, PA 19007, USA.
Australia: P.O. Box 6025, 83 Gilles Street, Adelaide, SA 5000, Australia.

Printed and bound in Great Britain by the Longdunn Press, Bristol.

Contents

Acknowledgements

I am particularly indebted to Penny Chandler for her tremendously diligent work commenting on an earlier draft of this work. Needless to say, the remaining inadequacies are all mine.

Thanks are also due to my wife and daughters for their enduring patience and support.

Introduction

More Than a Book on Testing,...and a Complement to Books on Overall Research Design and Statistics

Numerous books exist, usually with 'language testing' in the title, that deal with how language is measured primarily in the language teaching sphere. And there are of course numerous scattered articles and parts of books which say something about categorising and measuring language in particular separate areas of language research such as sociolinguistics, dialectology, foreign language learning, child language and psycholinguistics. There is also a branch of linguistics actually called 'quantitative linguistics', which concerns itself primarily just with counting frequencies of words and other linguistic units in text, and ensuing statistical manipulation of these figures, especially in connection with stylistics.

The present book attempts, seemingly for the first time, to survey and interconnect the principles and problems of language quantification that arise in all these domains within the general study of language. In doing this obviously I cannot cover every kind of quantification in every field, but the aim is to say something accessible and introductory about many of the important and commonly used types of technique, and problems and principles that have general relevance.

Where they are available, select references will be provided that may be followed up for more detail in specific areas. Thus this account can be regarded as a nexus for accessing further information on all aspects of language quantification.

Excluded only is consideration of observation which is purely qualitative and leads to nothing expressible as figures. There is incidentally no intention here to discount the value of this sort of data, which is valuable on its own in some kinds of research, and virtually always worth gathering alongside quantitative information.

This broad study of language quantification/measurement I have adumbrated does not have a recognised name. If one is felt necessary, I would propose *linguometry*, on the analogy of the established labels

1

'psychometry' and 'sociometry' in neighbouring disciplines (though the last in fact labels a rather specific type of sociological measurement only — see e.g. Hopkins, 1985: 76f.).

This book then is for anyone interested in how aspects of language are categorised, measured, tested or assessed, whether they be a researcher or student in higher education, teacher or therapist. If you are going to turn some aspect of language into numbers yourself in some connection, or have to read reports of what other people have done, or just want a guide to thinking in this area, this book is for you. Specifically:

Undergraduates doing linguistics courses increasingly these days not only have to understand how researchers measure, test and survey language e.g. in sociolinguistics or psycholinguistics, but are themselves set practical projects which require measuring something to do with language as part of a mini-investigation, rather than just the traditional essay or linguistic analysis exercise. This follows essentially from the greatly increased interest recently in the fully 'empirical' branches of language study. For them this book should be a useful companion to whatever topic-related course texts they use in these areas, and any more general books on language research methods and statistics (see Chap. 3 for how this book relates to these).

Undergraduates doing language-related work as part of courses in other disciplines such as psychology, sociology and education may also find this book a useful specific adjunct to general courses in research methods and statistics which they may be taking there.

Language teachers and speech therapists, especially those doing further training of the MA Applied Linguistics type, may find this book a help to clarify some concepts, heighten critical awareness of techniques they are called on to use, guide them when they assess pupils/patients, and even suggest things to measure and ways of measuring them that had not occurred to them. For them this book should extend what they derive from specifically pedagogical sources on language assessment like Heaton (1975) or Hughes (1989).

Postgraduate researchers in linguistics and applied linguistics, whether from a teaching background or not, increasingly work with empirical data. There are still too few courses and books available that provide training in the know-how to do this properly. The present work is a contribution to filling that gap and complements books like Hatch & Farhady (1982) or Woods *et al.* (1986), which focus on methodological and statistical aspects of investigations as wholes, but say little about the measurement/

quantification component which provides the grass roots figures to start with.

Different readers may want to focus on different aspects of the book. In particular some parts may seem to be more of interest to the teacher/therapist, others more to the researcher. However, I am confident that so much is common to both interests that in this instance the familiar barrier between books for pedagogy and books for research needs to be dissolved. Furthermore, nowadays increasing numbers of language teachers and therapists also get involved in research, either in-service, or when they go on advanced training courses.

Very little is assumed in the way of prior knowledge. The linguistics in much language measurement is in any case not very sophisticated and discussion of techniques which draw on anything of great theoretical complexity has on the whole been avoided or simply referred to in passing. Similarly, the more statistically and mathematically complex aspects of reliability and validity work in measurement are left to further reading. Some readers may already have some wider knowledge of how research is planned and executed, and the many statistical tests and measures that can be involved. For their benefit some linking references are included also.

A book of this sort is not the place to put forward radical ideas on the nature of the subject, hence I have tried to stick to a consensus view. Many examples are cited, and these are either from actual classic studies or syntheses of typical kinds of quantification used in the last twenty years or so. Inevitably the selection used is a personal one. However, I have attempted to innovate modestly in the organisation of the account, and in the coverage given to some topics often neglected.

1 Basic Terms: What Do People Quantify?

1.1 Basic Terms to Get Straight

As might be expected, there is a certain amount of technical terminology used in talking about turning things into figures. Part of the purpose of this book is to enable you to understand this when you read it in reports of others' work, and to use it yourself appropriately.

First, *quantification* is used as a cover term for any way in which aspects of language or speakers are *observed* and turned into numbers by *measurement* or *categorisation* or any other means. It is meant to include not only, say, the activity of giving people a test and obtaining numerical scores, but also, say, classifying the words in a text and seeing how many verbs and nouns there are.

A useful general term for the people or things that are quantified on any occasion is *cases*. Cases can be words, sounds, children, or works of a literary author. When they are people, which they often are when talking about language, they may be referred to for various purposes by all sorts of more specific label. In language learning/acquisition study they are often *learners*, in the study of language pathology *patients*, in sociolinguistics *informants*, in psycholinguistics *subjects*.

If we speak of measuring or categorising cases, we mean, of course, that we measure or categorise some property or behaviour of the cases, not the cases as wholes. The usual term for such an attribute is *variable*. Properties of people, such as reading ability or nationality, or of words, such as length or part of speech, are all variables, though in special circumstances we will also encounter variables referred to by other labels like *factor*, or, especially when they are more intangible, and one's measurement of them rather indirect, *trait* and *construct*. So we can speak of quantifying (linguistic) variables.

4

1.2 What Sort of Things do People Quantify?

I here attempt an overview of all the multifarious variables which are, or could usefully be, quantified across the breadth of language-related research or teaching. Many specific ones will be mentioned later, but there are a few general dimensions of classification of the 'content' of variables (and hence of measuring techniques for those variables) which are frequently used in labelling them, and serve to demonstrate something of the range you will come across.

1.2.1 Variables of different level and skill types

One simple distinction concerns what *level* (or levels) of language a variable is related to. It may be something to do with sounds (phonetics/phonology, including intonation), orthography (including punctuation), vocabulary (lexis/lexicon), grammar (inflections, syntax), definitional meaning (semantics), overt text/discourse structure (including cohesion and rhetorical structure), or pragmatics (including coherence of text, indirect speech acts, and overtones of word meaning). Or more than one of these may be relevant, or *all* these at once 'globally', perhaps with some strictly non-linguistic element involved too. For example, if you try to quantify communicative ability in English you are concerned with all levels of language and some world/cultural knowledge as well.

Besides this pure linguistic kind of classification, you can *also* distinguish most linguistic variables by which of the 'four skills' (in language teachers' parlance) is involved in what is measured, corresponding to types of language 'processing' in psycholinguistics. Variables may be to do with *comprehension* (passive, receptive language use), i.e. reading or hearing/ listening; or *production* (active use of language), i.e. writing or speaking. Again several or all of these may be involved together, as when you are globally quantifying how often a Moroccan would speak/write/read/hear in French as against Arabic in various kinds of communication situation. Or in some instances what you are quantifying is in some way an impersonal aspect of language, or at any rate neutral as to the comprehension/production distinction — e.g. the lengths in letters of English words.

The above two classifications, by level and by skill, together clearly define a large number of possible variables that can be quantified: you can have a measure of some cases' spoken 'r' sounds, or of their receptive vocabulary, their written question constructions, and so on. However, there are some other general characteristics of the 'content' of variables that are often referred to when talking about them. Though there is no real consensus on the details here, I shall regard them as falling in two other dimensions that largely crosscut the level and skill ones (and each other): the *epistemic* and the *instructional* (my terms). So potentially any variable to be quantified can be labelled in at least four different ways.

1.2.2 Variables of different epistemic types

The 'epistemic' dimension I so call to reflect the fact that it deals in some way with the *character* of the cases' language-related capability or knowledge that is being quantified. Approximately, a variable may relate to what people can do, what they know about what they do, or what they feel about what they do. This needs a little more explanation.

(i) A great deal of language quantification is intended to be of some aspect of what a person actually or potentially can 'do' in one or more of the skills and levels, i.e. something to do with their linguistic *performance* behaviour or *competence* knowledge or (cap)ability. A child's or foreign learner's or dialect speaker's spoken production of the third person -*s* inflection on present tense verbs in English is of this sort (*That tastes nice* versus *That taste nice*). Slightly less obviously, counting the number of times an author uses a particular word is measuring an aspect of that author's (written, vocabulary) performance. A psycholinguistic test of speakers' associations with certain words is no less a measure of this sort.

Something has to be said about the terms 'competence' and 'performance', which are usually distinguished by linguists, following Chomsky. The former is typically regarded as 'a mental phenomenon...indicative only of *potential* performance or capability' (Wiemann & Backlund, 1980). That is, competence is a somewhat idealised notion — that of the 'true' linguistic knowledge/ability of speakers that underlies their actual speech, comprehension, and so on. It only appears imperfectly in the latter due to slips of the tongue, memory limitations etc., and the fact that even in a speaker's entire life there is not time or opportunity for speakers to use everything they are linguistically capable of. Much variability of language as superficially encountered is often put down just to performance factors over and above underlying competence. For some, competence admits of no variation and so is largely beyond the scope of quantitative research. Furthermore, competence is often regarded as in some way neutral to, or 'above', the evidence of psycholinguistic and other fully empirical research and so again not requiring to be measured in the sense of the present book. For a discussion of the range of slightly different interpretations some have given these terms see Lesser (1978: 45ff.) and Garman (1990: 111ff.).

These days it is widely felt that it is useful to regard there as being such a competence underlying not only speakers' grammar, pronunciation and so forth, but also their wider communicative performance. That includes knowledge of *what* to say when, how to be polite or not, how to deal with misunderstandings, and so forth (Canale & Swain, 1980) — matters that are strictly on the pragmatic borderlines of language. This wider competence as a whole is referred to as *communicative competence*, though specifying *exactly* what should be included under that label is a continuing bone of contention (Bachman, 1990: Chap. 4). A special instance of communicative competence is that appropriate to teachers.

Given the above characterisation of competence, you might ask whether you *can* quantify competence variables separately from performance ones even if you want to. My own opinion is that you only really ever measure performance. It could of course be argued that some ways of measuring language get *closer* to tapping speakers' 'competence' than others. Thus measuring people's production of the -s inflection on verbs in writing done in conditions where there is time to reread and correct would yield in some respects more competence-like performance than measuring in the hurried speech of someone phoning for help to the fire brigade, but at the cost of accessing a totally different variety of the language. Some argue that self-directed introspectional judgement (7.4), especially by a trained linguist, directly accesses competence, or that underlying abilities can be identified by sophisticated statistical analysis. But what you can *directly* quantify (cf. Chap. 23) is performance under varying conditions of use and by different means. In any event the terms are used fairly loosely in the measurement literature and I shall not try to separate them hereafter. Thus testers often talk of measuring communicative *competence* though it is often done in simulations of real life where you might feel it was very much 'performance' that was being got at.

(ii) There is an increasing interest in quantifying *metalinguistic* competence/performance, sometimes called *language awareness* or 'knowledge about language' (*KAL*), especially in research on learning and teaching. This arises where it is not so much any direct linguistic capability of cases that is of interest, but rather their explicit knowledge *about* language, e.g. of the part of speech classification, or phonemic transcription of sounds or just their ability to talk and joke *about* usage in informal terms. Indeed this can be extended to knowledge about, say, the relative politeness of different ways of apologising (an aspect of 'metacommunicative' competence) and of how the subject him/herself learnt, or taught, a vocabulary item ('metacognitive' awareness).

Arguably meta-type ability can be of varying degrees of sophistication. Thus asking someone to judge if pairs of words rhyme accesses a lower, more 'tacit' level of such competence than asking someone to provide a phonemic transcription of them, requiring more 'reflective' knowledge.

(iii) Also of concern, and usually distinguishable from the preceding by their evaluative element, are language *attitude* variables, often pursued by sociolinguists and in the study of foreign language learning. Examples are cases' judgements about acceptability, annoyingness, attractiveness of what they or others say or write, or of a language in general. Measures of 'interest' in learning a language and of 'motivation' are also of this general *affective* sort (to do with feelings). Compare the other epistemic types which are more *cognitive* (to do with thinking).

1.2.3 Variables of different instruction-related types

What I call the 'instructional' classification mostly arises in the learning and teaching sphere. It has to do with whether the variable you are quantifying is being approached regardless of any learning or instruction, or with an eye to such instruction, which may be either previous or to follow. It must be admitted frankly that in some instances it becomes quite difficult to distinguish this from a classification in terms of *purpose* (Chap. 2).

(i) In most language research, and a good deal of language teaching, you are interested in quantifying language or communicative abilities irrespective of what teaching the cases may have experienced. This is often termed *proficiency*, which can of course be global, or in some specific skill or bit of language at some specific level only.

(ii) On the other hand *achievement* or *attainment* variables are defined in terms of how much cases know of something they have in the past specifically learnt/been taught e.g. via a school language course. Quantifying such things is particularly common in language teaching and the study of the learner, of course. However, something of this sort occurs often also in psycholinguistic work on language learning and memory where subjects are set to learn something in some specific way, and then tested almost at once to see how effective that way was, though the term 'achievement' is most commonly used for longer term instances of this sort ('retention' often being preferred by psychologists). The term 'attainment' seems to be widely used as a synonym for 'achievement', but is perhaps coming to be more associated with achievement measured specifically in a criterion-referenced way where the term 'mastery' is also common (Chap. 10).

It must also be noted that achievement as a variable is not always easy to distinguish from language ability of the proficiency type. Where a person has learnt to speak a foreign language through instruction, we may measure their linguistic achievement by a test specifically related to aspects of the syllabus that has been followed. But where he/she has learnt through natural immersion, or by instruction we know nothing about, we could only use a proficiency measure. But of course in many ways it is the same sort of 'thing' about the person, viz. some aspect(s) of their linguistic ability, that is being quantified in both instances. The difference lies in the different ways in which we are able to characterise and define the ability in the two instances. Achievement variables are essentially 'artificial' or man-made in some sense.

(iii) Finally, quantifying *aptitude* is essentially measuring what degree someone has of whatever ability is needed to benefit from some future activity such as learning a foreign language, in some specific way perhaps, or undergoing a specific kind of speech therapy, should they do it. Measures of 'readiness' such as the reading readiness of a kindergarten native speaker child are of this sort too. Strictly speaking you can attempt to quantify either aptitude for future proficiency or aptitude for future achievement, the former where unspecified instruction or immersion is envisaged, the latter where a known course of instruction is to follow. Aptitude is a complex variable and language learning aptitude, for example, is often taken as embracing not just readiness to perform in a language, but also attitude to speakers of the language, since this may affect motivation to learn, and potential language awareness capability, if instruction of a formal sort is envisaged.

1.2.4 Variables of other types

Other possible independent classifications of linguistic variables could be made by reference to: what languages are involved; what variety or varieties the variables are in (e.g. a specific dialect, legal language, everyday spoken language); what kind of cases are being measured — children or adults, native speakers versus foreign learners, normal versus language-impaired speakers, monolingual versus bilingual, and so on.

Potentially any given variable could be named by quite a long list of labels, one from each of the above classifications, reflecting its nature. For instance you could speak of wanting to quantify learners' attainment in knowledge about standard English tense uses, or East Anglian adult speakers' performance in pronouncing a certain vowel sound, and so on. In fact this is not all, since variables are often also labelled by the purpose in quantifying them (see Chap. 2 and 3) and the means used to do so (see Chap. 4ff.).

One other important point is that, particularly in language research, often *non-linguistic* variables have to be measured as well as linguistic ones because they enter into the comparisons you are trying to make. They usually appear in the role of what will be described below as 'explanatory variables' (Chap. 3). In sociolinguistic work social class and gender are obvious examples. In psycholinguistic work general 'cognitive' characteristics such as nonverbal intelligence, field independence (Oltman *et al.*, 1971; Witkin *et al.*, 1971) and learning style (Fitzgerald & Hattie, 1983) may be of interest in relation to some linguistic variable, or more 'affective' ones like introversion/extroversion of personality. In the study of language learning often age will be relevant, and learning style or method of instruction (e.g. using group work versus whole class practice), or self-worth attitude. In the study of language pathology it is often important to record the precise site of brain damage in patients, or the kind of event that caused the damage (e.g. stroke, car accident). And in the study of language quantification there are the variables of the means of measurement itself (so-called 'facets of observation' see Chap. 4ff.).

1.3 The Logical Stages in Quantifying Variables

Quantifying variables can be seen as involving three basic steps, each with its own range of problems and principles (cf. Bachman 1990: 30–50).

(a) Specify carefully the nature of the variable you want to quantify.
(b) Use or invent an explicit technique to gather observations relevant to it.
(c) Turn the observations into figures.

The first stage (a) usually comes first, and involves specifying what you want to quantify in terms like those above (but more detailed), with due attention to the pedagogical or research purpose of doing the quantification. The exception would be only in certain kinds of naturalistic research of the ethnographic type where you might gather data first, e.g. by extensive taping, and *then* decide from examination of it what variables are interesting to quantify.

One problem at stage (a) can be that of choosing to quantify an inappropriate variable. The simplest way this happens is in research projects where the tyro researcher routinely records variables like age and gender of subjects even though they are irrelevant to what he or she is researching. Or a teacher may use a test of a particular variable where for the desired ulterior purpose something else would have been better quantified. Purposes of quantifying variables are pursued briefly in the next two chapters.

A harder problem can concern disagreement over what some variable really 'is', and hence how it can be quantified. It particularly arises for the more *global* variables, like communicative competence in English, which are clearly 'complex' in nature. They are more difficult to decide how to quantify than specific 'simple' ones, like competence in producing the -*s* verb inflection, which intuitively feels more like 'one thing'. The former may be quantified unanalysed, e.g. simply by asking 'judges' to globally rate cases for this ability, but this is unsatisfactory in many ways (19.3.2). Often rather the concept is broken down into a number of simpler variables to be quantified separately and the results combined in some way to produce a more or less full measure, but there may be disagreement on exactly what constitutes the ability in the first place. Additionally, for some purposes, a single simple measure may be accepted as an adequate 'indicator' of the more complex one.

There are also problems with the more covert variables — like the types of process that go on in people's minds in order to recognise an English sound or the strategies used to learn a word. These are relatively more problematic to measure than the overt ones — like whether speakers can produce a certain sound. These covert variables are particularly important in psycholinguistic work and recently in the study of foreign language learners where some of the emphasis is switching from studying their competence as seen in the 'product' they produce to studying the 'processes' that underlie that product. There has to be some agreement on how such variables are to be *operationalised* in the form of something down to earth and observable which will serve as an 'indicator' of the hidden variable or 'construct' before you can begin to quantify them all.

Unsatisfactory specification of a variable (a) may be difficult to distinguish from specifying a suitable variable but then choosing an inadequate technique to gather observations reflecting it (b).

For instance, suppose you want to measure some subjects' spoken 'fluency'. You may define for yourself fluency simply as speed of utterance, and proceed to obtain recordings from which this can be derived. However, other applied linguists might object that this is an 'underspecification' of the notion ('construct') of 'fluency', which is really more complex and should also embrace degree of hesitation and error rate. This is obviously a theoretical issue over the nature of the variable, and so what overt behaviour should be taken as reflecting it, and has to be hammered out in the subdiscipline concerned. Alternatively you may define fluency in the wider sense but argue that observation of speed of utterance alone is a satisfactory indicator measure of the 'whole' variable. Disagreement here would then turn rather on what sort of data is minimally satisfactory to obtain a reasonable measure of fluency.

Theoretical issues about the detailed specification of particular variables are not pursued extensively in this book. Often a proper understanding of the substance of a variable and such issues can only be obtained from a textbook in the relevant subject, where it is seen in the context of knowledge of that subject as a whole: see the further reading below. There is some further coverage of complex and indicator variables in the discussion of validity (Chap. 22–23).

After the chapters on the purpose of quantification (Chap. 2, 3), the progression of most of this book is related centrally to the 'operational' stages of quantification (b and c above). I shall generally talk in terms of 'simple' variables, since most matters of practical quantification have to be considered at that level, even if the scores obtained for a simple variable have to be later added to scores for others as part of a more complex measure, or if the simple measure is due to be interpreted as an indicator of something other than what it superficially appears to be.

Further reading

The following is a small selection of useful references which give overviews of particular areas of language study and some impression of the kinds of variables that it is crucial to consider in each, whether quantitatively or not. If you are not familiar with the range of variables relevant in the branches of language study generally, or with the 'levels of language' mentioned above, start by reading a good general book on linguistics, e.g. Fromkin & Rodman (1988). On particular sub-areas of language study:

Psycholinguistics: Clark & Clark (1977), Paivio & Begg (1981), Taylor (1990).
Language Pathology and Remediation: Lesser (1978), Crystal (1980), Caplan (1992).
First Language Acquisition: Anisfeld (1984), Ingram (1989), Wells (1985), Fletcher & Garman (1986), Romaine (1984).
Foreign Language Learning and Teaching: Faerch et al. (1984), van Els et al. (1984), Stern (1983).
Sociolinguistics: Trudgill (1974), Dittmar (1976), Hudson (1980), Wardhaugh (1986), Fasold (1990), Holmes (1992).
Dialectology: Trudgill (1983), Chambers & Trudgill (1980).
Stylistics: Crystal & Davy (1969), Turner (1973).
Bilingualism and Bilingual Education: Baetens Beardsmore (1982), Baker (1993).
Language Attitudes: Ryan & Giles (1982).
Lexicology: Carter (1987), Aitchison (1987).
Phonetics: Ladefoged (1982).

2 Why Do People Quantify Language? The Teaching/Therapy Reason

2.1 Why Quantify Language?

2.1.1 R and T: Two distinct purposes

It is valuable in much discussion of language quantification to make a broad distinction between *two* general kinds of *purpose* measurers may have. This applies primarily where the cases are people.

First there is what I shall call *T quantification*, where T stands for 'teacher' or 'therapist'. Here the focus of interest is typically on measuring or categorising *individual* cases, and often on some ensuing *evaluation* or *assessment* of those individuals, not just measurement of how much of some variable is present in each person. I am thinking here for example of the language teacher giving his/her class a reading test to see who is best, who worst, or the speech therapist recording a child in conversation and analysing the tape to assess the extent and nature of the child's language deficiency. On occasion teachers themselves are the objects of this kind of evaluative quantification, in respect of their own language or teaching ability. Note that, though in the first example the teacher does measure a group, his or her main interest is in the scores obtained by individual cases separately.

Then there is what we might call *R quantification*, where the R stands for 'researcher'. Here typically the focus of interest is on *groups* and, if any evaluation ensues, it is not of the individuals measured. An example would be giving a reading test of English as a foreign language to two classes of children who were comparable in age, number of years learning English and so on, but had been taught reading by rather different methods. The interest here would not be in the scores of individual cases, but rather in whether *collectively* one group differed from the other. Indeed usually the aim would be to derive conclusions about much larger groups than those

13

actually studied, by ensuring the cases measured were in principle sampled randomly from the larger group of interest and applying 'inferential' statistical methods to the results. In this instance you would hope to generalise conclusions to a large number of people who might use one or other reading method. Of course such random selection of cases would be nonsensical in T measurement where the interest is in *particular* cases.

Furthermore, any evaluation would be of the teaching methods, not the children. Of course some such research *is* done on individuals, as when a researcher interested in how people learn foreign languages follows the progress of a single learner measuring him or her every so often in what is termed a 'case study'. But it remains true to say that the focus of *interest* in this sort of work is still a group — learners of the same general type as the one case studied (an exception being perhaps stylistic research on individual authors). And in general no evaluation of the individuals would be relevant here.

In short, *whenever* quantification occurs there must be both at least one case and some variable involved, but you could say the emphasis is different. In T measurement the focus is on cases. In R measurement you are primarily measuring language, and whatever potentially affects it or relates to it: focus on variables. Whether making measurements yourself, or considering those made by others, it is as well to be clear which standpoint is the relevant one.

2.1.2 How variables and cases are talked about in R and T work

The same measurer can, usually on different occasions, be interested in either purpose. Teachers who usually measure their classes to 'assess' individuals may also on occasion measure them as part of some classroom research into the effectiveness of the teaching process itself. However, they will (or should) talk differently in these two instances.

Since T measurement is typically tied to evaluation, the variables measured are often talked about in the parlance of *correctness*. You talk of *good* and *bad*, *correct* scores and *wrong* answers, where in R measurement of the same variable you would often talk rather of *high* and *low* scores. So, for example, suppose you were measuring how often some people add the *-s* to third person singular present verbs in English, and say *He likes it* as against *He like it*. If the purpose were T measurement, and the cases probably children or foreign learners or language disabled people, you would almost certainly talk in terms of 'How many verbs they got wrong', or 'How well they did'. On the other hand if the purpose were R measurement, and the cases again learners, or perhaps normal adult speakers of a nonstandard variety of English, then it would be appropriate to talk less judgmentally in terms of 'How many native/adult/normal/standard forms were observed' or 'How many interlanguage/developmental/abnormal/nonstandard forms' ('interlanguage' being a term for the specific, idiosyncratic, dialect of a language spoken by a learner of it at some point).

Further, if we said we were measuring an aspect of someone's 'competence' in a T context, this might be felt as an evaluative term, opposed to 'incompetence', rather than just a neutral term for someone's language capability, as it is in linguistic research (1.2.2). The fact is that the same variable can often be talked about both ways (and will be inevitably in this book) depending on the purpose of the measurement.

Cases also are often referred to differently in the two types of approach. People who might be labelled 'pupils' or 'patients' or 'teachers', and identified by name, for T measurement, become anonymous 'subjects' or 'informants' for R measurement. And whereas they may often be said to obtain *marks* in a T context, they will receive *scores* in an R one.

2.1.3 What is quantified and how for R and T purposes

To a considerable extent the same variables can be and are quantified for either purpose, and the same range of observation techniques, survey types, tests etc. are available to measure them with. Hence much of the contents of this book is relevant to both. However, it is perhaps true to say that the majority of standard, published ways of quantifying language that are available have been created with T measurement in mind: e.g. many language tests and exams for foreign learners and native speakers, and clinical assessment procedures for pathological cases. After all, this function of language measurement has been around for some considerable time.

Researchers on the other hand more often find themselves needing to develop their own ways of measuring things, for particular pieces of research. Many of the empirical subdisciplines of the study of language such as sociolinguistics and psycholinguistics have only blossomed relatively recently. They are 'young' areas of enquiry in which there is now a lot of interest, but which lack much in the way of established techniques. But this is only a weak generalisation: teachers, for example, quite often make up their own classroom tests to see how their pupils are progressing, and some research uses standard published tests of IQ, language proficiency and so on.

2.1.4 R and T in different areas of language study

As may have become apparent from the examples used up to now, T quantification is largely restricted to two particular realms of activity where language measurement occurs. One is language learning and teaching, which could be subdivided into first language, second language, foreign language, and bilingual. The other is language disability and its treatment, embracing deafness, dyslexia, aphasia, speech retardation, and so forth. These areas are regarded by most as the core of what is termed *applied linguistics*. On the other hand R measurement ranges much more broadly. It can occur not only in all the fields just mentioned, but also in sociolinguistics, dialectology, stylistics, psycholinguistics, historical linguistics, language typology, lexicology, or instrumental phonetics. In other words, R measurement is needed anywhere in the study of language where empirical work is pursued, and linguistic variables need to be quantified.

If we look yet more broadly at the kinds of activity of which quantification forms a part, we find further contrasts between these T and R functions. I shall now look at these in brief.

2.2 What are the Functions of Quantification in the Teaching/Therapy Process?

2.2.1 Quantification as part of the overall T enterprise

Quantification with what I have characterised as the T purpose is often in itself a fairly limited activity. On any particular occasion when measurements are made, the measurement of one or two variables for some individual case of interest, or group of cases, is all there is to it (contrast R measurement Chap. 3). For example, a language class takes a half hour end of term exam, or a therapist administers a vocabulary test to a new patient.

However, quantification with the T purpose is not usually pursued in isolation. It occurs as part of a larger enterprise, usually dedicated to changing the linguistic capabilities of the individual cases measured. Thus there exist wider pedagogical considerations, such as past or future language objectives of a course. These in principle decide what exactly is to be quantified (but see 2.2.4), and also often lead to some positive *action* being taken with respect to some individuals when the results are known. Incidentally, there are in fact some other fields where action also may follow quantification of individuals' language, not pursued here: such is forensic linguistics — which may attempt to establish an individual's identity in the courtroom by measuring aspects of their speech, for example.

Often the pedagogical process is analysed into steps such as *selection* (of what is to be learnt, what omitted), *sequencing* (of what is to be learnt into a sensible progression), *presentation* (by the teacher of what is to be learnt in a palatable way), *practice* (of what has been presented), *testing* (i.e. quantifying by a suitable means what has in fact been learnt) and *remediation* (to deal with what should have been learnt but wasn't). As this scheme indicates, then, a prime role of T quantification is to assess what has been learnt at some stage in the process and to be the basis for 'feedback'. In principle, what occurs at all the stages may bear on what is quantified at the 'testing' stage. Selection is, effectively, of what variables to focus instruction on. Presentation and practice deliver the instruction intended to improve learners' or patients' performance on the selected variables.

However, this is a somewhat oversimplified view. As can be seen from the common roles sketched now in 2.2.2, there are a number of T functions of quantification that do not fit this paradigm of achievement testing to assess progress. They are best seen as related to a wider range of possible types of decision that will be made and action that will be performed in the light of the measurement, by a wider range of 'consumers' of measurement information. Though not dwelt on here, many of these functions apply mutatis mutandis to instructors themselves as cases assessed in teacher training and so on.

2.2.2 Some reasons for evaluating people in the T context

Screening function. This occurs especially in speech therapy, to check large numbers of people just to see if any in fact have a native language disability/delay of *any* sort that has not been noticed and so might be in need of special attention. For this a broad spectrum of language performance variables needs to be measured, in a non-time consuming way. Cases sifted out would then be further tested, e.g. for classification purposes.

Classification function. In speech therapy this is to establish which of the conventionally distinguished kinds of language disability someone has. For instance do they have a form of 'aphasia', and if so is it Broca's or Wernicke's or what? This would most often be done when a case first comes to the attention of the professionals, e.g. just after someone has a stroke which appears to have impaired their language. Usually a selection of aspects of proficiency are quantified for this purpose — especially those which are used in the definition of particular named pathological conditions. Such measures are often expected to serve prognostic and/or diagnostic and/or placement functions as well.

Prognostic function. This is to see how well a person might do if he/she took language instruction/therapy, usually starting from scratch, perhaps with an eye to deciding whether it would be a good idea for that person to start at all (assuming there is a choice). An example could be measuring the foreign language learning aptitude of American college students by a standard test such as *MLAT* to help decide which might do well on a German course. Alternatively, if it is embarkation on a particular *known* course that is envisaged, the function is more of an *entrance* one, and the variables quantified could be directly prompted by the content and nature of the specific course.

Placement function. This is to see what a person knows already from some unspecified previous language learning/teaching before entering on a particular further course of teaching/therapy, especially in order to decide at what *level* of a course they should come in, or what sort of course would particularly suit them. An example would be the sort of quick quantification of overall proficiency in using English that has to be done by private language schools in Britain on their monthly intake of students from Europe, who know varying amounts of English and have come for short further courses. Done more thoroughly to give a profile of what the person's strengths and weaknesses are prior to some new instruction, this could be referred to as a *base-line* test or assessment. Again, more specifically, placement tests can also be designed to measure prior knowledge of things known to come at various levels in the course to be taken.

Progress evaluation function. The most well known T use of quantification, this is to see which people have learnt more than which others, at some point in a course of teaching or therapy, perhaps with an eye to promoting some and not others to more advanced work, or perhaps just to supply a source of motivation to the learners or 'expected' information to their parents. To provide a basis for this, achievement is quantified either just in itself at a point in a course, or relative to some previous 'base-line' quantification of individuals' ability (cf. 15.2.1). An example would be the French teacher in Britain giving a quick 'teacher made' test of achievement in mastering the French irregular verb forms which have just been taught, as an end of term assessment, or the first language English teacher using a test supplied with the materials he/she is using, such as the *Science Research Associates (SRA)* graded reading scheme. Often only a small sample of what had been covered is tested for this purpose. Nowadays quantification by student self-assessment questionnaire is also practised.

Progress assessment is sometimes divided into what is called *formative* versus *summative* evaluation. For some the difference is just that the former is done *during* a course of instruction, the latter at the end. However, particularly in UK first language assessment, the difference is defined more usefully in terms of more detailed purpose. Formative assessment is designed to provide some degree of useful feedback to the learning process of the individual case: hence it has to be during a course, and may have a strong qualitative element (e.g. comments on particular errors), not just be an overall mark. Summative assessment is often to inform the parent or institution about progress, may be more formal, and records achievement more as a summary score. Such assessment may then be during or at the end of a course (Gibbs, 1989; DES, 1989). The progress evaluation function is clearly central to the pedagogical process (2.2.1), and to some extent the teacher gathers data relevant to it all the time informally in class. On the other hand, precisely because it arises so much in the instructional process, yet usually has to serve the information needs of a variety of consumers, difficulties can arise where, say, an externally imposed end of term exam does not afford the opportunity for useful detailed feedback to the individual learner.

Diagnostic function. In foreign language teaching this is to see precisely what each person had learnt, and what they have not, from preceding instruction, perhaps with the aim of informing the learner as to where he/she is weak and doing relevant remedial work with some on certain select points, or just to provide a record of what they do and do not know at that point. Again an achievement measure would be appropriate, but much more detailed than just to check progress. In speech therapy an example could be the sort of comprehensive 'profile' of linguistic proficiency that can be made of a language-retarded child during therapy, to see which areas of language still particularly need to be worked on. Note that the term diagnostic is often used as here to refer to detailed description rather than, as in medicine, establishment of causes.

Selection function. This is to see what a person knows already, from some unspecified previous learning/teaching, of aspects of language that are a prerequisite for some, often *non*-linguistic, course or job, in order to decide whether they are up to an acceptable linguistic level or not, or what remediation they need before being acceptable. In short, are they linguistically 'qualified' for it? A general assessment of relevant proficiency by a published test is often used here though, as Yule (1980) indicates, often you really need a narrower test tailored to the specifically envisaged communicative needs (which he calls a 'sufficiency test'). An example could be quantifying the English academic writing ability of Sri Lankans coming to Britain to pursue postgraduate studies in Forestry, or measuring the French conversational skills of a potential salesman for a firm wishing to expand exports to French speaking countries.

It is worth pointing out by the way that T purpose quantification also occurs where the cases are not, as in the rest of this discussion, people, but bits of language. The commonest reason for this is again a kind of selection or screening. Thus teachers or course writers may quantify the readability of different passages of text to decide which would be best for a given remedial class, or the frequency of vocabulary in English to help decide which items to teach at a given level of learner. Once again the focus is on individuals and evaluation: which specific texts are suitably 'readable', which particular words 'best'. Other approaches to the selection of materials, and indeed of teaching methods, rely on surveying learners themselves about what they like or what language skills they think they will need in future ('needs analysis' cf. Munby, 1978).

Certification function. This is to see if, from whatever a person has learnt/been taught, they have reached a certain standard of language competence that allows them to be awarded some recognised qualification — which may be an end in itself. This role is exclusively performed by standard exams (and maybe continuous assessment measures) prepared by institutions which have public status and accountability — e.g. government ministries, or appointed boards. They usually aim to quantify language proficiency of an overall sort. An example is, for learners of English overseas, the *Cambridge First Certificate Examination*. However, where such exams are tied to officially prescribed language teaching syllabuses, as is the British *GCSE* French assessment, they might be regarded rather as a form of summative achievement measure. In such situations indeed often the perceived function is to show schools, government etc. the success of the teaching program more than that of the learners, though this is something that can only be properly demonstrated by research with a proper overall design (Chap. 3).

2.2.3 Indeterminacy over what is quantified and why

The distinction between some of these functions is somewhat subtle, and the labels are not all used consistently as I have above. Often a particular measurement will be made or test used, with varying appropriacy, for several particular purposes at once. Lesser (1978: 19) comments on how the *Boston Diagnostic Aphasia Exam* has been used for classification and diagnosis, but does not really quantify enough variables to do either properly. More broadly, sometimes one and the same T measurement is expected to provide a basis for evaluating not only the learners, but also the teacher *and* the course materials.

Also there can be some confusion in thought and nomenclature over the distinction between type of *variable* quantified (especially 1.2.3) and the *function* intended to be performed by quantifying it, since there are intimate connections between some of them. Thus aptitude almost inevitably is measured for prognostic purposes (though the reverse may not be always true), and to assess progress you can hardly avoid quantifying achievement.

Still, in quantifying language with the T purpose, you should generally think *first* about the *reason* for doing it and *then* about *what* variables it is appropriate to try to quantify. Quantification in the T context may be unsatisfactory *either* because variables are quantified that are inappropriate for the desired function *or* because the quantification of those variables is itself unreliable or invalid (see Chap. 19–23). Similarly, whenever we come across or use a test or other measure labelled an *X Test*, we must try to be clear if X is labelling the kind of variable the test is supposed to be quantifying, the proposed function of the test, or indeed something else about it (e.g. how the measurement is made or scored, see later).

As an example of how confusing multiple functions and shifts in *what* is quantified can develop, take the *Test of English as a Foreign Language (TOEFL)*. This can primarily be regarded as a general measure of English proficiency, used by American universities in a selection function to check the English competence of non-native speakers wishing to take their courses. However, knowing that this is a test their students will have to take, many language schools and courses round the world are now geared to do work precisely matched to the sort of areas of English competence and types of question covered by the *TOEFL*. Hence, for those who have done this sort of preparatory course, the *TOEFL* becomes more like a measure of their achievement in relation to the work they have just done than a measure of their general proficiency. And the role of the test is as much as an indication of their progress on that course as of whether they possess the minimum required standard of English to pursue courses in an American university.

2.2.4 Backwash: A further effect or function

The *TOEFL* example also illustrates how measurement in the T context can have a *backwash* (US *washback*) effect on other things that go on in the T situation, particularly the selection, presentation and practice phases of instruction (2.2.1), and cease just being an independent quantification of the effects of what happens. Wherever a prior syllabus does not control the content of the exam or other ensuing assessment, and the latter does not straightforwardly and comprehensively quantify achievement/attainment on what was taught, thus reinforcing it, the exam may get to control the teaching syllabus. This particularly applies where those in charge of the assessment are different from those doing the rest of the instruction, and where, as often, far fewer variables are quantified in the assessment than were actually targeted in the instruction. The latter limitation is often of course decided by what is quick and easy to measure, such as written rather than spoken performance.

In general, aware teachers/therapists, wanting their pupils/patients to 'do well', will often concentrate just on what seems to be most relevant to the coming test/exam or other assessment. The story is told (Steadman & Gipps, 1984) of the UK Primary English teacher who, knowing the class was going to take the *Schonell Graded Word Reading Test*, which contains an invariant list of 100 words to be read aloud, put the words up on cards round the class well in advance for the pupils to learn. Depending on what and how much the test covers, how measurement is made, and so on, this may or may not suit the actual language needs of the learners. As Mukattash remarks (1981), where foreign language assessment is a written one of specific vocabulary and grammar items, the pupils themselves may not take seriously any efforts made by the teacher to do work on, say, aural comprehension, however important this really is.

On the other hand, Hart *et al.* (1987) found one of the best things about their communicative language test of French was actually the impetus it gave to more communicative language work in class. This points to a potential positive and deliberate use of the backwash phenomenon (cf. Hughes, 1989). It invests quantification with a further possible function, which might be called *directive*, and which it tends to have whether you intend it or not: to influence teachers and learners to concentrate on one thing rather than the other, in the foreknowledge of the kind of variables that will be quantified later for assessment. This can be a more effective way of determining what is taught than setting out conventional detailed syllabuses and lists of objectives, and tends to make those who decide what to quantify in the T context the masters rather than the servants of the overall pedagogical process.

Further reading

Most books on language testing and assessment for teachers and therapists contain brief sections on the T functions (and side-effects) of language quantification.

Foreign language teaching: A. Davies (1977: 38ff.), Bachman (1990: Chap. 3). Also Whiteson (1981), Harris (1990: Chap. 6).
More general educational perspective: Spooncer (1983), Rowntree (1977: Especially Chap. 2, 3 and 7).
Language disability: Caplan (1992: 403ff.).

3 Why Do People Quantify Language? The Research Reason

3.1 The Functions of Quantification in a Research Investigation

3.1.1 Quantification of variables as part of the overall R enterprise

Like T measurement, R measurement is just one element in a larger enterprise, but of quite a different sort. In the most exploratory and ethnographic work, including some kinds of 'classroom research', it may *seem* that there is little more to the investigation than gathering data from one or more cases for quantitative — and qualitative — analysis, but even here the perspective is different from the T activity (2.1.1).

R quantification is most often clearly done as one integral part of an investigation which involves several groups of cases (or the same cases on more than one occasion) and several variables, and will be carefully designed to answer some research question, or evaluate a hypothesis. And a particular investigation may itself be just one step in a series of such investigations to explore some language-related area.

It is the objectives of the research, of course, that ultimately decide what variables are to be measured, and I cannot begin to enumerate here what those objectives might be. But unlike what often applies in the T situation, the same people are usually in charge of the whole process of which the quantification forms a part, so a better integration is normally achieved. Nevertheless a sort of backwash effect may arise (cf. 2.2.4) in that researchers can tend to become fixated on R issues for which the relevant variables are easy to quantify.

Research investigations typically involve recognised steps, corresponding to the headings often used when reporting on them. Considerations relevant to the quantification of variables come in at many points. Thus standard empirical research begins with a *literature review* by researchers of previous work, either empirical or theoretical, that is related to what they are investigating. One thing that should emerge from this will be what relevant variables have been quantified before and how, what cases were measured, what scores or categorisations were obtained.

This will typically lead up to formulation of the *research question* or *hypothesis* dealt with in the current investigation. This also inevitably involves some reference to *what* variables are involved. Thus 'Does deprivation of auditory feedback affect stuttering?' implies that some quantification of the amount of stuttering a stutterer produces will be involved. Auditory feedback is simply the ability to hear yourself as you speak, and whereas the speech of non-stutterers deteriorates when they cannot hear themselves speak, e.g. when they are drunk, it does seem that the speech of some stutterers is improved. Again, a promise to '...test the hypothesis that there is no difference between working class and middle class children in their pronunciation of *-ing* as [-in]' entails that the research will include quantifying the extent to which children say [-in] as against [-iŋ] in words like *eating, walking*, etc. In inexact everyday parlance, this is measuring how far the children 'sound their g's'. Alternatively, in more exploratory, 'hypothesis-*finding*' research, the researcher may simply decide to gather data, e.g. of language activity in the classroom, and quantify everything he or she can think of just to see what emerges.

The next major consideration is the *method* by which the research question can be answered, or hypothesis tested. There must be consideration of the cases — how they are selected, or sampled, who they are and so on (not pursued in this book). But, unless the study is purely qualitative a large amount of attention will also be paid to *how* to *quantify* the variables, including *materials* to be used (e.g. tests, questionnaires), *apparatus* (e.g. tape-recorder), *procedure* (e.g. instructions to subjects), *scoring and analysis* (e.g. how variables are filtered out of raw data and what scales they are quantified on). This all has to be as accurate as possible. These matters are the core subject matter of the present book. Thus in the example given earlier you would have to decide exactly how to gather information on children's pronunciation of the *-ing*. By a test? If so, when and where administered? By recording natural speech? If so, doing what task? Then you have to consider how to score it. Reduce to % of *-ings* pronounced as [-in]? What is the minimum number of instances of *-ing* that should be obtained from each child, and so forth?

The other crucial aspect of method to be considered is the overall *design* of the investigation, i.e. how the various groups of cases and variables quantified all fit together in the overall research 'plan' in such a way that, when the measurements have been made, an answer to the research question is actually obtained. Designs of psycholinguistic experiments can be quite complex; in other fields they are often simpler. Though again design is not something pursued in this book, we can usefully consider further the key functions of variables in these designs. These functions have conventional labels. Most simply you can distinguish the *dependent variable(s)*, the *explanatory variable(s)* (or perhaps *independent variable(s)*, see below), and other variables that have been *controlled* for. I shall refer to these as DVs, EVs and CVs for short.

A piece of research concludes when all *results* have been obtained and interpreted in relation to the initial research question/hypothesis, and there has been *discussion* of wider implications. A crucial part of this will be the visual presentation, summary, statistical treatment and interpretation of the scores/categorisations obtained when the relevant variables were quantified. This phase is not covered in this book (see references at end of chapter).

We now look in a little more detail at the three main design-related functions of variables in empirical investigations. It is convenient to do this separately for experimental and non-experimental research, both of which are common in language study. The essence of the difference ultimately depends on what sort of a variable the EV is, as explained below.

3.1.2 Explanatory and dependent variables in non-experimental research

Investigations often involve more than two variables, and may even only contain one, but the DV — EV distinction is easiest to see and explain in two variable ('bivariate') designs, disregarding CVs for the moment.

Our example of research on *-ing* actually involves two central variables, though it might not seem so at first. People are inclined to conceptualise such an investigation as involving a comparison of two groups of cases, each measured on the one variable — amount of [-in] pronunciation of *-ing*. However, it is also useful from the technical 'design' point of view to think of it as one group of people quantified on two variables — 'social class' and 'amount of [-in] pronunciation of *-ing*'. The investigation as a whole then comes down to a matter of looking to see if there is in fact a relationship between the two variables. Do people who are categorised a particular way for 'social class' tend also to score in some particular way for 'amount of [-in] pronunciation of *-ing*'? Or more concretely, do the working class informants really use [-in] more?

Now in such an example the EV is the variable which the researcher is looking on as potentially 'explaining' the DV. Since clearly you would think of differing social class as potentially being the 'reason' for any differing usage of the [-in] pronunciation of -ing, rather than the other way round, the variable 'social class' is the EV here and 'amount of [-in] pronunciation of -ing' is the DV.

The EV, social class, is by nature a variable that the researcher has to take as he/she finds it in the cases used for the research. It is observed and quantified in essence just like the DV. Hence this is a non-experimental investigation. If it were possible to impose the EV at will, i.e. to take people and randomly assign them to different social classes, it would be an experiment (see below 3.1.3).

EVs in linguistic investigations are often not themselves linguistic variables, indeed in this example the EV was not. However, if in an investigation of Welsh-English bilingualism you wanted to investigate whether Welsh-dominant bilinguals differ from English-dominant ones in their attitude to Welsh medium education for their children, then the EV would be language dominance. This is a more clearly linguistic variable that would somehow have to be quantified for the people used in the study. It is also worth noting that EVs, like social class in our example, are often quantified in the form of a categorisation rather than numerical scores. But this is not always so. If age had been chosen as an EV, that would lend itself to numerical scoring.

3.1.3 Independent and dependent variables in experimental research

In order to quantify DVs, you always have to observe, or record data for them in some way. However this is not true of all EVs. In the -ing example clearly the EV did need to be observed and quantified, in some broad sense, as well as the DV, as part of the overall investigation. However, there is a class of designs of investigations, referred to as, in the careful technical sense, *experiments*, where it seems odd to speak of 'quantifying' or 'measuring' the EVs. If anything the EVs here are 'made' or 'imposed' rather than 'measured'. It is just this subclass of EVs which, in careful usage, are referred to as *independent variables* or IVs, though you will also meet that term used broadly for any explanatory variable, whether truly experimental or not.

An example of a two variable *experiment* would be the investigation into the effect of auditory feedback on stuttering. Here the investigator is most likely to proceed by taking some stutterers and measuring their stuttering (the DV) both when they are speaking normally, and with the ability to hear themselves artificially removed. Thus the EV — 'presence or absence of auditory feedback' — is not simply observed and quantified by the researcher, it has to be imposed by him/her, making this a true experimental design.

Often in research you really want to know whether variation on one variable is *causing*, rather than just in a weaker sense 'explaining' variation on the other. The advantage of experiments is that, precisely because the EV/IV is imposed by the researcher at will, it is possible to find this out more certainly than in a non-experimental study.

Again, a psycholinguistic investigation might pursue whether people mentally process positive sentences faster than negative ones when they read them. Here the researcher might make up some true and false sentences of both types and measure how quickly people respond when presented with them and asked to say as quickly as possible whether they are true or not. Examples of the sentences involved might be:

The world is round	(positive and true)
Grass is not green	(negative and false)
Mr Major is Greek	(positive and false)
etc.	

The EV/IV — positive or negative polarity of sentences — again is not so much measured by the investigator as *made* by him/her as part of the experimental set-up stimulating the DV responses which he/she measures — here response time. In this instance it is clearly linguistic, and in order to *make* this variable, it is worth noting that the researcher has to be aware of what distinguishes a positive from a negative sentence just as much as if he/she were simply categorising this aspect of some sentences that had been obtained as DV data. Hence quite a lot of what is said in this book about quantifying variables in general is also relevant to fabricating this sort of IV.

3.1.4 Variables that are controlled for

In any sort of investigation it is useful to recognise a third way that a variable can feature in the design — as *controlled variable* (CV). CVs are variables that are picked on by the researcher as potentially interfering with the relationship he/she is trying to get at. He/she therefore often quantifies them as part of making a special effort to neutralise or eliminate them in some way. They may be linguistic or non-linguistic.

For instance, in the above example of the investigation of the pronunciation of -*ing* you might regard gender of informant, formality of the situation where the recorded speech occurred, and the nature of the topic being talked about as all potentially interfering factors (variables). They might affect the DV just as much as the EV you are interested in. Gender, for example, could be controlled either by deliberately restricting the study just to males or females, or by ensuring that samples of males and females in equal numbers appeared in each social class group. This illustrates two main ways in which you control unwanted variables. Either you eliminate the variable by making it a 'constant', or you ensure uniformity of its variation in all groups or conditions you are interested in comparing. In either instance, then, the investigator has to record the variable of gender or whatever for each case. Even if the researcher were gathering information in a way where it was impossible to *control* such factors, he/she would do well at least to record them so that they could be taken into account when interpreting the results.

Similarly in the sentence verification experiment the results would clearly be meaningless unless the sentences were all of similar length, and all the component words of a similar level of difficulty, and the same proportions of true and false sentences included in negative and positive forms. Or alternatively you would have to ensure that the same mixture of lengths and difficulties occurred in each type of sentence tested (false as well as true, positive and negative). Thus, to achieve all this again many variables would effectively be quantified apart from the one systematically varied as the IV, and the DV.

In practice, quite a lot of quantification in R work is for this purpose, and may involve measuring aspects of the cases, the materials, the situation where the research takes place, and even the researcher him/herself. Often some selection/screening of cases or test items on this basis is done as part of the preparation *before* the investigation proper is conducted.

Finally it must be noted incidentally that some people use the term 'controlled' more loosely to describe also the IVs mentioned above. To keep things clear, I shall refer to IVs and the like as 'imposed' rather than 'controlled', though there is obviously an intimate connection between the two activities.

3.1.5 Variables in more complex research designs

When you go on to consider quantitative research designs with more than two variables ('factorial' and 'multivariate' designs), the situation becomes yet more complicated, as there may be several EVs and/or several DVs as well as CVs. In the *-ing* investigation you could look at the effect of social class on the pronunciation of the *th* sound as well. Then you would have two DVs. In the verification experiment you could systematically vary both truth *and* positive-negative polarity, instead of *eliminating* one and varying the other. You could then see the effects on response time of both these separately and in conjunction. Effectively you would have two IVs.

However, this cannot be pursued further here. My only concern here is to give an inkling of how the topic of language quantification interlocks with the structure of research investigations as wholes. But it is important to realise that there is no straightforward connection between what sort of phenomenon a variable is, or how it is measured, and its place in the design of an investigation. The main thing, as always, is to try and be clear about what the relevant variables are in any investigation, and what part each is playing, so that they can then be quantified appropriately.

It is worth mentioning here that in *any* piece of research, however complex, it is well worth paying more attention to the quantification of the relevant variables than often appears to be paid in published versions of investigations. No investigation, however clever the design or complex the statistical analysis, is any use if the 'grassroots' measurement of the variables involved is unsatisfactory in some way.

3.1.6 An analogy between quantification of single variables and full research designs

The purpose of this chapter is to show how quantification of variables fits into the wider scenario of R investigations as wholes. However, there is a further point to understanding the wider R context in which quantification often occurs. That is that there are some loose *similarities* between what is involved in quantifying single groups of cases on single variables (the concern of this book) and what is involved in doing a full R investigation. Seeing these can help us understand better some features of *how* quantification is done (Chap. 4–8). In essence, measuring a single group of cases can often be seen as a quasi R investigation like that described in 3.1.2 in miniature. But instead of different groups involved there are different individuals: the latent EV is 'individuality', as it were, though it is usually only in the T context that you are actually interested in *following up* the comparison of individuals.

First the notion of 'sampling' applies in both. In typical non-experimental R investigations where you compare groups of people who represent values of an EV like class and so on, usually these groups have to be *samples*. You obviously cannot compare *all* upper middle class with *all* lower middle class speakers in how they pronounce *-ing*: you use samples, picked in any of a variety of ways that we will not pursue here, and generalise results to the larger 'populations' of cases. Now it may not seem so obvious, but when you are 'comparing' individuals by quantifying them again you are really only using samples. You cannot actually observe *all* the instances where a given person has a chance to pronounce -*ing* this way or that and give him/her a score based on them to combine or compare with other people's scores. We shall see how different techniques for quantifying variables often involve using a sample of more than one observation from 'within' each case to arrive at a score for that case. In effect you generalise from a sample of bits of language behaviour of a case to their population of behaviours of that sort. In both kinds of sampling issues arise to do with good and bad ways of sampling and what size samples should be.

Second the notion of 'controlling' for unwanted factors applies in both. We saw in 3.1.4 how you need to eliminate variables that might affect the DV in addition to the EV you want to know about. If you are comparing classes you don't want gender or formality of situation to interfere if pronunciation of -*ing* might be affected by those too. It would make no sense to observe and score upper middle class informants in a more formal situation than lower middle class ones, since it would then be impossible to tell if any differences in pronunciation were due to the EV (class) or the variable that should have been controlled for (formality of situation).

Rather similarly you need to try and control for many of the same kinds of thing *within* a group being quantified. If you are measuring some cases' reading ability, say, whether for T or wider R purposes, it obviously makes sense if possible for them all to do the task in the same sort of surroundings with the same tester and the same reading passages. Otherwise different cases' reading ability scores might be partly a reflection of other things than pure reading ability. We shall see how some approaches to quantification are more able than others to allow potentially interfering variables to be held constant or otherwise controlled for.

3.2 Can one combine the T and R functions?

I have been at pains to spell out the conceptual and practical differences between quantification for T and R purposes. However, it is not entirely impossible to combine the two. In other words, on occasion it is feasible to quantify variables and use the information, with care, both for a T and an R purpose at once.

In particular, teachers and therapists may undertake research simultaneously with pedagogy. For example they might try out a new way of teaching how to pronounce a difficult sound. When they quantify achievement afterwards, they could use this not only as an indication for each individual case as to how far they have mastered the sound and so how much more practice each needs, but also to compare the group as a whole with some other group still taught in the old way, or a group taught the previous year by the same teacher in the old way, to see if the results are on average better. Thus one and the same quantification is performing a conventional 'progress' evaluation function from the T point of view, and functioning as a DV in a bivariate R investigation as well.

However, 'classroom research' of this sort is a delicate operation. It is not easy to satisfy the wider conditions for good R and T at the same time, such as the former's need for control of extraneous factors and the latter's obligation to help individuals. It is also difficult, though vital, to keep separate in the mind the two conceptualisations of what is being done. But the fact that the same quantification often can be done for T and R purposes is one of the reasons for addressing both a T and R audience in this book.

Further reading

There are innumerable books for psychologists, sociologists and educationalists on the general structure of R investigations (and associated statistics). See for example Robson (1983), Langley (1979: Especially Chap. 5), Hopkins (1985) or, with greater thoroughness, Plutchik (1974), Christensen (1980), Cohen & Manion (1980), Pedhazur & Schmelkin (1991).

Specifically linguistic references on overall empirical research methods, especially overall designs and, in some instances, statistics (though in some areas what is available is fairly sketchy):

General: Butler (1985b), Woods *et al.* (1986).

Psycholinguistics: Prideaux (1984: especially Chap. 1 and Laboratories p. 211ff.), Garman (1990: 3.1).

Child Language: Bloom & Lahey (1978: Chap. II), Bennett-Kastor (1988), Wells (1985: Chap. 1, 2, 3.7, 3.8, Appendices), Dale (1972: Appendix).

Foreign language learning and teaching: R. Clark (1977: 105ff.), Brown (1988), Seliger & Shohamy (1989), Hatch and Farhady (1982).

Sociolinguistics: Hudson (1980: Chap. 5), Milroy (1982b: especially Chap. 1–3, and 1987), Downes (1984: 82ff.), Cheshire (1982a: Part I), Anshen (1978), Fasold (1984: Chap. 3–5).

Dialectology: Francis (1983: Chap. 3–6), Bagby Atwood (1986), Chambers & Trudgill (1980: Chap. 2.3, 4, 9), Petyt (1980: especially p. 44ff., p. 110ff., p. 145ff., p. 158ff.).

Stylistics: Kenny (1982).

Phonetics/Phonology: Ohala & Jaeger (1986: especially Chap. 1).

Grammar: Greenbaum & Quirk (1970).

4 Overview of Four General Kinds of Approach to Data Gathering for Quantification

4.1 Introducing the Four Approaches

Let us now turn to the methodologically crucial matter of *how* the tremendous variety of variables hinted at in Chapter 1 can be quantified, whether for R or T purposes. For convenience we treat this 'operationalisation' as usually involving two major phases, though sometimes one or the other seems so minimal as to be hardly noticeable as a separate activity. We look in this part (Chap. 4–10) primarily at the first phase — how relevant observable information on language or other behaviour is gathered from cases (=(b) of 1.3). This may be called the 'data gathering' phase, and is where any materials, instruments or apparatus for measurement are used and standard procedures applied. Later, in Part III (Chap. 11–18), we look in more detail at how this data is reduced to suitable figures (=(c) of 1.3). That is the 'scoring' phase, involving often some 'data analysis' where scores and categorisations for each case on variables of interest are extracted from the data as gathered, perhaps with further use of instruments or machines.

A useful way of getting an overview of ways of data gathering as part of what is necessary to arrive at quantifications of linguistic and other variables is to look at them in four general categories. By way of introduction, I shall first give an example of each type of technique applied to measuring the 'same' phenomenon.

Suppose we want to quantify the preference of speakers of English for saying or writing *needn't/need not* as against *doesn't need to/don't need to*. In terms of specification of *what* variable is being measured, we are in the realm of the measurement of a feature of the grammatical production performance of normal adult native speakers, for whom both types of negation, with or without *do*, are clearly possible. One interest here for the linguistic researcher is that the more *need* is treated the first way, the more it seems to belong to the set of English auxiliary verbs like *can* and *might*. These can be negated in the form *You can't come in* and so on, but not *You don't can (to) come in*. The more *need* is treated the second way, the more it goes with full verbs like *want*. These can be negated in the form *I don't want to come in* but not *I wantn't (to) come in*. Here are four general ways of getting quantitative information on this.

(1) You could sift written materials like newspapers, and tapes of radio and TV programmes, or just listen out for anyone you speak to using relevant forms, and count the proportions of each alternative way of putting *need* in the negative as it occurs.

(2) You could interview people for the purpose and try to get them to say the required forms in conversation, e.g. you might ask *Why don't you take the bus to work?* hoping to get a reply such as either:

> *Because I needn't. I've got a car.*

or

> *Because I don't need to. I've got a car.*

In this way you get a picture of people's general preference for one form or the other.

(3) You could present people with pairs of sentences like the following and ask them to choose which they would say:

> *You needn't wait up for me.*
>
> *You don't need to wait up for me.*

(4) You could give people a set of questions like: Put the following into the negative, using the verb *need*:

> *You must come before 8.0.*
>
> *George says he must go shopping today.*

In doing so they would be forced to come up with answers either containing *needn't* or *don't need to*, thus revealing their preference.

The example used here is, of course, of quantification for R purposes. However, the same four general types of approach are often, at least in principle, also available for T measurement. You could visualise using something similar to the above example when trying to ascertain the extent to which one or more learners of English express polite refusals like native speakers, in other words, 'correctly'. So instead of looking into usage of *needn't* as against *don't need to,* you would be trying to quantify usage of wording like *I'm sorry I can't do that* as against *No!* and the like.

These types of approach may be characterised as, respectively, 1. *non-reactive* and *fully naturalistic,* 2. *reactive,* involving *quasi-naturalistic interaction,* 3. *reactive,* involving people's *opinions,* 4. *reactive,* involving people's *manipulation* of some verbal material. Most quantification of language falls *fairly* clearly into one of these four types and for quantifying many aspects of language, but certainly not all, you have a choice which general type of technique to use.

Where there *is* such a choice, as also with more specific choices within these approaches, the decision over which approach to use may be guided at least in part by what is practicable with time and resources available, and what is easy for the measurer and familiar to cases. For instance, in a T context, an assessment method parallel to activities used in the course of normal instruction may be preferred both to save time — no special practice with something new will be needed — and to provide a backwash-type effect — justifying the normal teaching activities (2.2.4).

Often the choice is on the basis of custom — what previous researchers in the same field used, or what is 'traditional' or institutionally imposed in language teaching or therapy in a particular country. Also whether the method *looks* to 'consumers' like a proper means of measurement may be a factor — so-called *face validity.* Such considerations are often in practice decisive though it might be felt that the overriding consideration *should* be that of which approach most validly captures the essence of what you are trying to quantify, within ethical bounds (addressed in the following chapters, and see further Chap. 21–3). These four approaches to data gathering will be pursued in more detail in Chap. 5–8. However, a few general points can usefully be made in advance.

4.2 The Four Approaches as Different Kinds of Communication

First let us recognise that there is a loose analogy between the data gathering phase of quantifying cases and simple speech communication events in everyday life. In the latter, there are commonly two primary participants playing the roles of (a) speaker/writer and (b) hearer/reader. There is also (c) a situation in which the communication occurs, which may include onlookers, and there are (d) messages on some topic passing between the main participants. So also when measuring language where the cases are people there are (a) the measurer (or sometimes someone deputed to do the job) and (b) the case(s) being measured, as main participants. There is also (c) a situation in which the measuring event occurs and, as (d), the topic or test task — in the narrow sense the *instrument* — underlying the language and other behaviour that constitute the data from which variables are quantified.

These four components of the 'data gathering event', as we might call it, will be referred to frequently in the rest of this book. All contribute to how quantification is done and how successfully, whether or not they are formally treated as part of some measuring 'instrument' or technique as conventionally described. The data *analysis* phase is in this respect simpler, as it only involves the measurer(s) or researcher(s). Aspects of how quantification itself is done, such as these and more specific features (e.g. in 8.4), are themselves variables which can take on different values. In the more technical discussion of measurement, these variables, excluding those of the cases themselves, are referred to technically as *facets of observation*. Any specific means of quantifying language is defined in effect by a whole set of specific values or settings chosen on these facets.

For the present, we can note that the four approaches involve rather different communication between the main participants in this event. In the non-reactive approach (1), there either is no two-way communication between measurer and case at all, or it is entirely natural in manner and topic. In either instance the behaviour of the cases is presumably entirely authentic. In the quasi-naturalistic approach (2), there is communication approximating normal use of language, but the cases know they are being quantified in *some* way, so may not behave entirely naturally. In the opinion-based approach (3), there is interaction in which the topic of the communication is language itself. This is not entirely unrealistic as talk about language is a feature of ordinary discourse. In the manipulation-oriented approach (4), the interaction does not approximate normal language communication at all, since the sort of linguistic tasks done are essentially *only* ever done for measurement purposes (or, in a T context, as part of language practice in the classroom). Hence it is more appropriate to say language is 'manipulated' rather than 'used'.

One corollary of this is that we must in the end recognise that the four approaches don't ever really measure *exactly* the same 'thing', though this is often glossed over in practice. For instance people's opinion about whether or how often they use *needn't* (3) may well not coincide with their actual naturalistic use of it (1). The former is virtually a metalinguistic variable, the latter a straight language use one. Similarly, how they use it in conversation with a researcher may not be identical with their ordinary casual use when they don't think they are being observed. And what they do when asked to operate on a word in an artificial test sentence may not coincide with any of these.

Sometimes variation of this sort is written off as mere performance variation, with a single competence variable underlying it (1.2.2). But it is probably better to think of it as a matter of different styles, conversational strategies and so on being activated — i.e. different aspects of communicative competence. However such matters are designated theoretically it must not be forgotten that *how* you quantify — choice of facet values — and *what* you quantify — target variables/constructs — are actually related. Hence your specification of the target variable (=(a) in 1.3) may actually limit the 'choice' of means of quantification more crucially than the factors mentioned at the end of 4.1. For a discussion of this issue in a T context see Bachman (1990).

4.3 The Four Approaches as Degrees of Artificiality

The four approaches clearly move from the more natural to the more forced as you go from 1 to 4. Really of course this is a 'cline', and various intermediate types of technique can be devised. However, a number of things crucially relate to this.

Firstly, the more reactive and artificial the approach, generally the less is left to the measurer to do in the data *analysis* phase afterwards. Often it is just a matter of adding up total scores on a test, rather than actually doing the hard work of extracting information on a variable of interest from a lot of taped conversation and counting up instances of something. Correspondingly, the hard work in the more artificial approaches (3 and 4) is usually in the compilation of the test or questionnaire or whatever that constitutes the instrument used in the *gathering* phase, unless a ready made one is used.

Related to this is that the more artificial approaches to data gathering are also more 'a priori' in that they require a decision beforehand by measurers about exactly what they are going to measure: then the exact questions or test or whatever that they administer (the materials/instrument) are chosen. They are less likely to be able to refine the measuring process, for the data gathered, after gathering it, though they could next time round.

On the other hand the more naturalistic approaches allow for the teacher or researcher to adjust, or even decide, what variable(s) he/she is quantifying *after* gathering some data. You *can* go through written or taped material in a language without prior decision about what to look for and just see what suggests itself as being noticeable or interesting, and so worth counting up or whatever. Or you can begin with a *vague* idea of what you are interested in, but decide what exact categories might be relevant to classify things from the possibilities that actually seem to come up, as was done largely in 'communication strategy' research, for example (e.g. Tarone, 1980). Thus in the R context approaches 1 and 2 are a common feature of 'exploratory' work, where the researcher has no clear questions or hypotheses to start from.

Furthermore, the more artificial the technique, the greater opportunity there is for control of extraneous factors. We saw in 3.1.6 that control of unwanted variables is a key feature of any kind of quantification of individual variables, whether for T or R purposes. For example, you ideally want the scores or categorisations you ultimately obtain for cases just to reflect their differences on the variable you are trying to quantify. You don't want different cases' scores to reflect different circumstances in which the measurement was made (c), or different measurers (a), or different language tasks or topics of conversation (d). These things can far more easily be kept constant in 3 and 4 than 1 and 2.

Finally it is worth observing that often, particularly in an R context, many variables are quantified from the same cases in one study. Often they are *not* all approachable by the same general kind of technique 1 or 2 or 3 or 4. Where this is the case, it usually makes sense to gather data for quantification in order of naturalism of technique. That is to say, you would gather data for any variable you are quantifying by artificial items of means 4 *after* getting the cases to talk in conversation and be recorded for analysis (means 2), and so on. In this way the naturalism of 2 is not destroyed by having just done 4.

4.4 Alternative Labels for Different Approaches to Gathering Data to Quantify

A point about terminology needs to be made before looking at these four techniques more closely. There are a number of well-known terms that I might have used instead of the cumbersome periphrases for techniques 1 to 4, but all are used so variedly by different people that it is hard to pin them down. I shall now say a word about some of these.

Observation might be used for the more naturalistically based data gathering — especially for my 1 — and is sometimes opposed to 'testing'. However, *all* quantification, however artificial, really has to be said to involve *some* sort of observation of characteristics of cases.

Elicitation suits my 2 particularly well, but is commonly used more widely. At its broadest it would include *any* technique where the measurer prompts people to do or say something connected with what he/she wants to quantify, so it would include 3 and 4 and even some of 1. Labov's famous

New York department store study (1972), for instance, involved eliciting speech from shop assistants through 'staged encounters' *without* the shop assistants being aware they were part of an investigation at all. Labov, interested in the extent to which r's were pronounced, asked the assistants where he could obtain some item which he knew in advance was sold on the fourth floor of the store. In this way he obtained lots of instances of shop assistants saying the words *fourth floor*, with two possible occasions each time for them to 'sound' the r or not. This could be regarded arguably as in my terms *non-reactive*, but could still be labelled 'elicitation'.

Surveying suits my 3 obviously since we are familiar with opinion-poll surveys in everyday life. However, this label is commonly found used for quantification which includes some of the other three types of activity too. Thus what are called 'surveys' in sociolinguistic research often include relatively unstructured recorded interviews (2) and more test-like elements where the informants have to read lists of minimal pairs (4) — i.e. pairs of words which some speakers will pronounce the same, others not, like *God* and *guard* for US English speakers. Labov's department store study is referred to as an anonymous 'survey' too. The label *interview* can be used to include much the same range of quantification activity though, unlike a survey, it has to be face to face, and cannot contain a postal or take away element.

In fact, a 'survey' is often defined not as a kind of quantification technique at all, but rather as an overall method of R investigation. Any non-experimental piece of research is sometimes called a 'survey'. Others define it by reference to the sampling of cases involved: a survey is an investigation in which you generalise from samples of people. Or it is defined just by reference to the person who does it: anything done by a sociolinguist is then referred to as a 'survey', but a similar investigation by a foreign language learning researcher would not be so labelled. Thus 'survey' is such a variously defined notion that I have tried to avoid using it.

Questionnaire use is perhaps the closest to my 3, though not all opinion elicitation is as structured as this term implies.

Testing often equates approximately with my 4, but again we do not find it used also for some kinds of quantification in my other categories. Greenbaum & Quirk (1970) for example call my example of 3 above 'judgement tests', and my 4 'performance tests'. And in discussions of testing in the T context, often oral interviews and the like, of my 2 type, are included under 'language testing'. Some so-called tests can even be non-reactive (1) and not involve people directly as the cases. Counting up the average sentence length and average word length of a sample of text, to determine its 'readability' can be referred to as a 'test'.

Another problem with the label 'test' is that it is often associated in people's minds only with T measurement. They think of *school* tests whose aim is measurement of *individuals* with a view to *evaluating* them, e.g. finding out who did best in the French test (cf. 2.1). However, the term is in fact widely used in the R context with no evaluation of individuals in mind.

Most usually what are referred to as 'tests' in language study involve people, are reactive, need elicitation and are rather formal, using sets of test questions and perhaps machinery like computers. They are 'structured ways of observing' (Perkins, 1977), or instances of 'a standardised task which elicits a sample of the subject's behaviour, which can be objectively scored…' (Lovell, 1964).

One thing that is crucial is to keep 'testing' as a category of means of quantifying variables separate in your mind from 'testing' in the sense of designing an investigation to try and reject a hypothesis: 'hypothesis-testing'. There is a difference between a test as a measuring instrument used to quantify at least one variable in an R investigation, and the *whole* investigation viewed as 'testing' some prediction. In this latter sense, one example of the investigations described in Chapter 3 *could* be described as designed to 'test the hypothesis that removing auditory feedback alleviates stuttering'.

Hypothesis testing is done by R investigations which may or may not include variables that are quantified by 'tests' in our current sense. There is however some connection in that truly experimental research designs are most likely to involve some use of tests in quantifying the relevant variables, while the more exploratory research, with no clear hypotheses formed in advance, typically involves quantitative (and qualitative) analysis of more naturalistic data. Research which tests hypotheses but is not fully experimental (as defined in 3.1.2) — probably the commonest type in language research — frequently involves variables quantified in any of the ways characterised (1–4).

Clearly when any of these labels is used we need to look carefully at what is *actually* going on under that name. We also need to take care when we use labels ourselves. Quite apart from a general desire for clarity, you need to be aware of how a label may strike the human cases being measured. For R purposes, in psycholinguistics for instance, the word 'test' may put some people off and make them less willing to cooperate at all unless it is explained that they are not being evaluated as individuals. So you have to make clear that the purpose of measurement is R not T. You can say instead perhaps that some aspect of the English *language* or whatever is being 'tested', and stress anonymity. On the other hand it is also found that *some* kinds of subject only respond seriously if they think they *are* being individually assessed — otherwise they leave a lot of blanks on tests and questionnaires and give 'humorous' responses. The researcher needs to know his/her potential subjects/informants in order to judge this.

When doing research in areas usually dominated by T measurement, other reactions may be obtained. For instance children with speech defects, or their parents whose permission you should ask, may welcome a 'test' which they think of as being an individual assessment which will lead to new understanding of the child's problem, ensuing therapy and eventual cure. Now although this makes for very co-operative subjects, obviously it is not ethical even by implication to promise anything along these lines which you cannot 'deliver'. If you are not in fact testing people for T purposes, in a context where this might be expected, you must make this clear.

Further reading

The following are some useful sources of information on techniques of data gathering and quantification, often with examples of actual tests etc., and information on their construction, organised by particular sub-areas of language study. They are relevant to many topics of Chap. 5–10.

General: Seliger & Shohamy (1989: especially Chap. 8).

Measurement, especially of proficiency and achievement by discrete point tests, in foreign language learning and teaching: Ingram (1974), Heaton (1975), Valette (1967), Madsen (1983), van Els (1984: Chap. 15).

Ditto, by more integrative and/or communicative tests: Oller (1979), Ramirez (1984), Hughes (1989), Bachman (1990), Weir (1988).

Ditto, from interview and more naturalistic data: Dulay et al. (1982: especially Chap. 10), Faerch et al. (1984: Chap. 18, 19).

Measurement, especially of attitude, in foreign language learning: Gardner & Lambert (1972: especially Appendix A).

Quantification of child language performance, from both naturalistic data and tests: Dale (1972: 300–9), Potts et al. (1979: especially Chap. 2), Harris (1990: especially Chap. 7 and 8), Romaine (1984: especially Chap. 2, 8), Bennett-Kastor (1988: Chap. 3, 5, 6).

Measurement of child metalinguistic competence: Yaden & Templeton (1986: Chap. 12).

Measurement of language and other ability in normal and linguistically handicapped children: Bloom & Lahey (1978: Chap. 2, 11, 12, and appendices), Miller (1982), Crystal (1982), Bracken (1991: especially pp. 104–240), Berry (1969: Chap. 6–8 and appendices), Nicolosi et al. (1989: appendices).

Measurement by tests and machines in language pathology: Perkins (1977: Chap. 15), Caplan (1992: Chap. 10).

CHAPTER 4 41

Measurement in psycholinguistics: Carterette (1974: vol VII Chap. 2), Prideaux (1984: 3–15), Garman (1990: especially pp. 109–18), Anastasi (1988).

Measurement by machines in instrumental phonetics: Painter (1979).

Quantification, especially from data elicited in interview, in sociolinguistics: Labov (1972: especially Chap. 3, 8), Hudson (1980: 5.3, p. 144ff.), Cheshire (1982a: Chap. 2), Milroy (1982b: Chap. 1–3).

Ditto by questionnaire in dialectology: Francis (1983: Chap. 3, 5), Samarin (1967: Especially Chap. 2, 5–7).

Measurement of bilingualism: Baetens Beardsmore (1982: Chap. 3), Baker (1993: Chap. 2).

Quantification of attitude in sociolinguistics and elsewhere: Henerson (1987).

Quantification in stylistics: Kenny (1982: especially Chap. 5), Gibson (1970).

Quantification of general psychological and sociological variables: Cohen (1976).

5 Data For Quantification: Fully Naturalistic

5.1 Fully Naturalistic, Non-reactive Data Gathering Exemplified

Non-reactive observation/measurement is that where the people/things observed, the cases, don't or can't 'know' they are being quantified. Either there can be *no* communication between the cases and the measurer, because there is no direct channel of communication between them, or it is, from the case's point of view, entirely natural and not seen as involving measurement. Needless to say, the latter may not always be unambiguously determinable. Examples are:

Assembling texts of Old English (a *corpus* of *text data*) in order to count the frequency of, say, clauses with the basic order subject-verb-object, like modern English, as against subject-object-verb.

Taping unscripted material from English radio or TV, such as phone-in programmes, in order to quantify, say, the incidence of intervocalic written *t*, in words like *better* or *eating*, being pronounced as something other than [t] in spoken English. This is a variety of *third person observation*.

Stopping people in the street and asking them the way somewhere (apparently genuinely), in order to measure how often people use the different types of available 'strategy' to perform this communicative function of 'giving directions'.

Listening in surreptitiously to learners or linguistically backward native speakers talking amongst themselves, and rating each of them on a 5 point scale for fluency. This could be done with the use of a two-way mirror, for example.

Listening out for occurrences of Spoonerisms in spontaneous speech and noting them when somebody produces one, to see what types occur and in what proportions. A Spoonerism is when someone says e.g. ...*the next town drain* by mistake for ...*the next down train* (Fromkin,

1973). This noting down of rarely occurring things as and when they occur over a long period is known as *event sampling*.

Going through all Shakespeare's sonnets in order to quantify, say, the frequency of different types of departure from the basic metrical pattern of a line.

Going through several English teachers' class handouts, lesson plans, teacher-made tests, report cards etc. in order to quantify aspects of their instructional styles (a variety of *record review*).

Collecting samples of English text from authentic sources such as novels and using the *Flesch* measure of readability (15.2.4) on them to see what level of learner or age of native speaker child they might be suitable reading material for.

Getting hold of essays written in the normal way in school by learners of English as data to go through counting up errors of cohesion (faulty use of conjunctions, pronouns not referring back clearly to something already mentioned, etc.).

Getting a very young child's mother to keep notes of utterances the child makes, and what she thought they meant (a *diary record*), for you to categorise them for the kind of 'speech act' apparently involved in each (request, command, statement and so on).

Standing around in an Ethiopian market noting down surreptitiously how often bargaining for particular goods was done in particular languages (a *transaction count* — Fasold, 1984: 124).

A lot of R quantification in stylistics is of this sort, though, as the examples above show, sociolinguistic and other work can on occasion involve this approach too. In particular the more ethnographic R approaches often use these techniques, since their hallmark is prolonged participant observation with minimal disturbance of what naturally occurs, and data of this sort is also ideal for qualitative analysis. Quantification for T purposes is rarely done this way.

In addition, some variables used as EVs in pieces of research are quantified in this way. If you are comparing some aspect of the speech of men and women, you have technically to 'measure' the gender of your cases, as well as their linguistic behaviour. But the determination of gender can normally be done non-reactively. The researcher can (usually!) tell the gender of his/her informants without even asking them or making them aware he/she is recording this bit of information. Equally, if you were investigating the difference in average sentence length between high-brow and low-brow newspapers, again the classification of newspapers into high- and low-brow (the EV here) would be made as non-reactively as the measurement of sentence lengths (the DV).

5.2 Procedure and the Sampling Element

This approach to data gathering does not typically involve the measurer in a rigorous procedure of administration, with set materials involved. However, the observer may prepare in advance a checklist of things to look for that are relevant to the variables to be quantified. This could form the basis for a worksheet filled in in real time, e.g. while observing children playing and talking, or a language class in action. Or it forms the basis for what will be coded in a written or transcribed corpus (see below).

Most data-gathering as part of the quantification process contains an element of sampling (cf. 3.1.6). You cannot expect to observe or elicit *all* the information about a case that bears on how each scores with respect to some variable. You just hope to get a representative sample of data for this purpose. In doing this you in effect make a judgment about how variable 'within cases' the phenomenon you are observing is. If some property seems to be constant within a case, such as gender in people, then one observation per case is a sufficient sample (barring measurer error — see reliability 19.3). But language related variables, such as a child's ability to produce *wh*-questions, vary within the case. The more the variable varies, e.g. from situation to situation in individual people's behaviour, the more care is needed about obtaining a representative sample of observations from each case.

Often, too much data may be available. It is possible potentially to tape a very young child for long periods without it being aware of it and go through the material quantifying average utterance length and the like. However, this would produce far more data than seems practical or necessary for a representative sample from which to quantify this sort of variable reasonably accurately for that case. But how to limit it? The subjective choice of a parent of what to record in a diary study may be unrepresentative, since there may be a natural tendency to write down just the most unusual examples. Researchers for convenience commonly tape just one half hour block of talk, or about 150 consecutive utterances, but arguably this may be unrepresentative too, as it only represents one situation at one time with one addressee etc.

A *spread sample* of five or ten shorter recordings on different occasions would be a better reflection of the variation in average utterance length that might arise within the case due to varying *circumstances* and *topics* and which needs to be represented overall in any summary score for the child.

Alternatively you could specify the variable being quantified more closely as pertaining only to the language of a particular type of situation, and so forth. Some longitudinal child language research has followed stricter *time-sampling* or *interval sampling* regimes such as recording two minutes every twenty minutes between 9 am and 6 pm, or setting up apparatus that enables the researcher to record permanently thirty seconds of speech retrospectively after hearing it, whenever he/she decided something interesting had been said (Bennett-Kastor, 1988: 69). Of course, if the cases are young children, the time gap between observations that are supposed to sample a variable at one stage of development must not be too long (e.g. several weeks), otherwise they become observations of the *successive* stages in a longitudinal study.

Similarly in literary stylistic research you could potentially go through the entire novels of an author like Henry James analysing them in order to quantify something of interest, such as sentence complexity. Again for many variables this would be an excessive analysis effort. And again the most generally representative sample would often be a spread one, in this instance over text rather than time, not just one large continuous chunk of one novel analysed and quantified. For instance, you could sample 'systematically' and analyse five successive sentences from every fiftieth page. Or you could choose pages at random using a random number table (see e.g. Robson, 1983, appendix, for how to do this). This matter falls within the scope of 'quantitative linguistics' (see e.g. Tesitelova, 1992: 31ff.).

A rather different issue of representativeness arises in research on the relative incidence of different types of slip of the tongue. Many of these, such as the spoonerisms mentioned above, are rare in anybody's speech, and it can be a problem to gather enough occurrences to quantify the frequency of each type reliably. One solution is for the researcher to simply collect the largest possible sample, noting down every slip he/she hears or overhears from anybody for a long period, such as several years. A criticism of this procedure however is that the researcher cannot possibly *concentrate* on observing all the time. Hence the sample may be biased as he/she may miss instances of less prominent slips. A more careful procedure, though it produces less data, is for the researcher to set aside certain periods of only an hour or so at a time in which he/she consciously focuses attention on slips above all else, and only records slips noted in those periods.

If the data gathered is spoken, it is usually *transcribed* in some form and written down before any analysis takes place, since it is easier to handle the data in that form. Once transcribed, often many variables are quantified from the same 'corpus' of data, and much of the real work of quantification, e.g. by frequency counting, normally has to be done then (see 11.3, 12). What is thought of as 'the data' often shifts from the original tape, handwritten material etc. to the transcribed version, so it is important to do this sensibly, as verifying later·against the original may be too tedious to be ever attempted. Indeed in some instances, e.g. diary studies, the initial recorded version of the data *is* one that has effectively already been transcribed by the parent or other observer so no verification is possible.

Transcription brings with it the danger of unconscious 'editing' of the data, e.g. by removing performance slips and hesitation phenomena which may be valuable indications that the forms involved are in process of being acquired. Similarly there is the danger of imposing adult or standard language interpretations on what is said — e.g. transcribing what a child actually thinks of as *could of* as *could have*. Non-linguistic phenomena accompanying speech may be all important to understanding what is said, especially with children, learners and speech-disabled cases, but they are often not even recorded in the first place, unless video is used. Ideally a transcription would record the speech of each participant, and relevant non-linguistic gestures, objects referred to etc., in separate columns on the page.

If the data is handwritten it may pay to type it, again perhaps retaining markers of where misspellings or crossouts occurred. Whatever form transcription takes it is often a good idea to enter it in files on computer, since a certain amount of useful analysis can then be done automatically. However, the crucial thing is to be clear at this point about what variables you wish to quantify in the ensuing analysis phase so effort is not wasted. For instance, sometimes people think that because data is spoken it must be phonetically transcribed, but this is actually a waste of time unless the variables you are interested in quantifying are related to the sounds. On the other hand, especially when data is gathered in a more ethnographic R context where there is no narrow predetermined purpose in collecting the observations in the first place, it may pay to do as detailed a transcription as possible to start with. Increasingly in some fields, such as child language, collections of data are being published so that other researchers with their own research questions can skip the data gathering phase altogether and proceed directly to count instances of what they are interested in. In this context *standardisation* of transcription conventions becomes all important (Bennett-Kastor, 1988: 37).

Usually separated from transcription is *coding*, which is where the researcher, therapist etc. goes through transcribed or original printed material marking all the instances of items relevant to the variables to be quantified. For example, he/she marks all the nouns, or all the dependent clauses or whatever in each sample of text, so they can then be easily counted. This is dealt with under the analysis phase, though sometimes it can be done at the same time as transcription, or even instead of it.

5.3 Degrees of Naturalism and Control

In quantification of the present sort you should manage to get maximum 'naturalism'. Where the cases are people, they will speak or write or act as they would normally, which is usually what you most want to get at. This is the big 'plus' of this kind of technique. However, there are some problems. For instance, can you always be sure, when the people involved are contacted face to face, not in writing, that they do not suspect that they are being quantified or investigated? And language learners, in a T setting, may *never* really say or write anything, even when not in an apparent test or exam, without having some expectation that it may be quantified by the teacher as part of their assessment. Complete naturalness may be elusive then in the error analysis approach to quantifying aspects of learner language.

Then again 'natural' speech should not be unquestioningly identified with 'casual' speech, if that is what you are really after. Phone-in programmes on radio are a source of *natural* speech by the people involved, but it is likely not to be at the extreme end of the casual-formal scale of language variation that we vary along when we speak. We shall have more to say on this later. Many people have a distinct 'telephone voice' which, though to some extent formal, has to be regarded as their 'natural' way of speaking in that circumstance. It has been observed that the presence of a stranger, even when not perceived as a measurer, may change behaviour (Milroy, 1987: 185). For instance bilinguals talking in a shop may switch languages just because they detect a monolingual speaker in earshot. (For further discussion of the notion of 'natural' see Romaine, 1984: 2.3).

Another matter is the lack of control-like rigour often in such observation — the price paid for naturalism. In candid recording of strangers, asking directions in the street for a sociolinguistic enquiry, the circumstances may differ considerably in which each person is recorded, and the topic of the talk may be different, leading to some unreliability (20.2, 20.4). Some such factors you can at least keep a note of, even if nothing can be done to control them. In this way they can be given some consideration at least when interpreting the resulting figures and comparing with the results of others. Video recording also allows more to be recorded than audiotaping, though it is likely to be more noticeable and so not yield fully naturalistic data.

But there may be other aspects of people relevant to an R investigation, e.g. social class, birthplace, which you might want to try and keep constant for a particular investigation (CVs) or use as EVs, which there is no way of getting accurate data on by pure observation. These variables could only be measured, and if necessary eliminated, by standardising the situation and asking the people additional questions about their background, thereby almost certainly becoming reactive. Here you may perhaps choose to 'blow your cover' and ask some relevant questions of each case *after* the candid recording has been made. Only then can you discover that some of your subjects were perhaps unsuitable and eliminate them. In some instances the relevant information can be obtained reactively from people who know the cases being primarily observed, without disturbing the latter: e.g. you can find out about children from their parents.

A final problem concerns unanalysable data. With some variables in spoken material, both when non-reactively obtained and elicited (Chapter 6), there may be a substantial number of instances where it is impossible to decide which value of the variable is present, so these have to be excluded and the total number of possible occurrences is thereby reduced. For instance in L2 learning research if you are counting a learner's use of the correct (i.e. native speaker) past tense ending on verbs you have no trouble with examples like:

> He call in yesterday

which on tape will be clearly detectible as wrong, nor with

> He called in yesterday

which is OK. But where the next word begins with a [d] — an instance of 'back-to-back phonemes' — it is more difficult. On tape

> ...then he dive down

and

> ...then he dived down

are almost impossible to distinguish, so you have to leave instances like this out of the account altogether (Dulay & Burt, 1982). The only remedy is to elicit examples in controlled contexts where what is said will be unambiguous.

5.4 Limitations on What Variables can be Quantified this Way

As far as language goes, you can readily get evidence of what people say or write by this technique, at the levels of sound, and spelling, and to some extent grammar and vocabulary. However it is not so easy to establish what they intend, or mean by what they say, when there is doubt, e.g. when they are children. This sort of insufficiency has encouraged among some linguists the idea that corpus data is not worth using *at all* and that individual introspection is the only real source of data (7.4).

Nor is it easy to quantify comprehension (whether or what someone has understood from hearing/reading), nor any other more 'hidden' variables, such as attitudes, or features of the language learning or performance *process* which interest psycholinguists and acquisition researchers. These would require obvious questioning or testing. So, although you might well prefer a non-reactive approach, often what you want to quantify rules it out.

In addition, even in the area of language production, some elements of language occur pretty infrequently and in practice are harder to study non-reactively, given real life constraints of time and money. Examples are particular vocabulary items and some grammatical constructions, like those where the English 'subjunctive' might be used — as in *If I were you*. You might have to record or go through far more material than is practicable to get any/enough instances of what you are trying to observe. Or you have to try and find a way of getting the information by non-reactive elicitation (along the lines of Labov's department store study, 4.4). Or you try to find a situation that naturally favours what you are after — e.g. to quantify questions you attend a courtroom.

Something that is increasingly widening the range of what it is practical to quantify naturalistically is the availability of large corpora of language transcribed and entered on computer. These can then be gone through automatically by concordancing computer programs seeking occurrences of particular words, syntactic constructions and the like that you wish to quantify. This is particularly easy in those corpora which have already been *tagged* with codes for things you are interested in counting — i.e. where special symbols have been inserted in the text to show where particular types of phrase or clause or the like occur. Such tagging either has to be done by hand by someone, or in some instances sophisticated computer programs can achieve nearly as accurate a tagging automatically (Leech, 1986).

Large corpora of *written* English are already available on computer, such as the *Brown Corpus* of a cross-section of varieties of adult American English and its British equivalent the *Lancaster-Oslo-Bergen (LOB)* Corpus. Others are the *International Computer Archive of Modern English (ICAME)*, the Birmingham *COBUILD* Corpus and the currently being assembled *British National Corpus*. Many literary texts are available on computer from the *Oxford Text Archive* (see further Butler, 1985a). Also of interest are the

Longman Corpus of Learner English, with written material from learners of English round the world, and the *CHILDES Corpus* of spoken language of normal and language disabled children, mainly American (Macwhinney & Snow, 1985). But both these probably contain a mixture of naturalistic and elicited language. The main shortage, of course, is of large corpora of naturalistic *spoken* language of all sorts, transcribed and put on computer. On the horizon are multimedia computer systems which may in the end enable researchers to manipulate and switch at will between original video recordings, transcriptions and data analyses all on screen.

5.5 The 'Avoidance' Problem

Then there is the matter of 'avoidance', which arises particularly with foreign learners of a language. It is known that, to varying extents, learners avoid using words, grammatical constructions and so on which they realise, or think, they don't fully know and might get 'wrong', from the native speaker's point of view. How much someone does this depends partly on their personality (natural caution, as against drive to express themselves at all costs) and partly on the sort of learning environment they are in — one where correctness is insisted on, or one where the emphasis is more on communication.

These instances of avoidance are hard to detect when there is no constraint on what learners have to say/write, which there can hardly be in naturalistic data gathering. You can only reveal their lack of knowledge of a particular word if you make them talk or write about a subject that requires that word — otherwise they may simply avoid topics for which they know they don't know the words. If learners of French know or think their grasp of the inflected future forms is weak, they may either not talk about the future, or use the periphrastic forms with *aller*. Instead of *Georges le fera* 'George will do it', they will produce *Georges va le faire* literally 'George is going to do it'. The latter is often as acceptable as the former, but is easier to learn. The learner only has to remember the six irregular forms of the present tense of *aller* to be able to make the future of any verb, whereas to produce the former version he/she has to remember not only the six future inflectional endings but also the irregular forms assumed by many verbs such as *faire* when used in the inflected future. Again you need a more reactive approach to force out some inflected future forms (see also Dagut & Laufer, 1985).

Of course you might argue that it is natural for learners to 'avoid', so you should not try and force them to say something they wouldn't normally attempt as you are then deliberately destroying naturalism. It depends what you decide you want to quantify in the end. 'Forced errors' can be very informative about how someone's underlying *ability* in a language is developing. We have to admit that there is more even to people's *productive* language ability than just what they actually say/write. It includes what they can or could produce as well as what they *do* (cf. the competence versus performance distinction, 1.2.2).

5.6 Ethics

Finally there is the ethical matter of privacy, rarely discussed in language study. This mainly arises in the gathering of spoken data to quantify. The most *casual* natural speech people produce is likely to be in private circumstances talking to friends and family. Obviously it would be an invasion of privacy to use hidden taperecorders, bugs and long-distance microphones recording such material, quite apart from which the recordings may be poor.

If young children are to be recorded this way it is necessary to obtain parents' permission, though of course if the children are then taped talking with a parent, as often is desirable, full naturalism is partly lost. Parents who know their children are being taped have been found to talk to them differently — e.g. providing more explicit expansions than usual of what the child says, to make what the child is trying to say more explicit for the benefit of the researcher who will listen to the tape (Fletcher & Garman, 1986: Chap. 6). In diary studies the point has been made that it may be unethical to occupy the time of the parent or caretaker writing the diary rather than attending to the child.

Is it ethical to use hidden taperecorders when talking to people in the *street*, or in shops and so on? Or indeed to candidly tape or video others talking in such 'public' places, if they are kept anonymous? Does it make a difference if they have a public function — e.g. shop assistant — as against just being an ordinary member of the public? This remains a grey area, similar to the issue of whether candid photography is acceptable. In both instances the problem is that people may feel their self-esteem damaged when a permanent record is made of them in what they may feel is not their best light.

One solution is to tape first and ask permission afterwards, thereby preserving naturalism of the actual data gathered. This is essentially the policy being used in the collection of a spoken English Corpus as part of the British National Corpus. Volunteers of a cross-section of social classes and regional origins in the UK are being asked to carry small taperecorders switched on in all spoken interactions they participate in during their everyday lives for a fixed period. After each interaction they seek the permission of the interlocutor to keep the taped material. Of course in a sense the result is again only *half* naturalistic, since one person in every interaction is aware from the start that they are being taped.

The analogous ethical question in the T context is whether it is right to collect spoken or written material from learners/patients in normal classes and use it for assessment (or indeed for research only) when you have not beforehand *told* them it will be so used. Probably most teachers and learners would feel this was at least 'unfair'. This may be a real issue in relation to the proposals for the assessment of first language English in the UK National curriculum (DES, 1989: 15.43), which states 'the assessment of speaking and listening should, where possible, be informal, continuous and incidental, applied to tasks carried out for curricular purposes'.

Further reading

Bennett-Kastor (1988: especially Chap. 5).
Seliger & Shohamy (1989: especially pp. 158–66).
Frankfort-Nachmias & Nachmias (1992: Chap. 9 and p. 79ff.).
Sommer & Sommer (1991: Chap. 2 and 4).
On transcription of child language: Bloom & Lahey (1978) and Wells (1985: 45–110 and appendices).
On ethics: Seliger & Shohamy (1989: 195), Milroy (1987: 4.4), Plutchik (1974: 309ff.).

6 Data for Quantification: Quasi-Naturalistic Interaction

6.1 Quasi-Naturalistic Data Gathering Exemplified

This general approach involves the cases knowing they are being quantified, but usually not exactly for what, and the whole thing being done in a conversational form very much like an ordinary interaction between people, or analogously in reading/writing. It is 'communication oriented' or 'message oriented' interaction (to borrow Dodson's (1985) term), with the focus on what is being talked about, not 'language oriented' or 'medium oriented' interaction where the focus would be on the words, sounds etc. being read or uttered.

The nature of 'authentic' communication has received much attention recently, especially in connection with foreign language teaching and testing, and the characteristics highlighted there are maximised in the present technique. *Ideally* the language activity would involve a genuine interchange of information and opinion rather than just provide data for measurement. It would be interactive between measurer and case, or one case and another, it would be contextualised in a natural situation, and it would have an element of the unpredictable. It represents the most naturalistic you can be, given the exposure of the fact that you *are* observing and measuring *something*. Examples are:

> Interviewing New Yorkers for half an hour in sociolinguistic research and using the tape of the conversation as a source for counting up, say, how many r's are pronounced.

> Talking to children in turn about some toys, designed to make it easy for you to elicit certain vocabulary/grammatical structures from them to see if they produce the adult forms or, if not, what others. The children are aware that they are being assessed in some way, the proceedings are videoed and each child's speech sample analysed. This

53

is commonly done for R and T purposes with normal and language disabled children (e.g. Karmiloff-Smith, 1979).

Using the *Bilingual Syntax Measure* (BSM, 1975) with foreign learners of English. This is in effect a set form of finding out about a learner's grammatical ability via conversation with the researcher about a set of pictures (explained with illustration in Oller, 1979: 308ff.). Questions are asked which should elicit certain grammatical structures in the reply, unless the learner is particularly clever at 'escaping'.

Asking adults to describe their apartment for you — in order to analyse the general rhetorical structure of their replies — e.g. how many describe it as if they were taking you on a tour of it? (Clark & Clark, 1977: 233ff.).

Setting some foreign learners to write an essay to help you with your research, in the normal course of a lesson. You do use the material to do an error analysis of selected linguistic variables e.g. faulty use of the articles *a* and *the*, or count up how many complex sentences are used. Or this could be used for T purposes as an 'informal' assessment (Rowntree, 1977).

Collecting a quasi-naturalistic corpus of videoed conversations between language learners and investigators/measurers as a source for categorising and counting occurrences of 'communication strategies'. Faerch *et al.*'s (1984) *PIF* corpus is such.

Setting children to talk with each other in pairs about how to get from A to B on a map, as a task overtly to be used for analysis. Problem-solving communication between members of each pair is analysed and rated.

Sitting in the back-kitchens of working class homes in Belfast chatting and, with permission, taping all the conversation that occurs. A form of *participant observation*.

Sitting in on a class of non-native speakers who are being trained to be English-speaking air hostesses. They have to 'role play' — taking the part of an air-hostess dealing with a passenger who refuses to stop smoking in a no smoking seat. You rate them for their communicative performance in English, including tact, persuasiveness etc. (Sometimes referred to as using a *job sample* to measure/assess people, or a *performance test*).

Observing teachers teaching French in the normal classroom in order to assess them.

A number of standard exams for T measurement now contain elements of this sort. For instance the *Royal Society of Arts* English proficiency exam involves an interview, as does the *Foreign Service Institute Oral Interview* (Bachman & Palmer, 1981). And of course the *BSM* is often used for T as well as R purposes, as is the *LARSP* profiling instrument for language disabled patients (Crystal, 1982), which usually relies on data gathered in this way. Hart *et al.* (1987) describe a test of communicative ability in French (*A Vous la Parole*), stretching over 4–5 class periods, consisting of a gamut of 'authentic' tasks — writing a formal letter and an informal note, informal discussion with peers, a job interview and so on. A teacher could use the same approach to measure *achievement* on some specific aspects of language just taught too. This approach is also popular in sociolinguistic and child language research. In the latter some elicitation done this way by mothers from their children is clearly on the hazy borderline between the present approach and what you would regard as fully naturalistic (Chapter 5).

A special instance of this approach is found in some kinds of so called 'action research', which can be conducted by teachers and therapists in the course of their normal work. For instance a teacher might tape or video him/herself in action in some normal classes, or get a colleague to sit in and take notes. Afterwards the data gathered is gone through with a critical, objective eye by the teacher with a view to finding new hypotheses about his/her own teaching, interactions with pupils etc., or testing some prior suspicion about what was going on. Such data may be examined purely qualitatively or may be quantified in some way. But the essence of it is that it is effectively obtained by a form of quasi-naturalistic *self*-observation (Hopkins, 1985).

In addition, some EVs for R measurement can be obtained in this way. For example in a sociolinguistic interview it might be relatively easy in the course of natural conversation to get the informant to coincidentally reveal his/her occupation or place of birth, both of which the researcher might then in fact use as EVs (or CVs) in his/her actual study.

6.2 Procedure and Sampling

As with the fully naturalistic approach, often many variables are measured from each recorded interview or whatever, either by counting up various specific things, with potential diagnostic usefulness, or obtaining overall ratings. In addition *open* observation may be made of anything of interest, not necessarily quantifiable. Similar issues may arise to do with transcription and sampling (see 5.2). But often 'materials' are more prominent in this approach than the former — e.g. dolls, pictures, videoed material and other stimuli created or introduced to guide talk or writing this way or that. Also the measurer may follow a set procedure, introducing predecided tasks and topics in a particular order. Or he/she may have preset questions but introduce them in any order, depending on what seems natural at the time (Milroy, 1987: 72).

One broad distinction to be found in work that obtains data for quantification in this way is between that where the measurer or his/her proxy, such as an interviewer or teacher other than him/herself, communicates (in speech or writing, by telephone etc. or face to face) *directly* with the case(s) being measured, and that where he/she predominantly observes communication *between* two or more cases. Clearly the former allows for more possible manipulation and control of the communication (see 6.3), especially in the one-to-one interview. The latter, characteristic of much participant observation, is often more realistic (9.9).

As in the naturalistic approach, regimes of time-sampling are used both in classroom research and for T purpose screening and diagnosis of individuals (Hoge, 1985). This is designed for the situation where the observer/measurer either cannot note down fast enough every relevant bit of communication or other behaviour as it occurs in a group, and full videoing/taping for analysis later is impracticable, or it is felt that there is no need to try to analyse and quantify everything.

What the observer does is to sample ongoing language-related behaviour strictly to the clock. For example he/she might note down, in a predecided set of categories on a prepared sheet, what the case of interest is doing/saying once every 40 seconds over a period of twenty minutes, e.g. the kind of speech act being performed at the moment (Brody *et al.*, 1984). If the interest is in all members of a group being observed, such as a class of fifteen in school, he/she may record the activity of a different person after each successive 40 seconds, in a set order, and after fifteen observations return to the first person and start round again in the same order (see Hopkins, 1985: 90ff. for examples of worksheets). Nerenz & Knop (1982) used this approach to quantify how much time was spent by different language classes on different kinds of activity, both 'engaged' and 'non-engaged' — the former being classwork, which might be in the native language or target language, reading, writing etc., the latter including categories such as waiting for the teacher, or 'off-task' (i.e. fooling around).

6.3 What Can Be Quantified

Clearly the quasi-natural approach can vary from being almost as natural and 'open' as non-reactive elicitation to being almost an artificial test (Chap. 8). Sociolinguistic researchers can just let the interview/conversation run more or less naturally on football or the price of things today and so on, or try and manoeuvre it without making it too obvious to make the person being observed use certain bits of language they are interested in. They can introduce set tasks and materials/stimuli and a more rigorous procedure to obtain what they want much more readily than in the purely non-reactive approach. A lot depends on the skill of measurers and their ability to think on their feet. They can choose to make the conversation/interview relatively *structured* or *unstructured*. Indeed sociolinguists commonly conduct interviews which contain both unstructured parts — conversation, getting the informant to tell a story etc. — and (afterwards) structured parts — such as getting the informant to read a passage aloud.

This shows one of the advantages over the purely naturalistic approach — you can ask questions designed to get at rarely occurring items and to stimulate particular genres of discourse. You can also prompt a reticent person to talk at all, though for some types of case, the greater formality of the situation may reduce how much they say. You can make efforts to stop a learner 'avoiding' (5.5), and ask people what they mean by something (assuming they can tell you!). Or you can simply use your prompting skills to get information you want in a shorter overall time. Also, if on analysis of a tape it seems that you after all have insufficient data from which to quantify a target variable, it may be easier in this approach to revisit cases to gather further data.

However, the variables you are able to quantify are still mainly overt, production performance ones, as so much of people's normal receptive response, e.g. to what they read, is covert. Also some linguistic elements remain hard to get people to use, even prompted by carefully worded questions (Milroy, 1987: Chap. 7). Such are pluperfect tenses like *I had already arrived*, questions, and particular vocabulary items. This can be seen just by thinking about how to formulate, in a quasi-natural conversation, questions that would elicit *needn't* or *don't need to*. Everything you can think of allows alternative responses, equally good communicatively, but which don't require use of one or other of the forms targeted. These alternative responses are called *escapes*. You may work in questions like *When is the latest you can get up in the morning?* in the hope of answers like *On a working day I get up at seven, but on a Saturday I needn't get up at all* (or *don't need to get up at all*). However, there are numerous escape responses possible, e.g. not mentioning Saturday, or using *have to* instead of *need*.

Finally, what you get by the quasi-naturalistic approach is not guaranteed to be so casual and spontaneous as what you may get by the pure naturalistic approach (see Romaine, 1984: 23). Milroy (1987: 3.2) discusses the differences between interviews and real life conversation — e.g. that, in the latter, narratives are usually offered spontaneously by a speaker, not embarked on in response to elicitation. You can never be quite sure how much those you communicate with, or that you are observing communicating with others, are adjusting what they say in accordance with the fact that they are being measured — this is a major issue in sociolinguistic research especially. This adjustment or 'accommodation' takes various forms. Partly it consists of increased formality of language, since 'being measured' is not an informal event. Partly it involves people thinking more about what is said and altering it to suit what they think is correct (conscious reference to rules), so the variables you get to quantify may be partly metalinguistic. Or possibly there is a deliberate adjustment of speech *away from* the interlocutor.

Brody *et al.* (1984), working on child discourse, in fact did an experiment just on this point. They put children in the age range 4–8 in groups in a room with a two-way mirror. Some groups were left alone to perform a play task of building a barn out of bricks for a toy horse, approximating the pure naturalistic approach of Chapter 5. Others had someone posing as a detached observer (who said nothing) in the room while they did the same task i.e. the quasi-naturalistic approach. All were actually observed through the two-way mirror. Significant differences were recorded in the frequency of children's use of different kinds of speech amongst themselves. With the overt observer present there were fewer 'directives' (commands and requests), less task-related talk generally, but more non-linguistic on-task play. The implications for anyone observing and quantifying language are clear. See Chapter 9 for more on these issues.

Particularly in a T context, data gathering of this sort often involves *simulation* or *role play*. How naturalistic this is may depend on the personality of the individuals involved. Certainly there will be differences from 'real' communication. As Klein-Bradley points out (1991), the non-linguistic concomitants of verbal action are typically absent. In a role play complaining about a faulty watch the fist banging and anger of real life may well be absent, and a new watch will certainly not be received at the end.

6.4 Control

A clear advantage of the present approach is that you can standardise the situation in which the interview or written activity takes place, and find out about cases' backgrounds and so on. Children can be observed in the same play area, for example. In short, you have the option of introducing some element of control-like elimination of unwanted variation in some of the facets of observation.

A particular way which the modicum of control the measurer has can be valuable is in that he/she can dictate the topic of communication. Thus in sociolinguistic interviews you can get data from all informants talking about the *same* things (their holidays, ghosts, etc.), which would not always be so easy in a non-reactive situation.

This must be done even more closely when trying to quantify communicative competence for T or R purposes. There it is particularly important to be able to control the exact content that the cases are trying to communicate, so that you can then quantify how much of it they actually did communicate. Consider setting learners to write or talk about their last holiday or their family, as in a *GCSE* oral French exam. The measurer has no idea of the facts that should be conveyed — so the learner is free to describe something totally fictitious that he/she happens to know the vocabulary for. Compare this with setting the task of explaining carefully to someone who doesn't know exactly how to assemble a provided set of parts into a mincer (the *task based elicitation* of Brown & Yule, 1983: 112). In a written T assessment, learners can all be got to write the same story from pictures, or produce an argument from the same set of points. This also improves reliability (20.4).

6.5 Ethics

Finally, since with this approach you are bound to make clear in advance that you are quantifying *something*, the general ethical problem of privacy or 'consent' does not arise. But, to compensate, of course, you run the risk of having some informants in an R investigation refuse to co-operate! There can also be problems where several cases are involved at once in an interview event. What if, in a quasi-naturalistic situation, you and your interviewee, who has agreed to participate, are joined by a friend of the interviewee. Do you stop and renegotiate agreement with the new participant? (Milroy, 1982b). What if something embarrassing starts emerging in front of the co-participants? (Dorian, 1982).

A rather grey area with respect to what is 'right' concerns how far you conceal or mislead the cases as to what you are *precisely* interested in. It is commonly felt to be justifiable to say you are investigating or assessing cases' language and simply to be vague about what precise variables you are going to quantify. But how far is it fair to do this for T purposes? It is *certainly* rather different to tell interviewees in an R investigation, say, that you want to know their opinions about the town, when in reality you are going to use what you tape to quantify aspects of their accents. You would of course prefer not to tell them that in advance in case they adjust their accents as a result. As usual, perhaps a fair compromise is to be vague or even misleading initially and, after the data has been gathered, ask if you can use it to quantify what you are really interested in 'as well'.

A final set of issues, not pursued here, affect all data gathering where the cases are aware that data has been gathered (including Chapter 7, 8). How far does the measurer have an obligation to allow access by cases to their transcribed or analysed data, or to the results of any research based on it? Should they be consulted on what is done with it later? Who else should have access to it, even if cases are anonymous? Who 'owns' the data?

Further reading

Seliger & Shohamy (1989: 158ff.)
Bennett-Kastor (1988: especially Chap. 5)
Wells (1985)
Milroy (1982b: Chap. 2, 3; 1987: Chap. 3–4)
Allwright (1988)
Frankfort-Nachmias & Nachmias (1992: Chap. 9 and p. 79ff.)
Sommer & Sommer (1991: Chap. 2 and 4)
Hopkins (1985: Chap. 6, 7)

7 Data For Quantification: Opinion

7.1 Opinion Gathering Exemplified

The opinion or judgment approach is reactive, and often cannot conceal what exactly is being quantified. The form of the interaction between measurer and subject/informant may be more test-like or more conversational. It differs from the quasi-naturalistic interaction of Chapter 6 in that it is more overtly focused on language (or other variables being quantified). The talk or written response is about something language-related, so we could say this approach has the elements of normal communication — it is 'message oriented', but the message is *about* the medium here. What differentiates it from the more artificial techniques of Chapter 8 is that it is not totally removed from everyday interaction, in that things to do with language are a real life topic of natural interaction. Examples:

Interviewing Moroccans and getting them to say whether they would speak French or Arabic talking to their boss at work (a form of *self report*). Or you get them to keep a diary of what language they speak to who when (cf. Milroy, 1987: 187ff.).

Getting English speakers to judge whether they would ever say *None of them have arrived yet* or not. This is designed to measure the incidence of plural verb agreement with words like *none* which purists would say should have singular agreement (i.e. *None of them has arrived yet*).

Getting learners to keep diaries recording when, how and with what success they consult dictionaries.

Getting English speakers to judge whether they think *None of them have arrived yet* is 'normal' English. (Also called an 'evaluation test' — Greenbaum & Quirk, 1970).

Getting Welsh speakers to say what word they use for what in English is *gate*, as just one item in a long 'questionnaire' by post. (Or, less directly, asking them 'What do you open in order to go into a field?').

This elicits the range of dialect words used in different parts of Wales (e.g. *gât, clwyd, llidiart*).

Getting teachers to rate the 'gravity' of the learner's error in *He going to school* as severe, moderate or mild.

Getting stutterers to say in what circumstances they find their stuttering most severe.

Getting learners of French to say whether they agree or disagree with each of a set of ten statements about different aspects of their attitude to France. Their total of answers favouring France gives a measure of their motivation to learn French (an *attitude inventory*).

Playing a tape of someone speaking in a Birmingham accent and asking native speakers of English to rate the speaker for intelligence on a seven point scale. Often many accents are presented and judgments on several different scales obtained in one such study.

Giving English learners of French one by one a passage in French to read and asking them to tell you, as they go along, what difficulties they are having and how they are trying to resolve them. These *think aloud* verbal reports can be used here to explore what receptive strategies the learner is using and in what proportions (cf. Cohen & Cavalcanti, 1987). They tap short term memory (in contrast with the other more retrospective examples above, which involve long term memory).

The opinion based approach is popular in dialectological, attitude and bilingualism research. Often *questionnaires*, whether postal or gone through in an interview, are of this sort. It is becoming more important in foreign language learning work in the form of 'self report' and 'think aloud' studies, where often taping, transcription and subsequent coding may be needed. It is used for T measurement, especially where the variables measured are metalinguistic (i.e. to quantify 'language awareness'). But 'self-assessment', where cases rate their own proficiency or achievement, is also becoming more common (see e.g. Oscarson, 1989, and DES, 1989, where it is recommended for assessment of the writing process in the UK English National Curriculum).

The same approach can be used to get at some variables you may use as EVs in investigations of all sorts. Some of these may be non-linguistic. For instance you might ask informants their age, first language and occupation in a 'background questionnaire' before getting them to do a language task, so as afterwards to be able to compare results for people of different first languages and so on (cf. Milroy, 1987: Chap. 5). You would do the same if you intended to control for these variables, e.g. by only dealing with data from informants with a particular first language.

The approach may also be used in the preparation of a manipulated IV in an experiment. For instance, suppose you want to see if people remember actual wording versus semantic content of what they read to a different extent dependent on the difficulty of what they read. You need some easy and difficult reading passages to constitute the two 'conditions': you will then get the subjects to read passages of both types, with questions after each to test what sort of information they have retained. A simple way to establish what *are* easy or difficult reading passages is to select some likely passages intuitively and get some competent speakers to read them and rate them for difficulty. You then use in the experiment the passages which on average are rated most or least difficult. Note that in this instance the focus of interest in doing the quantification initially has shifted from the people judging as the cases to the things being judged.

7.2 Procedure and Control

As with the quasi-naturalistic approach, the technique of opinion gathering can be relatively unstructured or 'open', or more structured. In the former instance, such as the 'think aloud' example, there is usually a set task for cases to work on when giving their opinions, but no specific set of questions to answer. The data usually has to be taped and picked through afterwards and probably analysed into categories.

The more structured version usually involves not only stimulus material such as written or spoken examples of language to comment on, or statements to agree or disagree with, but also a structured framework for responses, such as a set of questions gone through in the same way for every case. The more artificial structured items, presented with the same instructions to all cases, are usually as straightforward to categorise or score as any test items (8.2). Indeed many of the formats of manipulative item reviewed in 8.4 can be used here (Chambers & Trudgill, 1980: 24ff.). Needless to say, open and structured items are often intermingled.

In addition to obtaining uniformity in that everyone can be asked identical questions, you can also of course readily control the kind of person you ask, and the circumstances in which you ask (cf. 20.2). This means of course that you have to know what you are after much more clearly in advance of gathering data than with less structured approaches. This is despite the fact that, as the pioneer dialectologist Gilliéron is quoted as saying, 'The questionnaire, in order to be clearly the best, ought to be made after the survey' (Francis, 1983: 52).

An important thing to note and keep clear in your mind is the distinction between where several questions are used collectively to measure one variable, e.g. the attitude inventory example above, and where several questions are involved with each one designed to quantify something different, as in many questionnaires. The former is obviously best used where a sample of more than one response from each case seems appropriate in trying to quantify a variable. If attitudes to several things were being measured at once, with each attitude corresponding to four questions, it would be normal procedure to jumble the order of the individual questions so that the informant cannot so easily spot what attitudes are being elicited.

7.3 What is Quantified this Way

To compensate for limited naturalness of the structured opinion/ judgment approach to quantification, you have the advantage that you can elicit people's opinions specifically about a wide range of aspects of language behaviour without having to beat about the bush. But, of course, asking a straight question you may get a straight refusal to answer or reply. What I have called 'opinions' elicited in this way usually enable you to quantify one of three general kinds of variable. You need to be quite clear which sort you are after when using this approach, since the approach is harder to use properly for some than others.

Often cases are asked to comment evaluatively on the acceptability, friendliness and so on of something they or others say or write or do (e.g. examples of language use, or methods of teaching). This is straightforward quantification of attitude variables. Indeed this is the main approach used to get information on variables of this sort. It is however open to problems of truth or naturalism if cases do not report their actual attitudes but those they think the researcher wants to hear for some reason. Naturalistic and quasi-naturalistic approaches are not so often used, though it is quite possible to observe or elicit attitudes voiced in those modes.

Secondly, cases may be asked to speak factually about what they (or others) actually say (or write or do), so you can quantify their ability to talk about these things in some way. This is for quantification of metalinguistic (and metacommunicative) variables, including knowledge of linguistic terms and general awareness *about* language. Again this is the main way of getting data on this, and is especially suited to it since giving an 'opinion' inherently involves talking *about* something, so has a built-in 'meta-' element. However, it is also possible to approach this via the quasi-naturalistic technique of the last chapter, as when the researcher sits in with families at mealtimes and tapes their conversation with a view to quantifying the amount of wordplay and comment on language matters that went on.

Thirdly, cases may asked to speak factually about what they (or others) actually say or write or do, in order to find out about what they say, write or do. That is, the opinion approach is used to access natural perform-ance/competence variables or 'use'. This is the trickiest and most controversial of the three uses: it involves special assumptions that will not always be justified. Broadly these are assumptions about difficulty — that the required information is capable of being both accessed and verbalised — and truth — that people will report honestly.

Difficulty of access relates to what aspects of language behaviour are at a conscious level, or how far people can have their consciousness 'raised' by special training. Young children or seriously language disabled speakers may not be able to report about much of their behaviour. However, it is usually assumed that normal adults can report on many variables related to the fairly superficial features of production which more naturalistic methods also supply evidence on. The advantage here is that specific points can be targeted with no possibility of 'escapes'.

Furthermore, such cases can usually say something relevant to more covert variables, such as what they mean by saying something, what they understand or misunderstand receptively, and some deeper aspects of processing, such as what they do to try and recall a word they know but momentarily cannot get hold of (retrieval strategies). In some people's usage the term 'strategies' is reserved for aspects of language processing that are more or less conscious and so amenable to classification and quantification from self-report data (this is more the foreign language learning use of the term rather than the psychologist's, which is broader).

Currently this approach is being increasingly used with foreign learners, who seem often to show a greater ability than might have been expected to introspect usefully about their conscious learning strategies and commu-nication processing activities for the language they are learning, as well as what they say in it. There is however considerable variation between individual cases in the amount of information they are able to access. 'Anecdotal' information by parents about their children's speech comes in for heavy criticism, on the other hand (Bennett-Kastor, 1988: 26ff.). And with 'think aloud' studies there is always the possibility that the processing reported on gets done differently due to the very fact that the case is trying to think about it at the same time.

As far as difficulty of *verbalising* opinions goes, we have to try to eliminate problems for the cases in how to express their judgments, otherwise metalinguistic knowledge is being quantified as well as or instead of the language knowledge we are interested in. As an example, suppose we ask someone to supply a preposition which often goes with the verb *look*. If we are asking a non-native speaker of English who we happen to know has been taught in a way that makes him/her familiar with grammatical terminology, then this is a way of getting at their linguistic competence — do they know we often follow *look* with *at* and so on? But if we ask a normal adult native speaker, who can be assumed to know perfectly well the linguistic facts but may well know few linguistic terms like 'preposition', this is a measure of metalinguistic knowledge. What you quantify depends on what you can assume (cf. 22.2.2). In think aloud tasks the problems of verbalisation per se are particularly hard to remove as they arise at the same time as actually doing the task.

Finally the truth gap between opinion and actual performance may be different depending on what aspect of language you are measuring. It may be quite wide on sensitive grammatical matters which are often treated prescriptively in school, such as singular or plural verb agreement with collective nouns. Educated native speakers are likely to say they say *The committee has decided to agree* but to actually say *The committee have decided to agree* in natural conversation, because the latter is often cited as an 'error' by prescriptively minded grammarians. Thus what you think is a factual report of usage is actually tinged with an attitudinal element of what the cases think they *ought* to be saying. This can even work in reverse where working class men exaggerate claims of use of *non*-standard forms (Trudgill, 1974).

All this in turn means you may be quantifying metalinguistic knowledge again — this time of overt grammatical rules. However, research shows that in other areas there may be close correspondence between opinion and use. For instance native speakers' judgments of how often words are used in English have been shown to be systematically related to (though not identical with) frequencies determined from actually counting up how often the words are used in large masses of material (Carroll, 1971).

In short, there are many ifs and buts about using opinion data as evidence of actual performance variables. Opinion about use, though interesting to researchers in its own right, is not usually the *same* as actual use.

7.4 Individual Measurer Introspection

Finally, a special instance of this approach worth mentioning is that where the researcher acts as both measurer and case — i.e. he/she gathers *self* self-report, or reflexively introspective, data about language behaviour of him/herself or others. This has long been the staple means of gathering empirical information used by pure linguists, who tend to resolve problems like 'Can you say *It is apparent John will win*, or must it have *that* in?' by simply reflecting on it and coming to a personal decision. This goes along with Chomskian ideas about speakers having an underlying invariant competence (1.2.2). Though working well on clear-cut matters in the standard form of adult language, this approach has justifiably been criticised as not really being sufficiently objective for the tricky instances of marginally possible sentences that sophisticated theories of language often turn on these days, even given the special training of the linguist (cf. on bias and validity 21.2.1). At the very least you need the 'inter-subjective' opinions of several speakers of the same dialect, preferably not ones who know what hypotheses hang on the decision (see Prideaux, 1984: 4ff.).

A similar approach to variables in a different sphere was used by psycholinguist R. Harris (1984), in a piece of research conducted when he was lecturing for a semester in Brazil. Each day he wrote down three notable events he had been involved in on the preceding day — one where he used Portuguese, one where he used English, and one non-linguistic one. He also judged the amount of 'affect' (emotive involvement) he experienced during each (on a seven point scale). Amongst other things he found the Portuguese events scored higher affect ratings than the others. Both the key variables here, the language employed and the amount of affect, were therefore categorised from purely introspective data of the researcher.

Further reading

Seliger and Shohamy (1989: 166–76)
L. Milroy (1987: especially Chap. 3)
Henerson (1987)
Chambers & Trudgill (1980: Chap. 2)
Francis (1983: Chap. 3 and 5)
Prideaux (1984: 212ff.)
Matsumoto (1994)
Sommer & Sommer (1991: Chap. 8 and 9)
Frankfort-Nachmias & Nachmias (1992: Chap. 10 and 11)
Burroughs (1971: Chap. 12)
Gardner & Lambert (1972: Appendix A)

8 Data For Quantification: Manipulation

8.1 Measurement via Manipulation Tasks Exemplified

This approach to quantifying linguistic variables vastly overshadows the other three in terms of the extent to which it is written about, under the heading of 'language testing', especially in relation to T measurement. It is reactive, usually obviously focused on some particular aspect of language and, although it tails off into measurement of the types described in Chapters 6 and 7, is distinguished in principle by the fact that the measurement event does not involve 'communication' in any everyday sense between measurer and case. There is no natural conversational interaction or written communication nor any interchange of a message/content in the normal sense, except about the instructions for doing the task. As Lesser puts it (1978: 68) 'The communication is the act not the content': the measurer asks the case to perform a series of more or less artificial tasks *involving* language. The activity is entirely focused on the bits of language being used, so is 'medium' oriented. At best the message *is* the medium! Examples are:

> Asking a child to pick the right picture (out of four offered) to suit the word supplied by the investigator, to see if the child knows the meaning. The *British Picture Vocabulary Scale* (*BPVS*, similar to the American *Peabody Picture Vocabulary Test*, Dunn *et al.*, 1982) is a standard, progressively harder, set of such questions, designed to measure vocabulary knowledge. There are similar tests for foreign learners.

> Asking a child to exactly repeat some sentences which the tester speaks, to see what changes are introduced. This is also used with adults, when you ask a speaker of a non-standard dialect of a language to repeat sentences spoken to him/her in the standard. It enables you to detect and quantify features at all levels of language (sounds, grammar, vocabulary etc.) that may differ (or, with a T perspective, be 'wrong') in the testee's system.

Asking people to respond with the first word that comes into their heads when the tester speaks a word (*word association test*). This is used with adults, children, foreign learners and pathological cases. By classifying the responses in various ways and comparing them with the most frequent associates produced by normal adult native speakers you can measure aspects of the vocabulary competence of the cases (the semantic and pragmatic links between words in the memory).

Attaching electrodes to certain muscles in a native speaker's face and asking him/her to speak certain words clearly, in order to measure the electrical activity of particular muscles when particular sounds are spoken. In instrumental phonetics work various pieces of apparatus are available and can be attached to measure other things like pressure of air flow from the mouth and nose when particular sounds are uttered, and so on.

Asking people to listen to minimal pairs of words like *ship* and *sheep* spoken on tape and say if they think they are the same or different. This could be used with foreign learners, children, or people with hearing defects to see if they can hear the difference between distinctive English vowel sounds.

Asking people to fill the gap in sentences like *Coal is got out of a mine, but stone out of a* ___. This could be a test of foreign learners' vocabulary, or used with native speakers to elicit dialect words.

Getting native speakers to listen to a set of sentences like *The elephant chased the camel* and later offering them sets of alternatives like:

> *The camel chased the elephant*
>
> *The elephant was chased by the camel*
>
> *The elephant chased the camel*
>
> *The camel was chased by the elephant*

and asking testees to choose which they think they heard earlier. This is a typical psycholinguistic test of *recognition memory* which would usually be done as part of experiments involving IVs and DVs. For instance it could be involved in comparing whether more mistaken choices are made when the nouns in the sentence are of one sort versus another: what if the above sentences all contained *man* where the word *camel* appears?

Getting foreign learners to read as much as possible in the time given of doctored passage of English and cross out all the words that don't fit as they go along (an *intrusion* or *cloze elide* test of reading speed).

Getting native speakers to listen to two-syllable nonsense words like *kiki* and *toto* which have been artificially synthesised by a computer and press keys marked A or B on the computer depending on whether they hear stress on the first syllable or the second. The computer might not only record which key was pressed for each nonsense word, but how long the subject took to press it after the word was heard (*response time* or *latency*), as an indication of how doubtful the testee was. If the synthetic words were arranged to have only a slight difference of pitch between one syllable and the other, then this would measure the subjects' perception of stress in relation to what is actually just pitch difference.

Asking some bilingual speakers of French and English to write down in two minutes as many words as they can think of in either language that relate to the topic of 'travel' (or that begin with *li-*, or some such). The more words they come up with in one of the languages as against the other, the more that language can be regarded as the dominant one for them (a *spew test*).

Getting a child to act out the meaning of *Donald is easy to bite*, using two dolls to see if he/she thinks of *Donald* as the subject doing the biting or the object of that action, as in adult English (Chomsky, 1971).

Clearly much R quantification in psycholinguistics and phonetics is of this sort, as well that of children, foreign learners and language impaired cases. Often the 'instruments' have to be tailor made for a specific investigation. Also many 'standard' T purpose tests and exams exist designed to quantify various collections of variables (e.g. parts of the *TOEFL* and *Cambridge First Certificate* proficiency exams for English as a foreign language). These have been designed by professional testers and have usually been piloted and revised and had their reliability and validity investigated (Chap. 19–23). Other such instruments are often made up by particular schools or teachers to quantify achievement in a particular T situation.

In addition, some variables destined for use as EVs in research may be quantified in this sort of way, e.g. intelligence or field dependence of subjects. Or indeed language dominance in bilinguals, as measured above, might typically be an EV rather than a DV. Again, this approach may be used to control for a variable (CV), in the sense of eliminating its effect in the design of an R investigation. For instance Blanchard (1984), wishing to do an experiment where Kindergarten children learned words in different ways and were tested, to see which way worked best, gave them two other tests beforehand so as to ensure all his subjects started from a common base.

He got all the children to read out the list of words he was going to use in order to exclude those cases who already could read some of them, and he also excluded any children who could not name all the letters used in the words of the experimental list. This he took as an indication of 'readiness' to learn the words at all.

8.2 Procedure and Control

The hallmark of the present approach is control of many aspects of the measurement event which, though it could be introduced to some extent in the other techniques, is often carried to the extreme in the present instance. There is usually a careful explicit 'procedure' which keeps the situation in which the quantification data is gathered uniform. Cases all sit in the same room or laboratory to do the tasks, receive the same administration individually or in a group, have the same tester, the same wording of the instructions, the same amount of practice beforehand, the same time allowed, the same feedback as they proceed, and so on. This should improve reliability (19.3.3, 20.4).

The core of the measuring 'instrument' is a carefully structured set of 'stimuli' (items, questions etc.), and a standard 'task' to perform on them, perhaps with the involvement of some 'apparatus' — computer (J. Alderson, 1987), tachistoscope, audiometer etc. A lot of work goes into devising all this. But the compensation is that the 'data analysis' phase afterwards is often virtually nonexistent. All you have to do is apply a mechanical scoring and totalling procedure (Chap. 13, 14).

The uniformity implicit in this approach is often beneficially specific. If you want to know what proportion of the time Belfast speakers say words like *Catholic* and *bad* with the a pronounced [ɑ:] as in standard southern British English *cart*, as against some other way, and you use the approaches of Chapter 5 or 6 then you probably won't get examples of different speakers all speaking the *same* set of relevant words (J. Milroy, 1982). Only with a more artificial test procedure will you get them all to say the *same* set list so you can check what vowel they use in each, and hence get a more rigorous score and, incidentally, be able to compare individuals fully on pronunciation of all individual words. The price you pay of course is in that you cannot be sure to get very naturalistic speech. As McEntegart and Le Page remark (1982: 115) '...one has to choose between statistically comparable but dehumanised "answers" and linguistically and socially informative conversations'. Some language tests and exams used tradition- ally for T purposes do not retain this property anyway — those that offer a set of items but allow testees to *choose* from it their own smaller set of items to respond to.

The presence of these features of 'control' leads some writers to refer to any work involving such tests as an 'experiment' (e.g. Milroy, 1987; Bennett-Kastor, 1988), though I think this label is really best reserved for overall designs of R investigations of a certain type (3.1.3). A therapist may assess an individual's vocabulary with the *BPVS* test in reasonably controlled circumstances. A sociolinguist may compare the competence in Spanish of first and second generation Puerto Rican immigrants to the USA with a carefully administered cloze gap-filling task, but neither of these are strictly 'experiments'. The confusion arises simply because it is quite *common* for non-experimental research to be able to control for few potentially interfering factors, and to involve variables quantified by the means described in Chapters 5–7. On the other hand experiments normally involve high control, and DV data is often elicited by manipulative tests and suchlike procedures which are systematically made or done in different forms to constitute the conditions of an IV.

Often in this approach a large set of items or repeated tasks, scored separately and then totalled, collectively measures one variable: the term *objective test* is particularly applied to these 'multi-item' manipulative instruments. The large sample of separate bits of evidence thus collected from each case makes this approach very 'reliable' (Chap. 19–20). Once again, of course, you have to differentiate clearly in your mind where there are in fact items or subsets of items, perhaps intermingled, designed to quantify *separate* variables, e.g. in standard tests like the *TOEFL* which have subsections to quantify grammatical competence, comprehension, etc. separately.

Again, you need to be clear if a set of items in fact contains two or more *subsets* constituting the different conditions of an EV. For example, if speakers' speed of processing (DV) of two types of sentence (EV/IV) is being tested in a psycholinguistic experiment, then you would typically present subjects with a series of sentences of both types mingled but of course disentangle and examine the reaction times for the two sets separately after (see also the *elephant* sentences and pitch example above).

8.3 What you can Quantify by this Means

The examples above only illustrate a small sample of the types of language manipulation that have been devised, but they do show the great scope for various kinds of artificiality. The whole framework in which the language appears in such tests is often unreal, usually with disconnected questions and fragmentary responses. As a consequence, it can be said that with this sort of test you elicit not 'language behaviour' but 'language-like behaviour'. As Greene remarks (1972: 130): 'Subjects will try to develop problem solving strategies appropriate to the experimental task, some of which may be quite remote from linguistic skills as normally used'. Haertel (1985) for instance reports research showing there may be a special reading strategy used to read a passage when it is known that multiple choice comprehension questions follow.

Furthermore, tests of this sort are often done in impersonal surroundings with strangers and, having the rigorous procedure described above, can be stressful events. Often too they are written. So we are likely to get formal rather than casual language reflected, and unless we are careful all such tests will be partial tests of reading ability, whether we want them to be or not. And there may be possible conscious reference to rules rather than spontaneous language from the 'testees' — i.e. quantification of meta-linguistic knowledge occurs. Thus Dulay *et al.* (1982: 225) report apparent differences in the order of acquisition of various elements of English by foreign learners depending on whether they were measured by communicative elicitation (Chap. 6) or manipulative tests.

It is important to be aware of this in the T context where evaluation of individuals goes on. Unfortunately it is hard to generalise about whether cases assessed by a more naturalistic approach will do better or worse on an assessment of supposedly the 'same' variable by more artificial means. On the one hand Lesser (1978: 68) remarks in the therapy context 'There are patients whom, from their normal small-talk in the waiting room, one is surprised to find attending a speech therapy clinic, until the structured situation of a formal assessment shows that they cannot cope with this removed level of language unsupported by the natural context of appropriateness'. Similarly the superficially easy task of just repeating a stimulus sentence spoken by the tester can be quite hard for young children, because for them the utterance lacks a realistic source in an actual message they wish to convey.

On the other hand if you examine foreign learners' of English performance on conventional tests made up of a series of multiple choice grammar items like:

> Mary _____ her new dress

    like
    alike
    likes
    liking

it has been found that they often score higher on use of the correct verb form than they do if measured by naturalistic techniques. This presumably arises from the fact that in the unnatural circumstances of this sort of test these testees have less distraction (no need to think about content/meaning of sentences as in real communication), more time to recall overt metalinguistic rules they may have learnt and apply them, and of course the variable being quantified is not so concealed. Thus what gets quantified is something a bit off the linguistic variable we were (probably) interested in, and probably also reflects a non-linguistic variable 'ability to do m/c tests' which has nothing to do with real life speaking and understanding language (cf. further 22.2.2).

These characteristics of the present approach are not necessarily bad, however. There are some applications where you actually might *want* to quantify the somewhat artificial, language-like behaviour these tests tend to elicit. For example in much traditional foreign language teaching, e.g. until recently the teaching of French in the UK, there is little emphasis on learners learning to communicate naturally in the target language, but a lot of decontextualised repetition of sentences, rote learning of lists of vocabulary items and so on. Hence it would be 'fair' for the tests of language ability and exams which accompany this learning not to be designed to elicit and quantify natural language, but rather to test the sort of somewhat artificial language behaviour, tinged with knowledge of explicit rules, that the instruction has emphasised.

This leads to a more general point about artificiality. It must be said that some tasks of the manipulative type, though not involving natural communication, are nevertheless at least *familiar* to many native speakers and foreign learners in the form of language games and exercises which they may have encountered, either for pleasure or in school. For example, exercises involving supplying words to fill gaps in sentences are common in the foreign language classroom simply as *practice* material, and are the basis of the UK TV wordgame *Blankety Blank*. Supplying the word to fit the picture with the use of 'flashcards' is a common game for children in or out of class. Word association of various sorts is the basis of many TV word games for the entertainment of native speakers e.g. in the UK *Lucky Ladders, Three Little Words, Password*. In the same vein, much of what is available in computerised form as language practice material for the native speaker child or the foreign learner ('CALL' programs) is again in multiple choice and/or gap filling formats identical to those used for tests.

Furthermore, the range of manipulation tests/tasks is so great that it is hard to generalise about how well they reflect natural use of language.

Greenbaum & Quirk (1970), for example, constructed rather clever 'operation tests', as they called them, which seemed to give better evidence of everyday usage than their superficially more natural 'judgment tests' (of my 'opinion' type). According to Lesser (1978: 68) supplying a word in completion of a sentence is a *bit* closer to real-life language use than supplying the same word in an object naming test, and hence proves less difficult for aphasic speakers.

It is usually felt that tasks which are contextualised and *integrative*, i.e. involve connected speech or writing which has to be manipulated at several levels by the testee (meaning as well as form), are less distant from natural language use. At the other extreme are tasks that overtly focus on more disjointed bits of language (words or sentences in isolation) and are designed to quantify performance on sounds or words or a grammatical construction etc. (*discrete point tests* — see further 14.1).

Nearest to real communication are those integrative tests that Oller (1979) calls 'pragmatic' tests because they require real world knowledge as well. They involve continuous passages as stimuli and tasks such as filling a series of gaps left, say, at seven word intervals in a continuous text (*cloze* task), writing to dictation, or retelling a story back to the tester. Though such tasks do not involve a genuine transfer of unfamiliar information between testee and anyone else — the information gap 'message' vital to real communication — they do seem to require use of many of the linguistic and pragmatic skills of real communication. But there will always be some doubt about how far what is elicited in these tests reflects a person's actual everyday use of the language in normal communication and not just their ability to do that sort of task. They could only be regarded as 'indirect' measures of communicative competence compared with the more 'direct' ones of Chapter 5, 6.

Perhaps the main benefit of quantification via manipulation is that it enables you to force out of people at least *some* relevant evidence for things you would never get data on in any other way. It is usually essential in measuring variables that are covert and at the *sub*conscious level, such as any areas of comprehension, receptive processing and memory, certain aspects of production, and variables like language learning aptitude. Furthermore, repeated information on the same thing can be forced out of cases, and they can be made to attempt things they would not spontaneously attempt, arguably enabling some light to be thrown on their ability underlying their customary performance (cf. 1.2.2).

In production, for example, such manipulation tests can prevent cases escaping or avoiding (except by leaving items out). Cases can be forced to respond with forms they may realise they haven't mastered and would normally 'avoid', or that are totally new to them (though some would regard it as 'unfair' to test the latter). Nevertheless researchers still find it hard to elicit data on some specific structures etc. in production as real speakers have an uncanny habit of finding some way of avoiding using just the structure or word the researcher is interested in, however cleverly he/she attempts to elicit it (Garnham, 1985: 2).

In psycholinguistics a great deal of work has involved showing subjects sentences with carefully controlled, highly specific, structures, vocabulary etc. (like the *elephant* sentences above) and then measuring responses either in the form of how quickly they judge the sentences true or false or how successfully they later recall or recognise them, or the like. In various ways the resulting time and percent correct scored throw light on difficulty of understanding, or remembering or otherwise processing different kinds of structure or whatever.

Finally, if you wish, you can choose to rig a test to heighten certain 'field of reference' properties of your measurement which might or might not occur naturally otherwise — see Chapter 10.

8.4 Types of Language Manipulation

Many subclassifications of manipulative tests/tasks/instruments are possible, in addition to those by the variable or case quantified, or the T or R function (Chap. 1–3). Commonly they are grouped and labelled by some key feature of *how* they work — i.e., in the jargon, choices in respect of test method 'facets' (see further Bachman, 1990: Chap. 5 for a detailed analysis of test facets and, for an introduction to 'facet theory', Canter, 1985).

One such feature is the procedure by which they are administered, and the circumstances in which the task is done: so we have 'timed tests', 'group tests', 'blind tests', 'take-home tests' and so on. Also relevant are the type of materials/stimuli provided. The stimuli may be non-linguistic, such as a picture to say something about or objects to name, or if linguistic, as we have seen, they may be anything from single sounds or words to sentences or a connected passage or conversation. Further, stimuli may be either heard or read by the testee, and, for foreign learners or bilinguals, perhaps in a different language from the response.

The task, usually repeated in a multi-item test, also can be of a great variety of general types. Common ones are: *Completion*, i.e. filling a gap in the stimulus, in the loosest sense including completing a sentence or word, providing a rejoinder to a remark, or completing a cloze passage. *Substitution* of a word or phrase and so on for one in the stimulus, e.g.

changing a singular noun to the plural. *Order-change* of words or letters in the stimulus, including solving anagrams, reorganising jumbled sentences into a coherent text, and 'transformations' like turning a statement into the corresponding question (Greenbaum and Quirk's 'operation test'). *Deletion* of what does not fit in the stimulus is some way, such as spotting the odd word out in five given, or an intrusion test. *Matching*, i.e. indicating what matches a stimulus or set of stimuli in some way, e.g. matching opposite words, the sentence that describes the picture, the object that the sentence refers to, the answer to the question about a story just read, the definition to the word. Similar is *translation*, where individual words or whole texts have to be provided with equivalents in another language. *Imitation* or 'repetition' of some stimulus word/sound/sentence etc. is perhaps a special case of matching. It can be identical, where the stimulus just has to be repeated, or with a change of mode, e.g. something heard has to be written (dictation). After a time delay it is a matter of 'recognition' or 'recall'. *Monitoring*, i.e. watching out for something, such as a particular sound in an utterance or word in a text, and indicating as soon as it occurs.

In psycholinguistic research often tasks are more complicated. For instance in studies using 'priming' there will be a series of stimuli and subtasks for each test item, only the response to the last stimulus being of interest. In a typical experiment, after simply reading silently with attention pairs of words like *bark-dog* and *bang-doll* subjects are asked to say aloud *darn-bore*. A whole set of little series like this constitute a test that often elicits spoonerism data. There is a tendency, for example, for subjects to read out the last pair as *barn-door* (Baars, 1992).

Responses can be classified in similar ways to those described above for stimuli. They may be non-linguistic, such as touching or moving objects in accordance with verbal instructions (the *token test*); often in psycholinguistic work time taken to respond ('latency') is crucial. But additionally most manipulation tasks can differ in level of support provided for the response, and so how much the testee has to supply. Three degrees may be recognised in order of increase in the amount the testee has to 'add'. (1) *Alternative response* items require a choice from just two alternatives, including a yes/no or true/false (verification) response or, in a T context, a choice between the correct and incorrect answer. (2) Slightly less supported are *multiple-choice* tests with so-called 'fixed/closed-ended/selected response' items. They vary depending on how many alternatives are offered, though four is commonest (of which in a T context one will be correct — the 'key' — and the others 'distractors'/'foils'). (3) Finally *free/supply/open/constructed response* tests/items involve no prompt about what the response might be.

For foreign learners, children and language disabled cases, often these levels of support constitute successive degrees of 'difficulty' of item formats. For competent native speakers they simply represent a gradation from highly determined formats (testing 'convergent' ability only — Rowntree, 1977: 149ff.) to less determined ones allowing the case more scope for 'originality'.

The gamut of detailed facets of technique on which tests can be classified is considerable. Choices on any of them may have subtle effects on the precise nature of the data obtained about some language variable you are really interested in.

8.5 Ethics

Ethical questions arise in this approach where the real purpose of a task is not made clear. In psycholinguistic experiments, for example, quite often it is desirable for the real nature of a task only to be revealed in the middle of the activity. An example would be where subjects are set to perform some tasks on some words (e.g. saying what the opposite of each is), with the impression given that this knowledge is the variable being quantified. It only emerges later that this is only part of the story when they get an unexpected further test to see how well they can recall the words so the researcher can compare the effect on recall of the different kinds of task performed on them. Effectively what subjects perceived initially as the DV turned out to be the IV. Subjects will feel tricked, but at least they do find out by the end what was really being quantified. Opinions vary on the acceptability of, and necessity for, such 'deception' (Plutchik, 1974: 311).

A different sort of problem arises in connection with captive subjects, and applies also to data gathering as in Chapters 6 and 7. It is questionable, for example, if schoolchildren really *feel* themselves free to refuse to participate in data gathering for some research project, even if they can, when it is done in school time. Often a test or questionnaire is passed off as tantamount to extra schoolwork. Despite the possible inconvenience, cases should be convinced of their freedoms and encouraged to exercise them.

Further reading

There is no shortage of specialist works on testing in the language teaching sphere. Most of the considerations discussed in these works are equally relevant to the construction of tests for *any* T or R application. See for example:

Seliger & Shohamy (1989: 176ff.), Hughes (1989), Oller (1979), Heaton (1975), Valette (1967), van Els *et al.* (1984: 15.5f.).

Language pathology tests described: Caplan (1992: Chap. 10).

The test-like tasks used in psycholinguistic research tend not to be discussed collectively, but piecemeal, in reports of individual pieces of research. For partial overviews and further references see: Garman (1990: 110), Baars (1992).

A sociological reference: Sommer & Sommer (1991: Chap. 15).

Accounts of standard published measures, esp. American, mainly for T use with native speakers/foreign learners/language disabled cases: Buros (1978), Sweetland & Keyser (1986).

Accounts of English as a Foreign Language tests and exams: West & Davies (1989), C. Alderson *et al.* (1987).

Accounts of UK child and clinical tests: the catalogue of NFER-Nelson.

9 Maximising Naturalness in the Data-Gathering Phase of Language Quantification

9.1 Getting the Most Naturalness Out of Reactive Techniques

So far I have outlined four general approaches to data collection for measurement of language-related variables. Given that they range from the non-reactive approach, yielding 'natural' data but with little 'control', to reactive ones, with various kinds and degrees of 'control', but also artificiality, we may wonder if the ideal — a combination of the two — is possible. In pursuit of this idea I shall now briefly review some ways (mostly already touched on here and there) in which you can try to make reactive approaches (Chap. 6–8) give as much evidence as possible of natural behaviour. 'Natural' language, similar to what is termed in foreign language learning 'authentic' and in sociolinguistics 'vernacular', is a difficult term to define precisely. We mean by it here the type of language first acquired by a speaker and not the result of excessive self-monitoring, though it does vary in different situations.

In reviewing these me must bear in mind that there are of course some circumstances where you are interested in quantifying formal language, metalinguistic knowledge and verbal manipulative skills for their own sake and not just as indirect evidence for more natural use/behaviour. In that instance you will not need to apply these means. Also, trying to ensure naturalism is never the only requirement. Some wider aspects of good quantification are taken up later in discussing reliability and validity (Chap. 19–23): the points discussed here are not necessarily incompatible with some degree of controlled elimination of other unwanted factors.

Apart from choosing the least reactive techniques you can, given what you are trying to quantify and the control you need, eight fairly distinct ploys stand out. They are not all applicable in all instances, of course. They are each related to one or more of the key features of the 'measurement event' (4.2): the measuring instrument *per se* (materials and task), the cases, the measurer, and the circumstances.

9.2 Realism of the Instrument

It usually helps to make what the person being measured has to do as lifelike as is possible. This tends to happen anyway with the techniques of Chapter 5 and 6 above. But some tests, especially as used for R purposes in psycholinguistics, seem to carry artificiality to unnecessary extremes. So for example you might avoid using stimulus sentences which are barely English. Witness the psycholinguistic experiment in which the DV was quantified by having subjects indicate as quickly as possible the truth or falsity of sentences like *star is above plus* in relation to diagrams picturing stars and plus signs in various configurations. In real life you would at the very least say *The star is above the plus* (Clark & Clark, 1977: 102).

Similarly, from this point of view, in tests of word memory and the like, setting the subjects to memorise and be tested on real words from obscure languages or even realistic but nonexistent English words such as *stup*, or *boltion* is better than using, say, sequences of three random letters such as *SQG*. Again, reading tests using continuous text, gathered from authentic sources, will be closer to real life than those with sets of disconnected made-up sentences, and so on.

In dialectological research this matter arises in the issue of whether it is better to allow data gatherers to formulate their own precise questions to elicit the required dialect forms, or to follow a predecided uniform set of questions. The former 'free-collector' approach allows the gatherer to make the interaction with an informant much more natural, by altering the exact forms of questions to suit the circumstances, interviewee etc., though the latter 'rigorist' position has more control-like advantages (Francis, 1983: 86ff.).

In foreign language learning research, and T purpose measurement, this principle surfaces as a common requirement that tests of communicative competence, often done by quasi-naturalistic elicitation, involve spoken and written tasks which incorporate a genuine 'information gap' (e.g. Brown & Yule, 1983: 111). If information is to be conveyed by a testee about a picture, the *addressee* should not be able to see the picture too, or the verbal conveyance of information about it is not realistically motivated. Indeed young children may be non-plussed by a request to convey information which is patently known to the addressee, just to 'display' language, and say nothing. Furthermore it is desirable to make the content to be communicated lifelike and interesting (as Hart *et al.*, 1987, tried to do; cf. West, 1991). Compare the rather dry and unrealistic information to be transferred in Brown & Yule's suggested regime (1983: 152) where testees communicate about the precise relative positions of lines and shapes on a sheet of paper.

9.3 Familiarity of the Instrument and Setting

Cases' behaviour will be more normal if what they are asked to do is familiar to them. This will not necessarily coincide with what is realistic. For adult native speakers often it will, but not necessarily for foreign learners who, if they have learnt by instruction rather than immersion, may be familiar with less realistic language tasks.

To some extent familiarity can be achieved by ensuring that subjects have some practice with materials and tasks like those to be used for quantification purposes just before the real test. However, it is even better if what is involved is also familiar from general prior experience, which may differ from case to case of course. You can perhaps choose among the many specific manipulative task types in accordance with what you know cases are familiar with (8.3). Again, using the opinion technique, you can try to ask about things the informant might actually express opinions about in everyday circumstances. In a quasi-naturalistic interview you can let children play as well as talk (provided they do still talk!), get Creole children to tell a ghost story (McEntegart & Le Page, 1982), and so on.

In general it also encourages natural behaviour if you choose an environment familiar to the case(s) being measured. Cheshire (1982a) interviewed her teenagers in adventure playgrounds. Young children are often best talked to in their homes with familiar toys and mother present (e.g. Local, 1982), or, if this is not possible, a mockup of such an environment (Bennett-Kastor, 1988: 73ff.). This is obviously more conducive than using offices, laboratories or classrooms for the purpose. In a T context, where assessment usually *has* to be in classrooms, the UK English National Curriculum guidelines (DES, 1989) suggest not making the classroom more artificial by trying to tape oral assessment sessions despite the fact that a permanent record would be useful for checking on ('moderating') the scoring afterwards (19.3.4).

Sometimes of course the variable being measured implies a particular environment, like it or not. Assessing air-hostesses' communicative competence for their job would ideally be done in an aeroplane, to achieve realism (9.2). And of course it may be impossible to avoid strange surroundings if a test requires special equipment that cannot be moved (e.g. in instrumental phonetics). There may also be a balance to be achieved between improving naturalism and other kinds of validity. Using a special room with a two way mirror to observe children in may mean the environment is a bit strange to them, but removes the effect of an observer being present (21.2.1). Realism and familiarity are also crucially involved in the topics of 9.8 and 9.9 (q.v.).

9.4 Disguise

If you make it hard for cases to spot what precisely you are quantifying, any semi-conscious adjustments made by the cases are likely to be irrelevant to what you are actually after. There is an element of this automatically in measurement via more or less natural communication (Chap. 5, 6) as the cases being measured can't usually tell what exact aspects of what they say are being picked on by the measurer, unless they are told. But disguise or 'misdirection' is much harder in the opinion or manipulation approaches — it is often more obvious what you are after even if you don't say what it is in so many words. Putting aside here the ethical question raised at and 6.5 and 8.5, there are some useful things that can be done short of outright lying.

One standard procedure used in multi-item tests and opinion inventories, in addition to randomising the order of items, is to intersperse 'dummy' items which will not actually be scored. They do however provide a sort of smoke screen hiding what would otherwise rather obviously be the object of quantification. They make it harder for subjects to maintain a systematically unnatural response or see a repeated pattern in a set of items. Such items are sometimes called 'distractors' — in a slightly different sense from the 'distractor' alternatives in multiple choice tests (8.4).

Thus in psycholinguistic work you might be interested in the subjects' speed of verifying the truth of sentences with modifiers attached to the subject as against the object, all describing a picture: e.g. *The green car is following the bus* versus *The lorry is following the red car*. If *only* sentences of these two patterns were used, even if in jumbled order, the subjects might well soon spot the distinction at a conscious level (generally not desirable). But if miscellaneous other sentences with both nouns modified, or with other structures, are interspersed, this is unlikely.

Sometimes the task itself can be cast in a way that disguises the real point. A famous example is Greenbaum & Quirk's (1970) use of items such as asking people to change the sentence *None of my friends had arrived yet* into the present perfect tense. The testee here naturally will think it is his/her knowledge of tense forms that is in question, but in fact what Greenbaum & Quirk were interested in was not how successful the testees were at changing the tense, but what agreement with the subject they chose to make the verb form show. Unlike in the past perfect tense which the stimulus example above is in, there is a choice in the present perfect between *None of my friends have arrived yet* and *None of my friends has arrived yet*, depending on whether *None of my friends* is taken as being singular or plural. Putting the sentence into the present perfect you inevitably choose one or the other agreement (hence Greenbaum & Quirk call this a 'selection test').

How many testees realised they were making this choice when changing the tense and that this was really what was being quantified we can't tell, but certainly the results seemed to closely reflect natural use which favours plural agreement (*None.... have..*) and which you would get direct evidence of from non-reactive observation (Chap. 5). This was in marked contrast to the evidence of measurement via opinion, which reflected more the prescriptive, purist's rule that *none* is singular — *None.....has....*

In language attitude research commonly ratings are elicited *apparently* of a speaker or the cogency of what they say. However, the stimuli have been arranged so that it is really the same speaker putting on different voices, and the content of what they say is the same, so what subjects are really judging is the language or dialect the person is speaking.

From the point of view of getting more natural data, it is well worth exercising your ingenuity to try and disguise the point of specific quantification and, indeed, of entire R investigations, from the cases. Cases are naturally curious and if you tell them nothing about what you are measuring/researching there is always a possibility of them coming up with different imagined ideas of what is being quantified, and their consequent adjustments affecting reliability or validity of the results (Chap. 19–23). Even if you misdirect them all in the same way (as a sort of 'cognitive placebo' — Christensen 1980: 143), some may see through the disguise. It is anyway valuable to talk to them *after* the measurements have been made in order to check on what *they* perceived. This could lead naturally into a belated explanation of the real purpose, if you felt that ethical considerations required this.

9.5 Distraction

Another valuable trick is to distract cases. That is to say you make them *forget* or lose sight of what the point of your quantification activity is, though they do in fact know it. They may even forget they are being quantified at all. Thus they may lift any special adjustments they made initially. The difference from 'disguise' can be slight, and some of the same techniques can be used in both, but it is ethically crucial since, as defined here, 'distraction' rarely involves anything that could be regarded as *deception*.

For instance when getting children to do manipulative tasks you can heighten the game aspect. Keenan & Brown (1984), for example, wanted to test how quickly children understood and could recall sentences of different sorts. This required the subjects to read a series of sentences from a TV screen and press a button as soon as they had understood each: the sentence would then disappear and they had to repeat the sentence out loud as accurately as possible. However, to distract the subjects from the avowed purpose of the test, and indeed make the whole activity more interesting, the researchers represented it as a simulated space control centre. A subject was cast as a controller who had to read messages off a screen as fast as possible as they came in from spaceships and press a button to let the spaceship know it had been understood. The screen then had to clear, it was said, so as to be ready for important new incoming messages, but the last message had to be repeated into a microphone to be stored.

In opinion measurement, interspersed distractor questions (perhaps controversial ones) about things you have no interest in (and are not scored) can help focus the informant's attention away from the linguistic matters they know you are actually wanting his/her opinion about.

However it is in sociolinguistic efforts to elicit *casual* language in quasi-natural conversation that we especially see distraction. For instance one of Labov's techniques (1972) was to turn the conversation to something the interviewees felt strongly about, e.g. politics, football, or ask them to relate any occasion in their lives when they had felt in danger of death. This has the effect of engaging speakers' minds even more than is usual in normal speech on the *content* of what they are saying, so they cease to monitor the *form*, which on a neutral topic, a normal native speaker would have spare mental capacity to be able to do. Consequently they may relapse into a more casual way of speaking (in Labov's study, with fewer *r*'s pronounced) than they would normally in a rather formal interview situation. Similarly, in St. Lucia, McEntegart & Le Page (1982) found shy children talked much more informally about black magic than about school.

One other example worth noting is perhaps Labov's idea of having an apparent break as a distraction in a quasi-naturalistic sociolinguistic interview. The language that occurred in the break was still recorded and quantified, and often proved more informal. Again what was said in 'breaks' which arose naturally was also used, as when the interviewee had to answer the telephone or speak to his/her spouse during the interview.

Finally, a rather different kind of distraction can be achieved in both R and T purpose quantification by regulating the *difficulty* of a task (which may involve the time allowed — see later). Clearly someone may very well know what is being measured but be unable to adjust in any special way if all his/her faculties are occupied just doing the task. As we have seen (8.4), some test item tasks can readily be varied in difficulty by varying the amount of prompt. It is generally harder to *supply* the correct past tense form of *sing* than to *select* it from four multiple choice alternatives offered. Brown & Yule (1983: 107), talking about T purpose measurement of communicative competence, discuss how different kinds of talk seem to differ inherently in difficulty. For example describing something is easier than opinion-justification, even for native speakers.

However, as with time control (9.6), it is not easy to determine just the right level of difficulty to obtain the required effect without creating too much stress or making the task impossible. Also difficulty may be something you do not want to tinker with as it may be crucial to what you are trying to measure (the notion recurs in Chap. 10).

9.6 Time

Time can be controlled directly in order to achieve disguise or distraction, and deserves separate consideration. In particular, you can arrange not to give the people you are observing *time* to reflect on or 'monitor' what they are doing/saying/hearing. This means they don't have time to revise their 'natural' behaviour by reference to conscious rules they may have learnt or to adjust it to something other than their normal style and so forth. Having to process spoken language in 'real time' as in the approaches of Chapter 5 and 6 anyway limits the adjustment cases can make, though native speakers normally can make *some*. Natural reading and writing usually admits of a lot of such reflection, which you may rule out by limiting the time available for a task, though you must perhaps be careful not to be too unauthentic (cf. 9.2 and Hart *et al.*, 1987).

It is in the opinion and manipulation approaches to quantification that tight time limits can most often usefully be used (on individual items, or overall). You can control the *speed* at which the task is done, rather than allow it to be done *self-paced*. For instance in psychological tests like word association you allow only a few seconds after each stimulus word for the answer before going on to the next and you don't allow subjects to go back and revise earlier responses. Often a tachistoscope and/or computer can be used to control how long stimuli are available and how long is allowed to do the task.

You must distinguish carefully between this sort of *speeded test/task*, in which speed is controlled merely to have a favourable effect on the data obtained for quantification of the target variable by not allowing second thoughts, and a *speed* test where speed is itself inherent in the variable that is the object of measurement. The latter are required especially for some T purposes (e.g. tests of reading speed) and in psycholinguistic research (quantification of response times or *latencies*). Tests which are not meant to be tests *of* speed *per se* (which includes tests of the vast majority of variables quantified for R and T purposes) are referred to in some T circles as *power tests*. Logically both power and speed tests can be either 'speeded' or 'self-paced'.

In T measurement and with child, language disabled and learner testees generally, tight time limits are not so often applied. Often more time than is needed and 'looking over' an essay or answers to a set of questions is allowed, which arguably weakens the value of the results as evidence of the cases' spontaneous language ability. This may be preferred, however, in instances where there might be effects of applying time pressure that would be *un*favourable, as follows.

The ideal time limit *should* introduce just enough pressure to rule out unwanted reflection but not make the task so difficult that useful responses are not obtained, because the cases are not left enough time for the normal mental processing required and perhaps become stressed. Cases may then, in a multiple choice item test, indulge in blind guessing in order to finish (a problem for reliability, 20.5); or they may leave out items/part of the task, which can make the analysis phase difficult. However, the ideal time limit cannot always be found. It can be approximated for a specific type of case (e.g. adult native speakers versus intermediate learners) by *piloting* an instrument on similar cases to those to be measured for real. It obviously should also vary for different lengths of stimuli and complexity of tasks: with native speaker adults commonly something of the order of 5 secs. is allowed for yes/no type responses, 15–20 secs. for a simple operation like sentence transformation (Greenbaum & Quirk 1970: 8 and 11). However, the ideal time may also be different for individuals, and where tests or exams are administered to a group all together, usually one overall time limit for all has to be imposed and a time that allows some to just finish may not give others enough time to finish sensibly at all.

Finally, a rather different way in which time can be used to distract is by its length rather than its brevity. If quasi-naturalistic interview, or even a test, goes on long enough, the people involved may just forget the point of the exercise or, in some instances, that they are part of an investigation at all. L. Milroy's work in Belfast (1982a and b) illustrates this rather well. She spent so long sitting around in her informants' back kitchens that many seem to have forgotten she was there as a researcher at all. Clearly an inconspicuous tape-recorder and mike are invaluable for this to work. This is a key feature of the 'participant observation' approach to research in general, though of course not many researchers have the time to implement it.

9.7 Capacity of Cases to Adjust

Sometimes you can choose to use subjects/informants who are less likely to make artificial adjustments in respect of aspects of language you are measuring. However, this only works if there *are* such people who also exhibit the behaviour you are trying to measure and if you are not interested in measuring particular individuals (i.e. you can't do this for T purposes). In general probably pathological cases, very young children and beginning learners of foreign language are inherently least able to adjust.

For example, there is a case for using teenage native speakers rather than adults in much sociolinguistic work. They *would* by that age be masters of their natural variety of the language but probably less capable than adults of spotting what a researcher is quantifying, or using conscious rules or switching to formal varieties of English. On the other hand some research shows that some children as young as 10 years can shift style to some extent. Other advantages of young informants are that they may be more at home with audio and video recorders and in some circumstances may accept outsiders more and hence talk more naturally. Also, if out of work or 'bunking off' from school they may have time on their hands and so be generally more cooperative (Cheshire, 1982a).

9.8. How the Observer is Perceived

Another key ploy is to reduce the contribution of the measurer to creating artificiality. In the techniques of Chapters 6–8 he/she, or their proxy, usually has to be present and so interact with those being measured, either as a third person observer/tester or as a second person (participant) observer. The effect of this has been particularly discussed in relation to sociolinguistic interview-type work under the rubric of the *observer's paradox*, though it is really an instance of what is known in psychology as the *Hawthorne effect*. For anything to be quantified there must be an observer/measurer, but the very presence of the observer may alter what he/she is observing, especially the naturalness and casualness of informants' speech. As Labov puts it (1972) we want to 'observe how people speak when they are not being observed'.

Usually the more familiar the measurer is to the case(s) involved, the better for naturalness. This (together with sheer convenience) leads some researchers to specialise in studies involving cases they are well known to. For instance many sociolinguists study language of their home areas, where from their own speech they will be perceived as *insiders* (e.g. Trudgill in Norwich, 1974). Again, many linguists record the language of their own children. The effect of teachers and therapists quantifying the language of their own pupils/patients is not so clear, however. Where the quantification is for R purposes, an outsider may be better able to convince the cases that there really is no evaluation involved, and so may get a more relaxed and natural response for that reason. Also Romaine reports on 'positive stranger value' she experienced as an American interviewing Scottish school-children (1984: 25).

Can anything be done about the measurer when not a natural insider, and one seems desirable? One solution used is to choose a suitable proxy as insider observer. So in sociolinguistic work with Puerto Rican immigrants to the USA, if you are not a Puerto Rican you deploy a trained Puerto Rican as interviewer, and so forth for different ethnic groups. Analogously, with unfamiliar children you can depute the parent to make the recording which you later analyse, or to administer a test, again with some minimal training. Even gender may need to be matched in some societies if you propose to visit wives at home alone during the day while their husbands are at work. All this should enable you to get more natural data or, in some instances, to get *some* data versus none. The disadvantage is in the diversity of observers, with possibilities for unreliability of administration and recording (19.3.3, see also Bennett-Kastor, 1988: 70ff.). For these reasons in dialectology opinions are divided on the relative merits of insider and outsider data gatherers (Francis, 1983: 80ff.).

There remains the question whether the investigator can make *himself/herself* an 'insider' when he/she isn't naturally, or whether the insider then always has to be a proxy. It seems the answer can be 'yes'. Several researchers have used 'long term participant observation' which had this effect. For example L. Milroy (1982b) got introductions via her students, rather than via more outsider figures of authority such as priests, to members of families in the areas of Belfast she was investigating. These then introduced her to other informants as an acquaintance. Thus she gained a 'friend of a friend' status which qualified her very much as an insider in the social groups she was researching. Mind

you she admits she was probably helped in this also by being a woman —
less a target of suspicion in troubled Belfast.

Labov (1972) did something similar by renting a young people's
clubhouse in Harlem (New York) and assisting his teenage informants by
driving them round in a minibus. Thus he became a helping participant in
their everyday activities rather than a detached observer. Finally, Cheshire
in Reading (1982) reports steps she took to identify with her teenage
informants — dressing appropriately, travelling by motor-bike, and
passing herself off as a student doing a vacation job. In a similar way
strangers can make themselves familiar to children, if they play with them
long enough, and so perhaps improve on the monosyllabic responses they
might otherwise get.

Whether teachers quantifying young learners' ability or attitudes in the
foreign language learning sphere can achieve really high insider status is
not so clear. However, there are ideas current in this field, as seen for
example in 'Community Language Learning', which are dedicated to
abolishing the traditional 'teacher centred' approach to classroom lessons.
This would have the effect of in some measure reducing the 'outsider' status
of the teacher.

Lest it be thought that these ideas are not relevant in more formal testing,
let me mention one of Greenbaum & Quirk's (1970) experiences. Some of
their disguised tests ('compliance tests') involved asking people to change
tenses of sentences, put them in the negative, or the like, but were really
after the adjustments they made that were *not* strictly asked for. For
example, asked to alter *He* to *They* in *He hardly could sit still*, the researchers
wanted to see how often subjects turned it into *They could hardly sit still*, thus
coincidentally revealing their preferred position for the adverb *hardly*. If no
such extra, 'non-compliant', changes had been made, the test would have
suggested that the testees found the sentences they were asked to change
the tense of or whatever perfectly satisfactory in themselves.

Greenbaum & Quirk found informants made many such 'non-compliant' changes in sentences that on other evidence we might regard as odd
when, as they usually did, they administered these tests to students at
London University who *knew* that Quirk was professor of English, and
pursuing research on English usage. In other words, usefully natural data
emerged when the measurers were, if not exactly insiders, at least well
known and well defined in the minds of the informants.

However, on one occasion the test was administered in the usual way
except that those giving the test were people unknown to the testees and
dressed in laboratory-type white coats. It was found that, administered this

way, many fewer 'non-compliant' changes were made. The testees tended to treat the whole test as a more artificial, mechanical task, and just changed what was strictly asked for, perhaps interpreting it as having a psychological or medical nature rather than an English language one. Hence the test was less useful as a way of measuring acceptability of sentences as English. It seemed to imply the sentences were mostly acceptable. In other words, the testees' perception of the nature of the test, derived from who seemed to be administering it, affected the naturalness of the responses and hence what it measured.

9.9 Pair and Group Dynamics

Finally, you can sometimes exploit interaction between cases or between cases and onlookers to aid naturalness, particularly in the approaches of Chapter 6 and 7. The first of these is seen in Brown & Yule's recommendation for assessment of communicative spoken language of learners: 'The listener-role should never be taken by the teacher. Ideally, the listener should be another student, preferably of the same level of ability' (1983: 122). However, the event cannot be fully spontaneous as the listener 'should be strongly discouraged from "taking over" the transactions' (Brown & Yule, 1983). Indeed the main problem can be controlling the effect of the listener/interlocutor so it is more or less the same for every speaker whose behaviour is being quantified.

It is in sociolinguistic R work that the effects of onlookers are most often exploited. Essentially what you do is not to talk to each informant in isolation as is typical in oral tests, interviews and so on. If you interview a teenager in the presence of his/her fellows this not only makes the situation generally more realistic and familiar, but it has been found that those present can exert pressure on the interviewee *not* to shift his/her way of speaking or opinions to suit the 'interview' situation. An individual may be ridiculed by his/her *peers* if he/she 'talks posh' for the researcher (Cheshire, 1982a). However, this can have unexpected side effects. Dorian (1982) reports the embarrassment resulting from testing the productive competence in Gaelic of a woman in the house of a more fluent long-standing friend and neighbour, when it emerged that the case being tested was far less proficient than she, or the friend, had realised. She had up to then *appeared* more competent through being good receptively.

Finally, if you talk to and tape informants in a group conversation you get the dynamics of cases talking to other cases *and* the presence of onlookers all together. The event no longer seems like an 'interview'. Thelander (1982), researching use of certain dialectal forms in N. Sweden, taped groups talking about a local political issue amongst themselves, as well as later to the researcher. Sometimes also the researcher can initiate a discussion, then retire to the edge and let the normal forces of everyday conversation work to produce natural talk. He/she can even entrust the tape recorder to one of the group and retire entirely from the proceedings.

Clearly, however, there are problems with using this approach. For instance, as Romaine reports (1984: 22), the speakers may remain aware of the tape recorder and even address it as if it were a participant in the conversation in the absence of the researcher. And there may be a problem where some specific language points are to be elicited, or where peer induced adjustment would *damage* the validity of what is being quantified. For example in Wales many people might not report their true attitudes to the Welsh language to/in front of their peers. Technically speaking, you would lose the 'independence' of one person's response from another's. In formal T purpose measurement — e.g. public examinations — traditionally individual cases are always strictly segregated for assessment.

Further reading

Romaine (1984: Chap. 2)
Bachman (1990: 300ff.) discusses authenticity in relation to communicative language testing.

10 The 'Referencing' Dimension of Quantification

10.1 Absolute and Relative Value of Measurement: Introduction

The *referencing* dimension of quantification has not been touched on so far. Yet it has all sorts of implications for what exactly is measured (cf. Chap. 1), how data is gathered (cf. Chap. 4–9), and indeed for how you can use the subsequent information provided (cf. Chap. 2, 3). It also has an impact on the topics of later chapters, so it seems appropriate to deal with it at this central position.

The main distinction usually drawn is between quantification that has some 'absolute' value to it, as against that which is purely 'relative', though other possibilities have been suggested too (Wiliam, 1992). In T discussion the former is usually called *criterion-referenced* (CR), the latter *norm-referenced* (NR), or, more or less equivalently, *edumetric* and *psychometric*. This constitutes yet another dimension on which many kinds of quantification can be classified in addition to ones met already (especially in Chap. 1–4). In principle any variable that admits of different degrees could be quantified either way, though some consider, for example, that the CR approach is naturally suited to measuring achievement, NR to measuring proficiency (Haertel, 1985). As far as kinds of instruments go, though it is by no means only relevant to tests consisting of a series of items each scored right/wrong or the like (Chap. 8 and 13), we will first look at it there, as it is easier to see what the difference is.

10.2 Norm-referenced and Criterion-referenced Tests

When we measure a variable with a test, we probably think of ourselves as doing two things. One, we want to reveal how much of the relevant variable is present in each case we measure. Two, we want to distinguish how much more or less of the variable is present in each case than in other cases measured. Now, in a nutshell, the difference between the two approaches under consideration is that a CR measurement technique concentrates on the first aim to the neglect of the second, while a NR technique does the reverse.

Suppose we want to measure the knowledge of the irregular verb forms of English (e.g. *sing, sang, sung*) of some cases. We can do this by a conventional test, e.g. containing a lot of items like *Mary SING sweetly last night* and *John has EAT too much*, with the instruction to 'supply the correct one-word form of the verb in capitals in each sentence'. Now we have already seen that data gathering techniques normally have to rely on *samples* of behaviour to quantify variables and, in more reactive techniques where the measurer has control of the sampling, the precise method of sampling can be used to focus its 'reference'.

In the present instance, unusually, we could at a pinch make up items testing *all* the irregular verb forms of English. Or we could use a strictly random selection, say 30, from this *domain* or *universe* as it is called. Either approach would allow us to claim the test represented the whole target variable and would provide *absolute* evidence of someone's knowledge. We would then, when using a sample, interpret someone's score of, say, 20 as meaning that that person actually knows about two thirds of the verb forms. You can't say the *exact* proportion because of course common sense tells us that a random sample will never give the exact information that measuring the whole set would — it's likely to yield scores a bit higher or lower than the 'true' score (See Subkoviak & Baker, 1977). Hambleton *et al.* (1978) cite technical ways of estimating true or 'domain' scores — in effect the average score a case would obtain over all possible parallel tests made using samples from the full set of irregular verbs. But still the focus of such a test is on individual ability, and of course quite a lot of people we test might score 20 or thereabouts, if it so happened we were testing a group of a similar level.

A different approach would be rather to select irregular verb forms which experience showed were inclined to separate those who knew more from those who knew less — e.g. by excluding ones too 'easy' for those the test was designed for, or ones that nobody is likely to know. So items would not be made from a strictly representative sample of irregular verbs, but a subjective choice, refined perhaps by trial and error (see on 'item analysis' later). If someone scores 20 out of 30 on such a test we can't then even approximately say what proportion of all irregular verb forms that person knows — though you usually assume he/she knows more than he/she's tested on. Indeed whether we should say we are quantifying *exactly* the same variable as in the last paragraph is a moot point. But we *are* likely to end up with fewer people scoring the same score and the scores should be more stretched out over the scale 0 to 30 than in the version in the last paragraph. Thus the score reflects with some refinement how much more or less of the variable is present in the individual *relative* to the other cases tested with the same test. A number of corollaries follow from the differences just mentioned.

First, the interpretation of a single case's score such as 'Samir got 80%' will be rather different. If *absolute*, it 'means' something on its own, regardless of what anyone else scores, as it refers directly to amount of some ability or whatever — the content of the variable, which is what the 'criterion' is often conceived of as being in CR measurement. You can additionally compare one person's score with another's if several people do such a test, of course, but the score is meaningful even if all cases score the same. A CR score 'describes' rather than 'distinguishes' each case.

However, if *relative*, the score on its own tells you little — you *have* to know if it's high or low relative to others to get any information. The relevant group of others provide the 'norm' of NR measurement, and Samir's performance looks different if many of the others got 85% than if they got around 70%. Indeed it could look different if he put in the same performance in another year, when the group he was tested with was of a different calibre. To try to ensure that individuals' scores can be fairly assessed within a NR framework, *standardised* tests of this sort are tried out with large 'reference groups' so that Samir's score at any time can then be considered not just in relation to, say, the average score of the rest of the class he happens to be in, but to the average score/norm of hundreds of children of the same age and background (or same MLU etc. — cf. 15.1), approximating the population of such cases. A score from such an instrument is often converted and reexpressed relative to such a large scale norm as a 'reading age' or 'spelling age' or the like.

For instance the *British Picture Vocabulary Scale* (Dunn *et al.* 1982), designed for native speaker children aged 3 to 19, is in a way really a series of norm-referenced tests with a whole series of norms established, one for each three month age interval, by testing 3334 normal children of a whole series of ages. Thus when you use the test, you can see from tables provided how any testee has fared with respect to the relevant aged reference group. If you use the test, say, on a child aged 4 years 9 months, and that child scores 9 (on the short form of the test), you can read from the table provided that this score corresponds to a percentile rank of 28. That means, in the reference group of children of that age, 72% obtained a higher score than this. If you prefer to think in terms of average scores, you can alternatively derive the information that the score of 9 is below the average for the relevant reference group, which was between 10 and 11. One problem with large scale norms established in this way by test developers is that in practice the groups used are not always of *exactly* the same sort of person as the target testees. Often they are middle class white American children or the like. Is it then strictly meaningful to refer to these norms when testing, say, British children or black children — or even more when using the test on children learning English as a foreign language, as is sometimes done (cf. 23.3)?

Secondly, on a CR measure the ends of the number scale typically have some absolute value as it is not a 'sliding scale'. 0 can mean 'total absence of knowledge of all irregular verb forms', 30 (full marks) 'complete knowledge of all irregular verb forms', subject only to normal error arising from the fact that a sample has been used. In a NR test the maximum and minimum scores have no such possible meaning. If a case gets full marks, that shows they know all the items in the *test*, but not necessarily *all* irregular verb forms. And, indeed, how well they have done depends on whether the average score for some relevant group is near the top of the scale or further down. Related to this is the nature of the variable itself. For CR measurement it must have inherently fixed 'ends', matched by the range of scores on the test or whatever, or be limited by some criterion. English irregular verb forms are a finite set anyway, but it is not so obvious whether a variable like 'familiarity with American culture', which might be a component in assessing immigrant learners' 'communicative competence', has any fixed upper limit. In the latter instance you would decide on some way of setting a top limit for your purposes — for example specifying what the average native American knows of American culture as a top limit *vis-a-vis* learners, though this is not uncontentious (Bachman, 1990: 338ff.; Wesche, 1983). NR tests on the other hand may be used to measure variables regardless of whether they have inherent or imposed limits.

Hart *et al.* (1987) tried to use native speakers as a benchmark *criterion group* for a CR communicative test for immersion learners of French in Canada. However, they experienced some problems. One was that though the native speakers of Canadian French showed a narrow range (variance) of scores on pronunciation and some holistic measures of a very specific task (e.g. note-writing), they exhibited rather a wide range of scores for vocabulary, for example. That made it hard to identify a convincing single score representing native speaker competence and constituting a notional maximum for the learners' scale. Another was the practical difficulty of gathering certain kinds of information for native speakers, such as verb counts, which led the test-makers to fall back on norms derived from other learners as a basis to refer to (essentially NR).

Thirdly, with a NR test usually the population of testees you can use it on is more limited than with a CR one. If a NR test is designed to work for 4 year old children it may not be suitable for 7 year olds because question items that would differentiate well between some aspect of the language ability of 4 year olds might be too easy for 7 year olds and so not differentiate effectively — they might all get full marks. On the other hand a CR test, having no brief to concentrate on differentiation of this sort, will work for anyone for whom it is legitimate to measure the relevant variable. In this respect then, there is more effort in creating NR tests, as you or someone else needs to make up sets of them for different groups to be tested.

10.3 Functions of Absolute and Relative Quantification

At this point it might occur to you to wonder why you should want to measure variables in the 'relative' way. Many people's common sense seems to suggest that CR tests give superior information. The answer to this is that, for many T and R purposes, the NR method is actually positively better, and anyway there are often considerable problems in trying to construct satisfactory tests of the other sort (10.4.2).

For some of the T purposes outlined in Chapter 2 clearly absolute information about what individuals know would be valuable. Such are the diagnostic and selection uses e.g. to guide the precise nature of remedial instruction or therapy (Bloom & Lahey, 1978: 325ff.) or for a future employer's benefit. However, some T purposes are served better by well-discriminated relative information. A therapist is in this position when simply wanting to know who needs therapy at all. A teacher assessing a class in order to identify the fifteen who should go in the top French set (placement) only needs to know who has done better than who by how much, on the year's work, not exactly how much of the year's work each knows. In the certification function the UK shift in foreign language teaching to GCSEs from the old O Level exam was heralded as essentially a shift from NR to CR measurement. In English as a foreign language teaching, though the term 'edumetric' suggests a special place for CR tests, in fact psychometric/NR testing concepts, which are more widely known at a higher level of sophistication than CR ones, have heavily infiltrated and often been used where not necessarily ideal.

When it comes to R comparisons between groups, relative quantification of the DV with high discrimination is often the most desirable. For instance, in a typical hypothesis testing piece of research, suppose you want to compare two methods of learning irregular verbs by getting different groups to use each and then testing them. You can reject the hypothesis that there is no difference between the two methods if you find that those in one group learned markedly more than those in the other group on a test. You don't actually have to know anything about what *proportion* of irregular verbs, on average, or which actual ones were successfully learnt by each method, though that might be of separate interest. Indeed the property of NR tests of magnifying discrepancies between individuals is a positive help in such comparisons. Too many items that everyone gets wrong or everyone gets right will create respectively *floor* and *ceiling effects*. That is, scores will bunch against the ends of the score scale and it will be very hard to demonstrate, statistically or otherwise, if there is any difference between groups. In statistical terms, you want a measuring technique in this sort of instance to produce a lot of 'variance', and preferably variance within a special distribution of the results called the 'normal distribution' (see e.g. Robson, 1983). NR tests are rigged to do precisely this.

By contrast, absolute information is of interest in descriptive research and where qualitative information is at a premium. Particularly in the areas of first and second language learning and language pathology the CR tests would be valuable for their 'descriptive power'. In these fields you often *do* want to know exactly how much and what an individual knows of some feature of language, or the facts of their usage, irrespective of others, and follow its change longitudinally. Also you may wish to compare people of widely differing types — a learner not just with other learners of the same sort, but in comparison with native speakers (cf. Hart *et al.*, 1987, described above).

10.4 Principles of Construction and Improvement of the Two Types of Test

Tests and inventories of many kinds mentioned in Chapter 8 and 13, whether for R or T use, lend themselves in principle to being constructed either on CR or NR lines. In the interests of clarity, I have presented the absolute — relative distinction in a clear-cut way so far. However, the situation is really more muddled. For one thing there is disagreement on terminology and the exact terms in which to define the difference between the two approaches. But, more importantly, many tests in actual use are not clearly constructed on one of the two principles, and have some of the characteristics of both. With Carver (1974), we should really think of these two notions as being 'dimensions' on which a test can be placed. Tests have many 'facets' (8.4), and it is quite possible for some to be handled one way and some the other.

10.4.1 Mixed referencing of tests

An example of the more mixed kind of test is the cloze test in the form of a spoken or written text with gaps which a testee has to fill appropriately. One typical use of this is as a test of overall language ability for foreign learners. Commonly a text is chosen that is not too easy or difficult for your learners, then you delete say every seventh word to make up the set of items which the learner will fill correctly or not. Is this more in accordance with the NR or CR approach? Well, choosing the text on the basis described has the effect, whether deliberate or not, of differentiating between testees and avoiding floor and ceiling effects, so is norm referenced. On the other hand choosing the gaps on the above basis is effectively choosing them at random, and is more criterion referenced.

To make such a test fully NR you would have to choose to replace by cloze gaps those words of text which differentiate between testees most effectively. You could in fact do item analysis of gaps just like for questions in a NR discrete point test, eliminating those which no-one or everyone successfully fills. Also you could make the test easier or harder by making the number of words between gaps greater or smaller. And you could establish a wider norm by seeing what the average score on the test was when administered to a large group of learners.

On the other hand, to make the test fully CR, you would have to make the piece, as well as the gaps, a random selection. You would have to define what kind of spoken or written English you are trying to assess the learners' competence in (newspapers? scientific?) and select your piece accordingly from such a population. Better still you would use a random sample of several short pieces rather than just one (as in fact happens in the variant of cloze test called *C-test*). Also you would usefully establish, as a criterion, the average score of a large group of native speakers on the test. This would not be full marks, in this instance, since even native speakers cannot usually fill a random set of gaps totally correctly — the redundancy of language is just not that great.

In fact, even in their common mixed form, cloze tests have proved themselves good differentiators of testees — i.e. they have good NR properties. But not being usually fully random or with cutting scores calibrated to native speakers, cloze tests do not usually yield scores that 'mean' anything *per se*.

10.4.2 Problems of test construction

More serious, perhaps, is the difficulty of constructing tests convincingly for many variables, especially CR ones. CR tests rely on procedures to choose appropriate test items in the first place, before using the test at all, often of a somewhat a priori sort and having the effect of ensuring a certain sort of 'validity' for the test. NR tests rely rather on procedures of trying out the test — 'piloting' — and refining items on the basis of this experience, a more empirical approach that generally has the effect also of improving the 'reliability' of a test. In a sense, the properties are more 'designed in' for CR tests, through the systematic sampling of stimuli, more 'developed' for NR tests.

From what has been said already it is clear that items in a CR test have to be selected to test a random sample, if not all, of the bits of language or language skills/abilities etc. that make up the variable to be measured — the domain (a special case of a 'population'). Now the whole business of random sampling cannot be gone into here. The real problem usually is to define what the domain actually consists of, since you can't easily take any sort of sample from an *undefined* population — you will end up with what Popham (1974) aptly christens a 'cloud-referenced' test!

The example discussed earlier was simple in this respect, since irregular verbs form a nice limited and well-defined set — a 'closed domain'. This applies also to tests of broader variables, made up of subtests of, say, five items, each sampling a different 'subdomain' of this closed sort such as forms of the verb *be*, or irregular noun plurals. Such subdomains are easiest to define for tests of achievement, e.g. of types of words retained in a memory experiment, or what has been learnt from a T course text-book or syllabus, or perhaps, less directly, to course 'objectives' derived from a needs analysis (Davidson *et al.*, 1985).

However, even in these simple instances you might quibble about numerous details. What about the sentences the verbs or whatever are presented in? Should *they* be a random sample too? But then there are infinitely many possible sentences. And what exactly do we mean by such variables as 'knowledge of the irregular verb forms of English' — stated as an objective we are trying to quantify? In the end this is really a matter of what statements put forward by pure linguists, psycholinguists and others at the theoretical level about these matters we accept. So you might argue that the domain you should be sampling and making up test questions for is not 'all the irregular verb forms of English' but more like 'all the behaviours/skills/abilities needed to use all the irregular verb forms like a native speaker'. In reality most domains have *several* relevant dimensions and 'behavioural' or 'functional' objectives are often pertinent as well as ones formulated in linguistic units.

Problems like this are multiplied when you want to construct a CR test of less narrow things — such as language learning aptitude, or overall communicative proficiency in a language. Even if you overlook the artificiality of measuring aspects of people's linguistic ability with tests in the first place, many variables, like the first, just do not seem to present any obvious domain of things to sample for test items. Or else, like the second, the possible domain seems so vast you do not know where to start — everything a native speaker knows of a language: the domain is 'open' rather than 'closed' (Black & Dockrell, 1984: 46ff.). This remains an area of problem and controversy in the realm of CR testing in the present absence of established, proven and satisfactory theories of language competence and performance.

In practice for more complex variables one or more of the following approaches are often used. Domains are defined multidimensionally; characteristics of admissible items are specified rather than trying to list everything; there is reliance not so much on strict random sampling as expert judgment to ensure items are representative. For instance, for a test of overall achievement in French with a communicative slant, such as the UK *GCSE* exam, you might specify the domain in part in terms of a set of communicative functions cast in more 'behavioural' terms e.g. answering the phone, booking hotel rooms in advance, understanding newspaper advertisements etc., though of course each of these labels characterises an open set of specific events. In addition the domain would also be specified in terms of a set of grammatical structures, a set of vocabulary items, and so on as per the syllabus. To obtain particular test items, or subtests, you then simultaneously sample on *all* dimensions. So specific situations are chosen instancing particular sampled types of function, and involving samples of structures and vocabulary from the defined sets. Ideally such tests would be of the 'work sample' type 'representative of the actual conditions under which the intended performances will be carried out' (Haertel, 1985: 24). In general CR testing favours 'direct' measures which quantify performance and underlying ability together (a source of criticism by e.g. Bachman, 1990).

This approach often extends beyond specifying the strict 'content' of the variable to specifying dimensions that are more to do with the format of the test items, the administration, and linguistic aspects of the items that are, supposedly, not the focus of the test but just have to be there to make up test items — i.e. choices on test facets. Thus Arrasmith *et al.* (1984) specify the domain of a native speaker English test in Dallas by defining not only a prime objective as 'The student will identify and construct complete sentences' but also that this is to be done via multiple and open choice items using words contained in the first-, second- or third-grade vocabulary word lists. Thus the distinction between 'dimensions' of the target variable itself and 'facets' of the means of quantifying it gets blurred.

A final variant of domain specification involves the notion of 'ordered domains'. The above examples assumed no ordering in any sense of the verbs, communicative functions, etc. listed or otherwise specified: hence everything specified was on equal terms as far as any sampling was concerned. However, it is possible, usually again based on expert judgment, to specify subdomains/specific objectives with a built in order, usually of difficulty. Thus some irregular verbs, communicative functions, tasks or whatever may be specified as harder than others — e.g. on the basis that at a given point in the educational system some have been taught, others not, but may nevertheless have been acquired, or that some are linguistically more complex, or known from research to be normally acquired later (e.g. third singular present tense of verb -s after plural -s, by foreign learners of English). There are well-known developmental 'milestones' for certain things, like the age at which a child starts producing two word utterances.

This can lead to the sort of system of 'basic' and 'higher' subtests seen in the GCSE exam system, where 'moderators' decide the difficulty level of items and make up different levels of subtest (= different papers, orals etc.). A candidate's absolute level of achievement in, say, French is then derived from how well he/she did on basic and harder parts of the test, though the system is made more complex by the fact that not all candidates will take all parts of test (see Partington, 1988).

Assessment of the UK National Syllabus is being developed along the same lines (DES, 1989). At one stage in its evolution the English domain was broken down into around 159 specific 'statements of attainment' (SoAs), each assigned to one of ten levels of difficulty and to one of five 'attainment target' (AT) areas of English. An example is 'Produce, independently, pieces of writing using complete sentences, some of them demarcated with capital letters and full stops or question marks', which is a level two SoA, in the AT of writing. The corresponding level three SoA has the same wording except for *mainly* replacing *some of them*. Since the SoAs are fairly general, there is some burden on the teachers in the scoring phase to work out what they mean (see 19.3.2). Depending on his/her mastery of the SoAs of levels relevant to the year of schooling the child is in, as quantified partly from more naturalistic teacher assessment in class, partly from tests (called 'SATs'), he/she gets an overall assessment by precise means that are still a bone of contention (see further 15.2.2).

Despite the problems of defining and sampling the domain suitably in the first place, it is here that the emphasis lies in the creation of satisfactory CR tests. However, there are also various ideas about how to *check* on potential test items and revise them. They mainly rely on a priori judgment by groups of 'experts' of the suitability of items, identical to what is discussed under the heading of 'content validation' of a measure (see 22.4.1 and Bachman, 1990: 212ff.).

By contrast, the nature of NR tests makes their construction more straightforward (but more time consuming). Provided they can be shown collectively to actually measure the variable they are supposed to (a matter of validity, Chap. 22ff.) there is no requirement that they *randomly* sample any defined domain of items or 'behaviours', or that they relate so directly to what they claim to measure, so it is less difficult to quantify covert and broad variables. The emphasis is much less on how items are obtained, more on the 'item analysis' procedures for checking and refining them through successive *pilot trials* (referred to by some as 'pre-tests', though this term is better kept for another use — see 15.2.1).

NR item analysis is a process geared to yielding a set of items that accentuate differences between cases. When done fully, as it has been for many standard NR tests, this involves trying out over 100 items in 'pilot' trials on at least 30 people, ideally a random selection of the sort of person for whom the test is intended 'for real', then weeding out items which don't serve this purpose using the evidence of their scores on each item.

In detail the construction of NR tests has reached a high state of sophistication that I can only hint at. In general you: (a) retain any item which your trial testees do not show a very marked preference to score the same way on; reject items they nearly all get right or nearly all get wrong. Also you: (b) retain items got right by those testees who over the whole test scored high; and retain items got wrong by those who overall scored low; (a) are often referred to as items with middling *facility*, (b) as ones with good *discrimination*. A third approach is that of retaining items which are got right or wrong predominantly by the same cases when the test is repeated or scored by a second marker, and rejecting those that lead to disagreement. This is 'stability' — a kind of reliability.

'Bad' items are either rejected entirely or revised — e.g. a multiple choice question can be made harder or easier if necessary by altering the distractors: putting in an alternative that is only just wrong will catch out more testees, making a question harder, if that is needed to make it more discriminating. Changing the level of support will make a question harder or easier too (8.4) — e.g. a multiple choice question can be made harder by making it open choice.

10.5 Absolute and Relative Quantification Across the Range of Data Gathering Techniques

Referencing is not often discussed in relation to measurement other than by multi-item tests with right/wrong, yes/no, etc. answers, though much of what has been said applies directly to opinion inventories of agree/disagree items too (and other examples of Chapter 13 and 14.2.1). Beyond that we should probably think of quantification as not really *being* absolute or relative, but rather as having, either by accident or design, greater or less *properties* of either sort (Rowntree, 1977; Spooncer, 1983: 32). Hence, with varying degrees of justification, it is possible to *interpret* scores or categorisations as giving either sort of perspective on a variable. In particular, where data is gathered less reactively (Chap. 5, 6), the type of sample obtained is not so much in the objective control of the measurer. Hence it is harder to make such quantification have clearly distinct absolute or relative properties like those of 10.2 (see Bloom & Lahey, 1978: Chap. 11).

Thus if you wanted to be more naturalistic in your measurement of learners' correct use of irregular verb forms you would not test them, but might use unstructured elicitation via free conversation, and count up correct and incorrect instances that happened to occur (Chap. 12). It is common to use such scores both as evidence of how much a learner knows and for individual and group comparisons. In a different realm, discussion of Labov's (1972) naturalistically derived scores for [r] usage by shop assistants can focus *either* on how near zero or total use of [r] individuals and groups are, in an absolute sense, *or* on the relative differences between assistants from different shops (for whom norms could in principle be established). Similarly, Crystal *et al.* (1976) effectively proposes that his *LARSP* profiling instrument records variables that are *both* a guide on where remedial teaching may be needed (CR-like), graded according to developmental stages, such as when two word utterances typically emerge in the normal child, *and* chosen to discriminate between cases (NR-like).

But, as we have seen, in the instance of learner verb forms you would have little control of what verb forms each case attempted. For instance you couldn't stop them using mostly ones they knew and got right, if they were so inclined through avoidance, so they might end up with fairly uniformly high scores. It might be hard then to show any difference between individual learners or groups of learners on this variable. So you would not have the high relative discrimination engineered by a NR test, unless you could identify and exploit naturally occurring situations where differences showed themselves spontaneously.

If the sample was reasonably random, it would be a fair sample of the domain 'irregular verbs used by the individual case' but, again through lack of control, not 'irregular verbs of English in general', which a CR test would typically sample. Hence the proportion of correct forms you observe may give an absolute idea of what correct and incorrect forms the learner uses over the range of verbs he/she uses at all, in the setting/circumstances in which the data were obtained. But it will not be likely to be a reasonable estimate of the proportion of correct forms referenced to all the irregular verb forms of English.

Furthermore, this can be a problem when you are interested in comparing, say, a learner's or child's or pathological case's ability with a normal adult native speaker's as criterion. The former's *natural* output can perhaps be considered as samples of the same domain as another learner's etc.'s, but not of the criterion group's. Though this is often glossed over in practice, there is doubtful comparability of, say, a speech retarded child's % correctly formulated negative statements in free speech and the % of a normal child of the same age. What looks like the 'same' variable isn't quite, unless you ask them both the same set of questions requiring negative answers. It's a bit like trying to assess the technical competence of a flautist, playing a simple practice piece, on the same terms as that of another who chooses to play a Mozart concerto.

Though of some R interest in itself, this sort of absolute information would not serve the T purpose of showing how much the learner really knows, and what remedial teaching might be needed. Hence what seems to happen is that from counts of things more naturalistically observed you are more inclined to get absolute information, but not necessarily about precisely the variable required.

Finally one other way of measuring less reactively is where quasi-natural data is assessed by the measurer, or indeed cases themselves, globally rather than by counting up. He/she rates each case on a scale (14.1), or places him/her directly in some system of ordered categories (Chap. 17). For instance a teacher decides from experience of learners in class which have or have not acquired the German genitive case adequately, or a measurer rates speakers of different social backgrounds at interview on a five point scale for conversational communicative ability. Some standard measures like the *FSI Oral Interview* used to assess oral English proficiency as a screening for jobs in the US foreign service work this way. In this sort of instance the measurement may be made more CR or more NR simply by the way the measurer applies his/her subjective judgment within the limits specified by the definitions of the scales and categories involved.

If the instruction is to classify as, say, 'fluent' all those judged near native speaker fluency, and as 'non-fluent' any with less ability, regardless of numbers falling in each category, then this approximates an absolute categorisation. On the other hand, if the instruction is to divide cases equally between categories, or to place 60 cases on a 9 point scale according to a preset distribution like 2 3 6 11 16 11 6 3 2 (Cohen, 1976: 133ff.), then it is relative to the level of cases measured. Similarly NR in basis are instructions like 'Please try to use the entire 11-point scale' (Ohala & Jaeger, 1986: 244) or encouragement, when judging sentences for naturalness, to read them all first and anchor the ends of the rating scale from judgment of the most extreme cases (Prideaux, 1984: 270). Often of course the basis is not made explicit and, it is not clear if NR-like 'grading on the curve', as teachers call it, has occurred or not. What 'Samir got an A' really means heavily depends on this.

Even with clear instructions to categorise in absolute terms, there remains the problem that there is no explicit domain, and you cannot be sure if different 'judges' are applying the *same* 'absolute' standards. Indeed the same judge may not apply an identical supposedly absolute standard to different groups, such as native speakers and foreign learners. Once again the variable being quantified may not always be exactly the same one. The domain is in effect defined and sampled by the measurer, rather than by the case or the measuring instrument itself (test) as above. But obviously this can be improved if some care is given to the definition of labels of the different levels/categories on categorisation and rating scales which the measurers all use (19.3.2, 22.2).

Further reading

Cziko (1981, 1982) has a good review. See also Noll *et al.* (1979).

For detailed accounts of item-construction see: CR: Roid & Haladyna (1980); NR: Valette (1967), Heaton (1975)

For methods of item analysis as a step in test development see: Simple NR approaches: Allen & Corder (1977: Vol 3: 313ff.); Perkins & Miller (1984); Cohen *et al.* (1988: 169ff.). Sophisticated NR approach (latent-trait theory/item-response theory, Rasch model): Bachman (1990: 202ff.), Leonard (1980), Willmott (1980), Oscarson (1991), Henning (1987), Agrawal (1979). Possible CR approaches: Subkoviak & Baker (1977), Hudson & Lynch (1984), Black & Dockrell (1984: 82), Hudson (1993).

Other important consequences of the relative-absolute distinction relate to:
How change of ability can be quantified (15.2.1)

The way in which numerical scores can be reduced to categories like pass-fail or grades A B C D (Scholfield, forthcoming a)

The ways in which scores for different variables can be converted and combined additively (15.2.2f)

How formal checks on reliability and validity can be made (Scholfield, forthcoming b and d).

The journal *Language Testing* extensively covers more technical aspects of the referencing dimension of language testing, primarily in a foreign language teaching context. *The British Journal of Curriculum Assessment* is non-technical and includes coverage of how English and other languages are assessed in the UK national curriculum.

For other suggested kinds of referencing see:

Bloom & Lahey (1978: 329ff.) — communication referencing

Wiliam (1992) — self-referencing and construct referencing

Hambleton *et al.* (1978) — domain-referencing.

11 Overview of Scale Types: Simple Sources of Interval Scales

11.1 Scoring and Scale Types: Introduction

11.1.1 The scoring/counting phase of quantification

The output of the phase of quantification that we have reviewed (Chap. 4–10) is 'data'. Often it is in the form of what are technically known as *protocols* — the name for primary chunks of data, as obtained individually from each case, which may need processing to yield quantitative measures of variables of interest. 'Protocols' include: completed test sheets or questionnaires, compositions, observer's notes on each case from a time sampling observation (6.2), computer records of each person's response time on a series of tasks that were presented on screen, and recordings of oral interviews and 'think aloud' sessions (or transcriptions thereof). Though the traditional use of the term 'protocol' is quite general, there has been a tendency recently to speak of 'protocol analysis' in a narrower sense, just applied to recordings of oral 'think aloud' sessions and the like (7.1).

Turning the data as gathered into figures representing a score or categorisation of each case on a given variable or set of variables may be quite automatic, e.g. for a published standard test like the *British Picture Vocabulary Scale*, or require a lot of work under the heading of 'scoring' or 'coding'. Extracting such figures, whether for R or T purposes, may involve further procedures and instruments, usually used by the measurer alone. The output of this phase is essentially a table of figures, the most standard form of which has a row for each case and a column for each figure obtained from that case on a different variable.

This table should record figures in their most 'grassroots' form, e.g. giving how every person scored on every separate item in a multi-item test, not just the total (and entering some special symbol like a star for where an item got missed out). The reason for that is that separate figures can always be added up if required, but the reverse cannot be done, and you cannot often be sure initially that you will not at some later time need to look at the raw figures in some way. For instance you might initially only be interested in each *person's* total score, constituting their placing on a given variable. But later realise that there might be something to be learnt by thinking of the test items as the 'cases' and looking at total scores for each of *them* too.

Both the protocols or other observations and the basic table of figures derived from them are often referred to as 'data', or 'raw data'. But only the latter are *quantitative* data. They are also, in a very preliminary form, 'results', since they are usually the consequence of some very basic 'analysis'. Any purely 'qualitative' information desired can be derived directly by going through the protocols picking out evidence of interesting or new phenomena to comment on for particular cases.

For T purposes the basic quantitative table may be no more than a column of names and one column of figures, and often constitutes the end point of the process. Teachers and therapists can use the information in it directly to evaluate individual cases and pursue the purposes outlined in Chapter 2. However, further handling of the figures will take place if the measuring instrument itself is in process of development and improvement — e.g. item analysis (10.4.2) and quantitative studies of reliability and validity.

In an R context, though this table marks the end point of the quantification of the individual variables separately, there is generally much *further* 'analysis' to be done before the 'results', in the full sense, are obtained. That further analysis typically involves *summarising* information about different groups and conditions corresponding to values of EVs with *descriptive statistics* such as averages and percentages, and *presenting* this information in graphs and tables of various kinds. Where the research is not purely descriptive and exploratory, usually *inferential statistics* will also be used to generalise results for the interlocking EVs and DVs in the design from samples to larger groups of cases. Only then is it usually possible to throw light on the R question or hypothesis posed at the start of a typical investigation (Chap. 3). This further analysis is all beyond the scope of this book (see e.g. Butler, 1985b, Hatch & Farhady, 1982, Woods *et al.*, 1986).

A crucial aspect of the figures entered in the basic table is their scale type. This is only loosely connected with *how* the data was obtained, or *what* variable is being quantified. Though often neglected, it is important for two reasons more connected with the wider function of quantification (Chap. 2

and 3), and will form the basis for our review of how data as gathered gets reduced to data as raw figures.

First, when quantifying either for R or T purposes, the scale you build into a measuring procedure, or which comes with a ready made instrument used, determines a certain amount of what you can actually conclude about the variable and cases involved. Second, the scale type on which a variable is recorded has many consequences for what kinds of further statistical treatment can be done after the quantification of the variable is complete. This is particularly important where a variable is being quantified as part of a larger R investigation, as mentioned above.

11.1.2 Introducing the five main scale types

Consideration of scale type requires us to be familiar with yet another way of classifying quantification in addition to the ones introduced so far. We have already hinted at it in referring to quantifying variables in such a way as to yield a numerical score for each case measured as against quantifying by placing the cases in categories. Various distinctions can be made between kinds of measurement scale, but the following division is the most useful to grasp, and will turn out to embrace all kinds of scale-related terms used in relation to measurement — e.g. 'scoring', 'ordering', 'counting', 'categorising'. The 'relative' — 'absolute' distinction of Chapter 10 largely cuts across this.

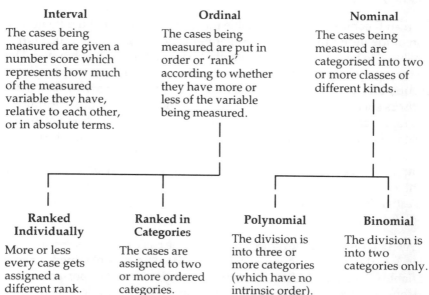

Interval

The cases being measured are given a number score which represents how much of the measured variable they have, relative to each other, or in absolute terms.

Ordinal

The cases being measured are put in order or 'rank' according to whether they have more or less of the variable being measured.

Nominal

The cases being measured are categorised into two or more classes of different kinds.

Ranked Individually

More or less every case gets assigned a different rank.

Ranked in Categories

The cases are assigned to two or more ordered categories.

Polynomial

The division is into three or more categories (which have no intrinsic order).

Binomial

The division is into two categories only.

These kinds of scale can be regarded as forming a hierarchy in that from right to left they record information about the presence of a variable in cases that is quantitatively successively more and more detailed. Clearly the more sophisticated scales (on the left) include by implication indication of the information the simpler scales give.

Binomial measurement involves just recognising whether each case you measure is the same or different from the others with minimal discrimination, since there are only two categories. Polynomial measurement still involves only recognising sameness and difference, but requires more discrimination since you have more than two categories that any case might belong to.

Ranking in categories involves recognition not just of sameness and difference but also of whether more or less of a property is present. However, only broad groups of high and low degree have to be distinguished. Individual ranking carries discrimination of 'more' or 'less' to its maximum in that ideally every case measured is distinguished as having more or less of the relevant variable than each other, so each case has their own category.

Interval or fully numerical measurement involves an additional element. You have to discriminate not just which person or thing has more or less of a property than which other, but also by how much.

As we have said, these types of scale do not correspond directly with classifications we have explored earlier. For instance, the right scale for 'readability' of a piece of written English is not obvious. Should you try and give all the pieces of text examined interval scores, like measuring a person's height in cms, or should you simply order the pieces relative to each other, like putting types of rock in order of hardness? On the other hand, it does seem natural to record the gender of your informants on a binomial nominal scale. You wouldn't normally think, for example, of ranking them in order from 'most male' to 'most female' (but see 12.1). Incidentally, the distinction I have drawn between the 'variable' property itself and the quantitative 'scale' it ends up as is referred to by some as that between a 'conceptual variable' or *construct* and an *operational variable*.

In practice measurers usually go for the leftmost scale on the diagram that seems at all reasonable, because of the point already made that more information is recorded by results of that sort and more can be done with them. Also, the majority of approaches to gathering language data, because they involve obtaining a sample of responses from each case, naturally yield interval scores. In addition, as we shall see, it is always possible where necessary to convert information about variables from a more detailed to a less detailed form, but not vice versa.

The main determinant of what is an *appropriate* scale is often the ulterior function or purpose of doing the quantification. In a T context, for example, many of the purposes outlined in ch. 2 really require only binomial scaling — they relate to decisions of a 'pass or fail' type about cases. Others, like the British GCSE examination system, require output in ordered categories 'A', 'B' and so on. So typically scores obtained initially as interval scores, either with absolute or relative status, get converted. In addition, there may be instances where scores recorded and exploited by teachers or therapists themselves in, say, interval form are translated into some other form, such as categories like 'doing well' and 'could try harder', for ease of consumption by parents and so forth.

In an R context it is the function of a variable in the overall research design that may dictate appropriate scale type. For instance, since experimental two variable designs typically require the EV/IV to be in categories, if originally quantified on an interval scale, it would have to be reduced to categories. But more of that later.

Finally, of major consequence especially in R work is the tie-up between scale type and the appropriacy of particular statistical procedures in the further handling of the 'results' of an investigation, especially 'inferential' ones. Indeed the implications are so strong that researchers may even choose to quantify variables with instruments that yield data on particular scales just so that they can then use particular statistical procedures afterwards — another form of backwash effect. Though other considerations also determine the appropriacy of statistical measures or tests, most statistical techniques are limited just to data on particular scale types. And choosing the right statistical measure or test is the main problem there, as usually a computer can readily do the maths, once you are able to 'tell' it which statistical operation to perform. In general the sophistication and complexity of what can be done is greatest for interval data and decreases down the hierarchy of scales.

In short, both for ulterior R purposes, and to ensure misunderstandings do not arise through wrong interpretation of what scores really convey in a T context, it is crucial to be aware of what sort of scale you are really using (covered from here to Chap. 18, inclusive).

11.2 Quantification on Interval Scales: Introduction

Here the scale on which the cases we are interested in are placed consists of numbers which indicate the presence of larger and smaller amounts of the variable being quantified. The crucial feature of this sort of measurement is that scores indicate not just that one individual has more of a given property than another individual, but precisely how much more. This is the 'equal interval' feature that gives this sort of scale its name. If person A takes 3 centiseconds (i.e. three hundredths of a second) to speak a given sentence, person B 3.75 centiseconds and person C 4.5 centiseconds, we know not only that C is slower than B and B slower than A but also that the difference in time between A and B is the same as that between B and C (viz., 0.75 centisecond).

But having emphasised the 'equal interval' assumption we must also note that many experts feel it is justifiable to treat scores as interval even if this requirement is not *exactly* met, or if, as often happens, it is simply not *known* if it is met. This is especially so if the departures from equality of intervals are thought to be random.

Interval scales arise from a very wide range of measurement techniques as I shall now review (up to Chap. 15).

11.3 Scoring on Straightforward Length-like Scales

The most obvious sources of interval scores in language work are measurements of variables that we are used to quantifying this way in everyday life, especially various forms of 'length' and 'rate'. For either R or T purposes people often measure things like the length in morphemes of utterances produced by a child. Here initially the cases are the utterances and the scale on which each sentence is measured is 'number of morphemes', a scale consisting of whole numbers 1, 2, 3 etc. Any particular utterance scores one number on the scale, and, of course, several may score the *same* number (for the derived MLU measure see 15.1). Again, as part of the data for a sociolinguistic investigation you might enquire the age of the people interviewed, in order later to try to relate age to the preference for a certain pronunciation. Here the cases are the people and the scale of the variable 'age' on which they are measured is basically interval. Similarly you might measure:

> The durations in milliseconds and basic pitch level in cycles per second (Hertz) of the vowel [i:] spoken by the same person in the word *sheep* 10 times, in controlled circumstances, and recorded. The scores on the two variables could be determined by sampling the continuous output of a spectrograph.

> The times taken by 20 people to verify the truth of sentences like *He wasn't sad* in the context of a particular scenario provided ('response times' or 'latencies'). These would have to be ascertained from analysis

of a tape of the administration of the test, or by getting a micro-computer to present sentences to subjects, and record automatically how long they take to press a key indicating whether they think the sentence is true or false.

The lengths in letters of 1000 words from *Nicholas Nickelby*.

Time taken to read a passage aloud by each of 20 linguistically backward patients, measured with an ordinary stopwatch (an example of a 'speed test').

Lung capacity of a child in litres of air.

Number of clauses per 'turn' of a child in conversation with an adult — i.e. length of each contribution of the child to the interaction, in number of clauses.

Time taken to learn 30 English-Eskimo word pairs by each of ten subjects in a psycholinguistic experiment — the 'criterion level', perhaps due to be compared with the time taken on a later occasion.

Air pressure in cms of water recorded for ingressive and egressive sounds in words spoken by Quichean speakers wearing a nasal catheter connected to a pressure transducer (Ohala & Jaeger, 1986: 127).

Notice that these scales generally start from an absolute value of zero (even where, as in the last example, negative values are obtainable) — hence they are sometimes referred to technically as *ratio* scales (Bachman, 1990: 29). The effect of this is that, for example, if the length of one word is five letters and that of another ten, we can say that the second is twice as long as the first (in letters). We cannot express relationships between different scores on *all* interval scales like this. For instance, if one person scores 40 and another 20 on a norm-referenced vocabulary test (e.g. *BPVS*), we cannot conclude the former knows twice as much vocabulary as the latter, because the zero score on such a test does not mean 'zero knowledge of vocabulary'.

Also many of these measures can be alternatively stated in terms of 'length' or 'rate'. One can speak of the lengths of utterances in words or the number of words per utterance. Where it is matter of linguistic units occupying a period of time, however, such measures can only be spoken of in rate form, e.g. oral fluency and reading speed will be quantified in a form labelled 'number of words per minute' rather than 'length of minute in words' (cf. 12.1).

Time duration measurement is involved especially in psycholinguistic and phonetic work, usually in artificial circumstances where time is recorded automatically with some 'apparatus' (computer, spectrograph etc.). In instrumental phonetics there are in fact numerous time-related and physical properties of sounds measured on interval scales. Some are fairly straightforward physical (acoustic) ones like duration of a sound, voice onset time, pitch, and intensity. Recently a host of more complex measures have been developed to quantify similar things in auditory/perceptual terms, i.e. on a scale that reflects how people *perceive* the phenomenon in question. The problem is that what are physically equal intervals on a scale of pitch, for example, may not be perceived by humans as equal, so one can attempt to develop an alternative scale that reflects human equal intervals. Thus beside pitch quantified acoustically in Hertz we have it auditorily in 'mels' or 'bark'; beside physical sound intensity in decibels we have perceived loudness in 'phons' or 'sones'. The conversions are quite complicated (see e.g. Ohala & Jaeger, 1986: 18ff).

The quantification of length or rate by simple counting of linguistic units arises particularly in work in stylistics (non-reactive) and for data obtained by quasi-natural elicitation in the study of child language, foreign language learning and so on. Standard linguistic reference books on phonology, grammar, discourse analysis and so on detail all kinds of units in which length may be counted. If the text or suitable transcription of an interview has been entered on computer, some of these things can easily and accurately be counted automatically. A word processing program like *WordPerfect* will count length of a written text in words, for example.

Something like length in clauses, say, would be more of a challenge for a computer to calculate, however. Either the measurer has to first mark the limits of each clause in the text on computer with special 'tag' symbols to enable a concordance program like the *Oxford Concordance Program* (OCP) to count them. This has been done, for instance, for the *Survey of English Usage* corpus at London University. Or, increasingly, there are 'parsing' programs available. They can run through text on computer and, with the aid of a built in dictionary of words' part of speech and some grammar rules, can work out the syntactic structure of sentences. At present, however, the latter method will usually end up being only approximately correct when compared with a count by a linguistically sophisticated measurer (see Butler, 1985a).

A crucial point about length is that these various measures of so-called 'length' are usually quantifying *different* variables, not the *same* variable on scales with different units in the way a ruler with length in inches and length in centimetres does. We can see this from the lack of translatability. We can convert length in inches to length in centimetres perfectly, but we cannot convert length in words to length in letters so readily, because there is no fixed number of letters per word.

A measure of length of text or recorded speech that has enjoyed some favour is the *T-unit* (or 'communication unit'). The label is short for 'minimal terminable unit', reflecting the fact that such units are definable as being capable of being separate sentences if any co-ordinating conjunctions are overlooked. In practice T-units are either identical with familiar sentences, with or without dependent clauses, or they correspond to unreduced co-ordinated clauses within sentences. Thus the sentences *The man I saw in the grocer's had just come out of the door when the lorry hit him* and *Fred is asleep* are both one T-unit: there are no co-ordinated clauses in either. *John came in and everyone laughed* would be two, since *John came in* and *Everyone laughed* could be separate sentences. But *John came in and sat down* would only be one, as *Sat down* could not be a sentence without special contextual support.

Some measurers of child and foreign learner language, both for T and R purposes, prefer to measure length in T-units rather than just sentences for several reasons. One is that they actually may be easier to spot in recorded spoken material, or writing with poor punctuation, where there are no full stops or capital letters. Another arises from the use of increasing average sentence length as an indicator of a child's degree of language development. This runs into trouble because some children at an early stage make very long sentences by simply joining up everything they say with *and*. Hence they appear more advanced than they really are on a measure based on sentence length — but not on a measure based on T-unit length. (See Presland, 1973; Gipps & Ewen, 1973; and for criticism O'Donnell, 1976).

Another way of putting the last point is to say that length is not to be confused with complexity. Lesser (1978: 23) cites two sentences used as stimuli to be repeated by cases in the *Minnesota Test for the Differential Diagnosis for Aphasia*:

I ordered a ham sandwich, a glass of milk, and a piece of apple pie

The office is on the twenty-fourth floor of the Merchant's Bank Building

Though of similar length in syllables, and treated as comparable in this test, they are quite different grammatically. The first features co-ordinated noun phrases following the verb *ordered*, the second a single more complex noun phrase in a prepositional phrase starting with *on*. Not surprisingly aphasic patients often find them of quite different difficulty.

Note that measurement of the length of things in the sort of units discussed here (especially words, sentences etc.) is often an integral part of other types of quantification (e.g. in Chap. 12). Also for many of the simple time and length variables discussed here (e.g. utterance length, vowel length) it is normal not to use just one measurement from each person quantified, but the average of a set of measurements. See Chapter 15 on this.

Apart from being measured as DVs, length is often controlled in the construction of materials for manipulation tasks and experiments. The aphasic test cited above is an example. In a memory experiment for concrete versus abstract words, it would usually make sense to make all the words subjects try to remember the *same* length (i.e. length is a CV). Similarly as we saw in 9.6, time allowed for people to respond may well be controlled. Again these variables may be varied deliberately as IVs in R experiments in subdisciplines like psycholinguistics. For example an experiment on memory for sentences might involve a comparison of memory for sentences of different lengths, so sentences have to be chosen and their lengths determined by the researcher as part of his/her preparation of the stimuli for the experiment, probably resulting in two or more groups of sentences being used, with the sentences within each group being of the same length.

11.4 Precision

A little thought shows that there are actually two kinds of scale involved in the examples above. There are *continuous* ones, where it is possible to get a whole range of scores between the whole numbers. For instance time duration can be 10 milliseconds, 10.3, 10.32 etc. with detail only limited by your measuring apparatus. Much of the output from phonetic instruments is information about how a case's airflow, pitch level etc. is scoring on a continuous scale. Furthermore, this information comes in the form of a continuous flow over time which has to be sampled to obtain scores at particular moments. But outside this discipline most scales are *discrete*, i.e. only admit of whole number scores. For instance the number of letters in a word can only sensibly be a whole number. Most of the interval scalings covered in Chapters 12–15 are discrete.

Obviously finer detail of information can be recorded if a scale is continuous but the distinction does not matter too much for most ulterior purposes. For instance, in the R context, though many interval statistical techniques are really based on continuous scales, this is regularly over-looked and the techniques freely applied to discrete ones which are much commoner.

Often measurers will find it easier to record a variable that is naturally continuous on a scale that is discrete because the amount of extra detailed information in scores on continuous scale is unnecessary. They can decide that it is enough to elicit age of adult informants in years only, so each case scores a whole number, rather than in more detail. The decision will depend, of course, on whether it is thought that the more precise measurement will enable a result to emerge that the simpler scale would not show. If the cases are adults, common sense suggests it is unlikely that it would be crucial to record age in parts of years as well as years. But in child language research obviously it might be crucial to distinguish children differing in age by months only.

If in doubt, of course, the best policy is to record initially in the more detailed way. It is always possible later to go over your figures, simplifying 23 years 4 months to just 23, or, on a more grossly discrete scale, to 'between 20 and 29', but not the reverse. The product of such simplification is known as *grouped data* on a scale with *step intervals* (cf. Cohen & Holliday 1982: 10ff). With interval measurement in general there are dangers in excessive grouping, if too much information is lost for the purpose in hand, or if it produces a misleading picture, which particular choices of step interval size may do. But also overprecise scores may be confusing and unnecessary, and certainly undesirable if retained simply for effect, to give an air of professionalism to a piece of research where, say, a fairly crude language test has scores reported to several decimal places!

Finally a mode of measurement used by Major (1987) is remarkable in a number of ways. Cases had to record their judgment of how 'heavy' a foreign accent they heard was by moving a lever connected to a computer to a suitable point between two extreme positions. This sort of task is normally quantified on a rating scale with few values (14.1), but here the potential 'precision' was far greater, even when the continuous scale of the apparatus was electronically reduced to number scale from 1 to 256 for the recording of scores. But we must ask if the hand-brain coordination of the cases, not to speak of the refinement of their judgment, made this procedure as precise as it seems.

Further reading

Choice of statistical measures and tests on the basis of number of variables in the design, their scale types and other considerations is dealt with in many general statistics books, such as:

Langley (1979: Especially brief guide at the end).
Robson (1983: Especially flowchart on the flysheet).
Cohen & Holliday (1982: Especially pp. 127ff).

Measurement scales are covered sketchily in many books, e.g.

Pedhazur & Schmelkin (1991: 15ff), Nunnally (1978: Chap. 1, 2), Hatch & Farhady (1982: 39ff).

12 Scoring on Interval Scales: Counts of Various Sorts

12.1 Scores that are Counts of Occurrences in a Continuum

Slightly different from measuring the length of a written sentence in words, is measuring, say, its 'degree of punctuation' by counting how many commas, semicolons, etc. occur within it. This might be done in stylistic analysis. Here you are counting the occurrence of specific isolated things within the continuum of the whole sentence as a way of quantifying it rather than counting something that occurs in every part of the continuum, like words, morphemes, letters and so on as in 11.3. It is common practice to take counts like these as interval scores, though technically observations of such occurrences in continua of time and space can be regarded differently (not pursued here: see for example Langley, 1979: 31, 399). Thus in our example we regard the sentences as the cases, each of which is getting a unitary score for 'degree of punctuation'. Similar instances arise by counting:

Numbers of exclamation marks per 1000 words in passages from ten newspapers — a measure of 'extroversion' of style.

Numbers of occurrences of [θ] (the initial sound of *think*) per minute in 20 separate one minute segments of recorded speech.

Number of hesitation phenomena (*em, er*, pause, etc.) per lecture in 20 different lectures.

Numbers of errors per essay in 50 different learners' essays.

Number of adverbial clauses per 50 sentences (or T-units) in a newspaper.

Number of SVC/O structures used by a child in half an hour's conversation. This is one of the many things recorded when using profiling schedules like the *Language Assessment Remediation and Screening Procedures* (*LARSP*: Crystal, 1982).

The above all involve counting what are sometimes called *tokens* — i.e.

119

every occurrence of something, whether it is a repetition of the 'same' one that has occurred before or not. However, where what is counted has definable subvarieties, as errors do, for example, you can choose just to count how many of these *kinds* of whatever it is occur. That is to say you count *types* rather than tokens. The following involve counting 'types' — i.e. repetitions would not be counted:

Numbers of associates to a word each of several people can produce in 60 seconds.

Number of new vocabulary items introduced per lesson in each of 15 textbook lessons.

Number of different kinds of adverbial clause per 50 sentences (or T-units) in various newspaper samples.

Number of different syllable types in each of 317 languages in the UCLA Phonological Segment Inventory Database.

Number of distinct phonetic variants for /a/ used by each of several Belfast informants in an interview (J. Milroy's 'range score', 1982: 41).

The type-token distinction is important as counts of each represent different variables, but it can often be unclear which is being talked about. If a child language researcher or a teacher reports a child as using eleven adjectives in a composition, do they mean eleven adjective *tokens*, perhaps six of which were *nice*, or eleven types — i.e. eleven *different* adjectives but perhaps twenty adjective tokens in all? Any T or R conclusions about the child would be rather different in each instance.

Counting of these sorts is commonly done in stylistic work, and analysing transcripts of interviews with children, foreign learners, and pathological cases. In much work of this sort and that to be seen in 12.2, 'errors' (*vis à vis* normal adult native speaker language) are counted, in what are called *error analysis* studies. Similar to this is *miscue analysis*, where slips, hesitations and errors in reading aloud are quantified (Pumfrey, 1985). This is back in favour in connection with assessment of first language English in the UK National Curriculum (DES, 1989: 16.47). These may be distinguished from what are sometimes called *performance analysis* studies where occurrences of items are counted regardless of whether they are erroneous or not. These do not focus on any sort of 'deficiency' of a child, learner or language disabled patient, nor impose any normal adult model of correctness.

Again, certain things, such as occurrences of particular words, can be counted readily by computer, e.g. using *OCP* (Butler, 1985a), while others, e.g. occurrences of a particular grammatical construction, would often require complex programs to spot them (amounting often to 'parsing' programs). Some things are not likely to be identifiable by computer at all in the near future, and a computer could only count them if a human had previously gone through the text stored on computer coding or 'tagging' it wherever certain things to be counted occurred. Such are many kinds of child or foreign learner error, and aspects of text which may be only 'there' pragmatically rather than overtly. 'Coherence' is an example: linkage of clauses and sentences by a 'cause-effect' connection of ideas occurs in *He dropped the vase and broke it,* but not in superficially similar *He dropped the vase and left it.*

One problem that can arise concerns the strict interval quality of counts. An example is the study of Crosby & Nyquist (1977) where the 'femaleness' of samples of speech was quantified by counting the occurrence of various 'markers' which Lakoff has suggested occur more often in women's speech than men's in American English: 'hedging' expressions like *and stuff, I guess, kinda;* adjectives like *divine, cute;* terms of politeness like *please, excuse me;* questions made by using a statement form with rising intonation like *You're coming?.*

Here we are counting a mixed bag of things, less obviously of one sort than, say, 'relative clauses', and hence we need to convince ourselves that they are really all indicators of the *one* variable we are trying to measure and of equal 'weight'. If, for example, we felt that an occurrence of *divine* was really a far stronger indication of femaleness in somebody's speech than, say, an occurrence of *please,* then the 'equal interval' nature of our total counts for each person would be in question. A ludicrously simplified example: in a given stretch of time:

person A has two occurrences of *please,* so scores 2
person B has two occurrences of *please* and one of *divine,* so scores 3
person C has four occurrences of *please,* so scores 4.

The difference between A and B is 1, as is the difference between B and C, but that 1 point only represents the same amount of difference in both instances if *divine* and *please* are really of equal 'femaleness'. Wherever the equal interval nature of seemingly numerical measurement is seriously in doubt the safest thing is to convert the results into a rank order. Thus above C would be ranked 1, B second and A third in femaleness — with the rank ordering by definition implying nothing about the differences between the three people being equal. Alternatively, you could weight the items counted (see 14.2.2).

A final consideration with this sort of data concerns the size of the continuum. Commonly occurring continua in linguistic work are stretches of time or text — pages, chapters, utterances etc. — in which something is counted. However, if we are measuring several people or whatever, we need to make sure the lengths of these stretches are comparable. If you are measuring ten learners' error-making by counting the number of errors made by each in an essay, you clearly need to be sure the essays are of roughly equal length so each has the same chance to make errors. In the femaleness measurement above all the conversations used were of approximately two minutes duration, one for each person, recorded in a police station.

Alternatively, scores can be adjusted in accordance with some suitable independent measure of the size of the continua. So, scoring lectures for number of hesitation phenomena, if one lecture goes on for 50 minutes and another for 60, you can either disregard whatever happened in the last ten minutes of the second lecture, or use the total score for the latter divided by 60 and multiplied by 50, to even things up. If one essay is twice as long as another in words, divide the number of errors observed in the longer one by two to get an error score comparable with the first essay. Note that either method requires calculation again of the sort of overall length measures discussed in 11.3. The second method does not waste information like the first, but may not be suitable if frequency of occurrence of what you are interested in is not straightforwardly proportional to size of speech or text sample (see end of 12.2.3).

12.2 Counts of Occurrences Where Non-occurrences are also Countable

12.2.1 Counts over the entirety of text or time periods

It is not far from examples like those just discussed to quantifying as follows (and indeed many issues raised above apply here and in 12.2.2 also):

Number of vocabulary words in each of three readers for foreign learners that are outside the range of a given wordlist, in 100 word samples of the text. Note, this could be done either for word types or word tokens.

Numbers of adjectives in each of 10 100-word samples from newspapers.

Frequency of, say, the perfect verb form in different texts, per 1000 words, or of *wh*-questions per 100 sentences.

Number of words containing an error per hundred words of child written composition.

Amount of Welsh TV watched by second language learners of Welsh, in hours per week.

The numbers of different words used in samples of 500 words of running text by different authors. This is often divided by the number of running words to yield the *type token ratio* (*TTR*) for that text. The resulting figure ranges potentially between 0 and 1 and is used in stylistics and elsewhere as a measure of the vocabulary richness of the text. A higher figure reflects a greater use of different words.

The difference from 12.1 is that the measure of the 'continuum' is in the same general kind of units as the phenomenon counted. Hence, unlike in the examples of 12.1, we could readily state non-occurrences as well as occurrences. For instance if 300 of the running words (i.e. tokens) in a 500 word passage are new, then we can equally say that 200 words are not new, but repetitions of words previously used in that passage: if it was 300 words in a page we couldn't. In effect we get proportions, not just frequencies, and any such counts can be re-expressed as percentage scores either for easier interpretation or to put on the same footing counts out of stretches of different lengths for different cases (see 12.2.3).

A consequence of this is that there is a definite maximum possible score in such examples, which may be chosen as a round figure, e.g. the first 1000 words, or the total in whatever text etc. is being examined, e.g. 582 words, or in percent terms is of course 100%. In 11.3 and 12.1 there was no *a priori* limit: a sentence or essay can be any length in theory — though in practice, its length is limited by what people want to say/can remember etc. Equally it is hard to pin down any fixed maximum to the number of *um*'s anyone can produce in an hour's lecture! However, the maxima in the present instance are often only theoretical. In *practice* we could never get a newspaper extract where every word was an adjective, for example.

It should also be noted that several complementary counts of the above sort in what are sometimes called 'taxonomic' studies may in fact nearly or totally exhaust the total of relevant units. E.g. we count:

The adjective tokens in a 1000 word text, or the speech sample of a child, and also, separately, the nouns, verbs, adverbs and function words. The text's scores for each part of speech will more or less add up to 1000. Equally, if there are 475 *different* words (types) used in this text, the scores for adjective types, noun types, etc. will more or less add up to this figure.

For each of several children, the number of utterances that are spontaneous, imitative, or both in a speech sample (Bloom & Lahey, 1978).

Word frequency. Conventional word counts, of which Johansson & Hofland (1989) is a recent example for English, count the frequency of every different word in several million running words of text of various sorts (e.g. newspaper, legal, novel).

Several language classes are observed, following a time sampling 'observation scheme' (6.2): e.g. the ongoing class activity is categorised twice per minute as involving either the NL or the TL or neither, and for whether the teacher is speaking/writing or the learners are, or neither. In a forty minute lesson of a particular class there will be 80 observation points, which will be more or less exhausted twice: the separate complementary proportions/scores of a class for a number of items each language was in use in a class will together approach 80, as will the proportion of occasions when the teacher was active added to that when the learners were. (See further Allen & Carroll, 1987).

The main factor that may make such complementary count scores non-exhaustive is the occurrence of unanalysable items, e.g. in a transcription of a recording of a natural conversation, or ones that could be categorised in several ways (5.3).

Such complementary counts closely resemble nominal classification of cases into several categories (Chap. 18). Indeed many matters relevant to nominal categorisation (18.1, 18.2) also apply here, and sometimes it can be difficult to decide whether it is best to think of your counts as complementary quasi-interval scores, as here, or as nominal classifications. This issue is mainly of importance only if you intend further statistical handling of results (see 18.2.3 and Scholfield, forthcoming c).

12.2.2 Counts over limited potential occurrences

In the above example the whole extent of each sample of language was involved, i.e. the proportions were 'out of' a number of some sort of unit that occurred in every part of the stretch of text or whatever being examined, usually words or sentences. However, a very common type of frequency score is where only certain items in a piece of language are looked at and treated as what the proportion is out of. Often then the theoretical maximum scores are obtainable in practice. E.g. you count:

The numbers of instances of post-vocalic *r* pronounced as a recognisable [r] sound of some sort in samples of different people's speech. In the sociolinguistic jargon the instances where an [r] sound *could* have been pronounced are the *loci* of this variable, the variables often being given an overall label in round brackets — here (r).

The number of correct uses of the perfect forms of verbs (e.g. *I have been here since 6 o'clock* rather than *I am here since 6 o'clock*) as a proportion of instances where the perfect form should have been used, calculated separately from essays written by different learners of English. In the child language/foreign language learning jargon the instances where a form should have been used are referred to as the *obligatory occasions/contexts* for that item.

The proportions of relative clauses in various texts that have overt relative pronouns, i.e. ones like *The play which we say yesterday...*as against *The play we saw yesterday...*

Adj + N phrases as a proportion of total NPs (noun phrases) of any sort, for each case assessed. This could be found from a profiling schedule like *LARSP* (Crystal, 1982), even though it does not actually require it to be calculated. The total can be deduced by adding all the figures for different types of NP, which have to be entered separately on the *LARSP* form.

Much data from both error analyses and performance analyses (12.1) emerges in this form. The former, together with similar sociolinguistic scoring of occurrences of dialectal pronunciations and grammatical forms, may give rise to problems in deciding where the loci/potential occasions are. Often you in effect have to provide, or hold in mind, a transcription of each protocol into some criterion form, usually the standard variety of adult native speaker language, with which comparison can be made to see where targeted sounds or words *could* have occurred. Milroy (1987: Chap. 6, 7) discusses some of the problems, e.g. in deciding what are the loci for *done* in Appalachian English. You can see where it *is* used, e.g. when someone says *I done forgot when it opened,* but it is hard to tell where a speaker is expressing the same meaning but *not* using it.

In general it is best to omit from calculation any item/locus/occasion where there is doubt either as to whether it constitutes a locus for the target variable at all, or as to which alternative has been used (cf. the example at the end of 5.3). Or where these problems are acute one may have to revert to counts in the style of 12.1 or 12.2.1.

As for 12.2.1 examples, you may generate complementary 'scores' of this sort for people, texts etc. by counting separately the proportions of two or more variants of the chosen unit.

The numbers of occurrences of *no* in several children's speech indicating respectively nonexistence, rejection or denial (Bloom & Lahey, 1978: 30).

The proportions in different texts of all occurrences of modal verbs like must in epistemic senses (as in *It's late — he must have missed the bus*) versus deontic (as in *It's late — you must go now*) versus some other meaning.

Of the instances where a sound should have occurred in a speech sample, the number of times it was correctly pronounced, omitted, and substituted by another (recorded on a *PROPH* profiling instrument — Crystal, 1982).

This does not arise when there are only two alternatives of interest — there is little point in giving a learner a score for correct uses of perfect forms, out of all obligatory occasions, *and* a score for incorrect ones, since one score is simply the total obligatory occasions minus the other. Here a simple 'proportion correct' score will do.

Similarly in sociolinguistics often 'binary' variables are used so that a single proportion score will represent each case on each variable. The variables may actually be chosen for study in part *because* only two main variants occur (e.g. J. Milroy, 1982; Thelander, 1982: 69), or the several variants of the variables chosen may be deliberately grouped into just two types, or one versus the rest (Anshen, 1978: 10ff). For instance Labov reduced the phonetic variety of simple and r-coloured vowels and r segments that can actually arise in the loci for his (r) variable just to [r] versus non-[r] pronunciations. Partly this is done just to keep things simple for presentation and further statistical manipulation, partly it may be justified if other considerations suggest that the different proportions of more detailed variants would be of no research interest. Thus Labov claimed that social prestige and the lack of it were attached only to a broad [r] versus non-[r] distinction.

However, it must be admitted that uneasiness has been voiced by sociolinguists about this sort of data reduction, especially where, as J. Milroy found (1982: 39) for the (a) phonetic variable in Belfast, the range of phonetic variants does not naturally divide into two obvious groups on sociological grounds. It is so extensive that just measuring the *number* of *different* variant 'types' of a variable such as (a) used by each informant may be of value. One solution then is to calculate complementary proportion scores for each person for each main variant, out of the total loci.

The problem with that is that you seem to be giving cases *several* scores for what you may have thought of as *one* variable. And, if you reconceptualise the variable as several — one for each variant scored — these variables are then logically mutually dependent in a way that separate variables usually are not, which must be borne in mind when doing more elaborate statistics. See for example Local in Romaine (1982) for a treatment along these lines (for other possible answers, see 14.2.2).

Finally, though mostly associated with naturalistically gathered data, frequency scores sometimes also can be derived from more test-like data. Chien & Lust (1985) set Chinese children to imitate a set of Chinese sentences and noted any changes they made. The number of changes of a sort the researchers were interested in was then calculated for each child as a proportion of all changes made.

12.2.3 Percentage and suchlike scores

Derived scores such as percentages are often calculated for cases, based on the raw frequencies each obtains in counts of the types seen in 12.2.1 and 12.2.2. This is often done even where the number of words/sentences/forms/etc. that each person's score is out of is by design the same for every case, though it is not so necessary there. However, it *is* essential in the situation that often arises — when the number of potential occurrences is different for different cases measured. This is often so where frequencies relate only to *certain* loci/potential occurrences in a sample of text or recorded interview, etc., so the number of these you get may be small and you will want to use *all* of them for each case rather than a flat figure (12.2.2).

As an example, consider Escure's (1982) quantification of several Creole speakers in Belize to see the degree to which each used zero past tense forms of verbs as against standard English forms, which are nearly always marked as different from present tense ones. Zero past tense forms sound just like present tense forms — e.g. in *Wi had wan o tu dat kech kramp…bot de get ova it* (= Standard English *We had one or two that caught cramp,…but they got over it*), *kech* and *get* have zero past tense form, *had* has not. So for each speaker she got a total of zero past tense forms out of a total of past tense forms of all sorts which happened to occur in the sample of speech recorded. Here are three of her results:

Person measured	Number of zero past tenses	Out of a possible
Errol	4	12
Joe	4	5
Alva	3	5

Now, assuming we want to treat these figures as a unitary score for each person, we can't use the 4, 4 and 3 directly because they are not comparable, being out of different possible maxima. There are several common ways of converting such scores which make them comparable, all yielding forms of what is called *relative frequency* (though some reserve this term for (i) only). For instance:

(i)   Turn them all into scores out of a maximum of 1 by dividing each score obtained by its possible maximum:

   $4/12 = 0.33$
   $4/5 = 0.8$
   $3/5 = 0.6$

Thus all the scores fall between 0 and 1.

(ii) Turn them all into percentage scores, by multiplying the preceding by 100:

   $0.33 \times 100 = 33\%$
   $0.8 \times 100 = 80\%$
   $0.6 \times 100 = 60\%$

Frequencies of individual words relative to *all* words in a text, because they are so low, are often given not as percent but as a rate per ten thousand or per million. So if *block* occurs 150 times in 500,000 words of text its relative frequency is $150/500,000 = 0.0003$, so its per ten thousand frequency $= 0.0003 \times 10,000 = 3$.

When figures like these are calculated, from data with uneven numbers of potential occurrences, the procedure succeeds in making each case's score comparable with each other's, but a problem is that you might query whether the scores really still have the 'equal interval' property. Is someone who gets 2 out of 4 'correct' forms the same amount better than someone who gets 1 out of 4 as someone who gets 6 out of 12 is? You might feel 6 out of 12 is more definitely better than 1 out of 4 than 2 out of 4 is, because there were more chances to score. Yet when converted, 6 out of 12 ends up the same as 2 out of 4, and so differing from 1 out of 4 by the same amount (cf. 20.4).

In fact many researchers disregard this and treat evened out scores like this as fully interval. A more cautious approach would be to put the results in rank order and use any further techniques appropriate for ordinal scores (Chap. 16). Anyway, it is always good practice to quote the number of potential occurrences for each case *as well* as relative frequency information when reporting such scores. Doubts about equality of intervals could also arise in the same way as discussed in 12.1 where the items counted are heterogeneous: e.g. if we measure someone's spelling accuracy by the number of misspelt words in 100 words, are all misspellings really equal?

A further problem is that it is known that some proportion scores vary systematically depending on the size of the sample they are calculated from for a given case. Number of word types is a prime example, as it does not increase in a simple way proportionately to the size of sample of running word tokens it is derived from. Rather the increase slows down. This is no doubt because the vocabulary available to someone in relation to a given topic is limited. So the more they say or write, the more they begin to run out of new words to use that they have not used already (unless they keep shifting topic). Hence it is unfair to calculate one person's TTR (12.2.1) from 500 running words and another's from 700. It used to be common to calculate it from a fixed number of utterances or sentences for all cases, but this is unsatisfactory because older children, for example, will use longer sentences than younger ones, so the number of tokens will *not* be even across cases. A flat rate of tokens is best, though some related measures that are supposed to be less affected by sample size have also been suggested, e.g. the Characteristic K (Yule, 1968).

12.3 Different Forms of Count Score Compared

In the work where this sort of counting goes on, often there is a choice between calculating figures in the manner of 12.1, or 12.2.1 or 12.2.2, though the subtle differences in the precise nature of the variable you effectively measure by each method are not often discussed. In stylistic work the approach of 12.1 or 12.2.1 is often preferred, in R and T measurement in foreign language learning, and in sociolinguistics, that of 12.2.2.

A clear example would be counting verb form errors consisting of omission of the third person singular present -s on English full verbs, often omitted by learners. Such errors could be counted, for example, per page or per 100 sentences (12.1), as a proportion of all words in an essay (12.2.1), or as a proportion of all verbs or of all errors or of all third person singular present full verb forms, erroneous or not (12.2.2). See also Thompson (1981) for a discussion of this issue in relation to errors made by native speaker children reading aloud: would self-corrected errors best be calculated as a proportion of all words read wrong, or of all words read?

In general, the approaches of 12.1 and 12.2.1 amount to much the same provided the lengths of continua in the former are matched up for size. They both give a measure of how often someone used whatever item is in question, and so how often the hearer/reader would meet it, in continuous text or time. However, the person's choice is conflated with the general frequency of items, their sheer possibility of occurrence in the language, and other choices (e.g. about what meaning content to try to convey) made by the speaker/writer. These methods do not usually give much of an indication of 'frequency' in the sense of how often a case chooses a given option against other logically alternative possibilities *where he/she has a real and relevant choice.*

Clearly if -s is omitted on verbs 15 times on one page, or if 2% of words in an essay are wrong in this way, we would probably judge this error as quite frequent, in a certain sense. But these figures also reflect how often the learner chose to use the present simple rather than some other tense of the verb, or how long a page happened to be. Indeed they are limited by the fact that of course every word does not anyway provide an opportunity for this error (as noted earlier).

On the other hand the method of 12.2.2 typically minimises reflection of how often items are able to occur, and so forth, and instead registers frequency in comparison with some sensibly chosen alternative, only. Take frequency in relation to 'all third person singular present full verb forms, erroneous or not'. Here a figure of 15 -s errors on verbs out of 30 'potential occurrences' tells quite a different story from 15 out of 18, say, and of course the theoretical maximum of 15 out of 15, or 100%, is clearly possible.

But, while this sort of counting can be made to reflect a more careful notion of 'choice', or 'opportunity', tied to what are real potential alternatives linguistically, it of course does not reflect how often that more limited choice actually arises in running text/speech. 15 errors out of 18 tells us nothing per se about how long you have to wait to get the 18 potential instances. In a sense, calculating proportions of several sorts of error on this basis and comparing the figures would give the error-types equal weight, regardless of how often occasions for error of a given type occur. Milroy's discussion of the research of Lavandera brings this point out (Milroy, 1987: 165ff). The latter's concentration on % scores for use of the subjunctive in obligatory contexts hides the exceptionally low frequencies of those contexts in the first place, due to avoidance (5.5), in some of the cases studied (speakers of Cocoliche and Spanish in Buenos Aires).

Further reading

Hudson (1980).
Labov (1972: 207ff).
L. Milroy (1987: especially Chap.6).
Bennett-Kastor (1988: 89ff).

13 Scoring on Interval Scales: Totals from Uniform Sets of Dichotomous Items

13.1 Totals of Correct and the Like Responses on a Uniform Set of Items

Many of the more reactive measuring techniques, especially manipulation tests, will be in the form of a set of items — often questions — each with the same two possible ways of being scored by the measurer — so called *dichotomous* items. This is true of many criterion- and norm-referenced 'power' tests, whether standard ones or made up *ad hoc* by the measurer, especially in T contexts and language learning and psycholinguistic research. Each case measured gets an overall score for the variable — the total of their answers of one type, typically 'correct answers' or 'known items'. Omitted, of course, are any items included just for practice, or as 'distractors'. In effect you give a numerical value 1 to each answer of one sort and 0 to the other alternative.

As with proportional counts (12.2) there is a definite maximum score — if you know how many questions someone gets right you know also how many the person got wrong. But unlike such counts there is a parallelism between each person's score and each other person's score in that the *items* are the same for everyone. Also the maximum will usually be the same for everyone (but see below on omitted items): so though results may be turned into percentage scores and so forth, as in 12.2.3, there is not usually any levelling out involved.

Examples:

Number of correct answers obtained by each of 105 testees in a reading proficiency test which involved reading a passage of English and answering 25 comprehension questions with multiple choice answers.

Number of words correctly recalled out of a list of 40 words set to be learnt under specific conditions earlier in a psycholinguistic experiment, by each of 15 subjects.

Number of past participles correctly formed by each pupil for ten French verbs recently covered in the course given by the teacher in a class test.

Number of words out of ten containing the [s] sound, spoken by the therapist, that a speaker with a lisp can imitate without lisp.

The number of 'objectives' mastered in a criterion-referenced test with subtests scored just for mastery or not of that objective. Such a test could have fifteen objectives, each tested with five items. An objective might be considered mastered if at least 4 out of 5 items relating to it are got right, yielding a score out of 15 for each case (10.4.2).

Number of irrelevant words correctly identified in an intrusion test of reading.

Number of correct identifications of pairs of spoken words as the same or different (e.g. *ship-ship*, *ship-sheep*).

Number of times the [θ] sound is correctly articulated by dialect informants (or children etc.) reading aloud a wordlist of words like *think* and *bath*.

Number of times a synthesised vowel sound is recognised as [a], out of six repetitions presented jumbled amongst other synthesised stimuli.

Quantification of this sort can often be recorded quite mechanically. For example a small computer can readily be programmed to put up questions on screen, accept an answer typed in by the testee/subject, compare the answer with the correct one it has been supplied with, and add up a total score for the testee accordingly. Also some published multiple choice 'objective' tests can be scored with a 'template': a piece of card with holes in is placed over the printed sheet on which the testee has filled in the answers e.g. by ticking a box opposite the multiple choice alternative they judged correct for each question. The holes in the template are so placed that they allow the marker only to see the boxes for the correct multiple choice alternatives. Hence it is a quick matter to count up which of these boxes have in fact been ticked by a particular testee and so get their total score.

This sort of scoring does not arise so often from more naturalistic data, because of the difficulty in obtaining parallel evidence from all cases on an identical set of items without being heavily reactive. However, of this type is quantifying:

The number of factual points, out of eight possible omitted by five children in retelling the same story originally heard from the re-searcher, to a third person. Note how the set of items need not be an obvious list of questions which the testee answers: here it is a set of points covertly identified by the measurer. Cf. the quasi-naturalistic communicative task involving transfer of information about mincer assembly of Brown & Yule (1983: 116, 122ff).

Number of words, out of a list of 100 provided by the investigator, that each of five sixteen month old children ever use spontaneously, in the opinion of their mothers, who went through the list ticking items used by their child.

Scoring of this sort is particularly associated with T purpose tests with 'correct' versus 'incorrect' answers. However, it can also arise from other of the more reactive techniques, often of the opinion survey type, used in sociolinguistic work and the study of bilingualism. Here the two possible values of the individual items are not usually 'correct' and 'incorrect'. Thus an attitude inventory consisting of a set of statements each of which is to be just agreed or disagreed with can be scored totalling the number of preferences shown by an informant that tend a particular way, e.g. those that show an integrative motivation to learn French. This will *not* usually be the same thing as totalling all the 'agrees' or all the 'disagrees', since probably you will not have formulated all the statements so that 'agree' always signals the same attitude. 'Polarity' is normally varied to provide some disguise. As with several examples below, the variable quantified here will often function as an EV in the design of R investigations.

Other examples show how the choice of score value for a given item is often decided by the case rather than the researcher in this sort of instance:

'Index of linguistic insecurity' scores (Labov). Two socially important American English pronunciations of eighteen words are offered — e.g. *vase* pronounced [vɑːz] and [veɪz]. Testees have to mark the pronun-ciation they think they use *and* the pronunciation they consider correct in each case. Testees are given one mark for each case where they claim their actual pronunciation *differs* from what they regard as the correct one (0 for the other items) and the total is their index of linguistic insecurity score.

Language dominance scores, where bilinguals are asked to supply the name of one of the two languages they speak — e.g. Welsh or English — in answer to a series of questions all basically measuring the same variable. For example:

Which language do you speak for more of the time?
Which language are you more often stuck for a word in?

Which language do you dream in?

Which language do you swear in?

The total number of times one of the languages is cited as a % of the number of questions, is a measure of the dominance of that language for that speaker (cf. also Hatch & Farhady, 1982: 41).

The number of times a subject chooses a word ending in -ness (rather than -ity) when presented with pairs of words like reflectiveness — reflectivity and asked to say which sounds more like an existing English word. This 'lexical decision task' throws light on the productiveness of different derivational morphemes (Prideaux, 1984).

Scoring like this can on occasion be based on nonreactive data, and be quite subjective. An example is where, in order to measure some property, the investigator him/herself goes through a checklist of points for each case measured. For each point he/she asks 'Is this feature present or absent?' and gives one mark for 'yes', 0 for 'no'. Thus each person/thing gets a total score between 0 and the number of points checked. The researcher as it were takes a test *for* the person measured, using knowledge he/she has acquired about them.

An interesting example of this is 'network strength' as a (non-linguistic) EV in Milroy's work on English accents in Belfast. Roughly, a person has a high 'network strength' (i) if the people he/she is socially linked to are also linked to each other (e.g. Fred knows George and Bill, does George also know Bill?) and (ii) if he/she is linked in several capacities, not just one, to the people he/she is linked with (e.g. if Fred knows George, is it just as a friend or also as workmate, relative etc.?) As a way of measuring these Milroy uses a five question checklist of points which yields a score between 0 and 5 for each informant (L. Milroy, 1982a). Compare also Cheshire's 'vernacular culture index' (1982b: 155).

13.2 Some Detailed Scoring Issues

Sometimes there can be an issue over the basis on which to decide what *is* the 'right' answer. For example in cloze tests (10.4.1) for each gap you can count as right either only the actual word omitted from the original text, or any word that native speakers regard as acceptable. Though the latter appears fairer, it is more effort for the marker than the former. Anyway it seems that there is little difference in the result as the same people will score relatively higher and lower on both systems. Though cases' scores will be lower on the 'exact word' marking system, this is irrelevant since cloze is generally norm-referenced anyway (cf. Brown, 1980).

Non-response can be an issue. Sometimes it is in fact one of the standard responses to test items, corresponding to 'wrong' — e.g. where a set of words has to be recalled. Elsewhere, non-response to items by testees needs some thought. In some instances, such as the sociolinguistic ones above, it does not seem right to score it in either of the two ways involved. Choosing neither agreement nor disagreement with a statement may be a legitimate indication of uncertainty. You can choose then to score each person out of the items they answered at all. Such totals will then have to be adjusted to be all out of the same total, e.g. by conversion to percent. Similarly, choice of a legitimate 'escape' response to an open choice item should not be counted wrong (6.3, 20.5 v).

However, in many instances, an absent response more likely counts as one of the two alternatives being scored — e.g. where items require past participles of verbs to be supplied in a school achievement test, items with no response would typically be scored 'wrong'. In general with items scored correct/incorrect the crux is: were the omissions due just to undue haste and lack of attention or cooperation, or perhaps lack of understanding of the task/question (so should be discounted), or to lack of ability (so to be counted as wrong)?

Again, some standard tests, especially norm-referenced ones for T use, are organised in such a way that cases are never even asked to respond to all the items in the test: these are called *graded tests*. Typical are the *British Picture Vocabulary Scale* (Dunn *et al.*, 1982) and the *Schonell Graded Word Reading* (Shearer, 1975), for native speaker children. The latter consists of 100 items — words to be read aloud. But since these are norm-referenced and item analysed to a series of age groups all the way from beginning readers to teenagers, there would be little point in all testees attempting all items. For most cases there will be many items too easy or too difficult.

Instead the items are arranged in order of increasing difficulty as determined from the norm-referenced item analysis performed by the test creators: e.g. *tree* in large print occurs early on, *campaign* in smaller letters later. A set procedure is then laid down, the essence of which is that the tester either starts presenting items at a point in the set of items related to the testee's age, or presents every fifth item in sequence from ten before that item. The test stops after a run of ten wrong answers have been made, and the testee is credited with a score as if they had answered correctly the earlier test items skipped over (see Shearer, 1975 for full details).

Another example of more complicated scoring arises with dictation tasks. Prima facie every testee has a chance to write down either correctly or incorrectly the same set of items — viz. all the words in the passage read out. However, in practice people may add and reorder words as well as get them wrong or just omit them. See Oller (1979) for discussions of possible scoring regimes for such tasks.

As we saw in 8.4, many tests consist of items where two or more alternative answers are offered to choose between. Obviously this leaves it open for some testees to choose responses more or less by random guesswork instead of omitting items where they are not sure. Practitioners have different approaches to this. One approach is to assume that testees will guess when they don't know, or actually instruct them to do so. An adjustment is then often made to all total scores that takes this into account. Since, in a 20 item test where two answers are offered, testees would on average, in the long run, get 10 items correct by dint of random choice with no knowledge whatsoever, a score of 10 is considered no better than 'chance'. Similarly would be five right in a 20 item m/c test with 4 alternatives for each item. The following is a common simple formula used to adjust scores for guessing:

$$\text{Score adjusted for guessing} = \text{Raw score} - \frac{\text{Possible maximum minus raw score}}{\text{Number of alternatives offered for any item, minus one}}$$

This makes scores equal to chance come out as zero, scores worse than chance come out as negative figures, and scores better than chance remain on a scale with the same maximum as the original one (i.e. up to max. 20 in the example).

Alternatively you can assume that testees will omit items they don't feel they can answer rather than guess blindly, or tell them to do so. Then you have to decide how to treat the omitted items, as already discussed. One major problem with all this is the uncertainty about whether cases will actually abide by the instructions or, with no instruction, all behave the same way. Would adults in an R context be more likely to conform than children in a T one, for example? And there is the problem of how far cases are able to assess their own knowledge. Often what someone thinks of as a blind guess is actually made non-randomly on the basis of some unconscious knowledge, so with an instruction not to guess, some cases may underscore (cf. 20.5).

Note that if there are only two alternatives, the formula above reduces to:

Adjusted total correct score = Total correct − Total wrong

This would be appropriate for a set of items offering binary choices in each item other than the special type now to be described.

Many tests scored right/wrong offer essentially the same two alternative choices repeatedly for each item, the choice being of some positive/ negative type, or where one alternative is clearly the more important one to focus the quantification on. For instance all the test items are words which have to be judged as real English words or made up, with of course some of the stimulus words in fact being real, some not. This is used in psycholinguistic research and assessment of vocabulary size. Here argu- ably it is ability to spot the real words correctly that is more 'important' than ability to spot unreal ones. Similarly a set of sentences may be offered some of which contain ill-formed relative clauses, some correct ones, and they all have to be judged as correct or not (used to quantify grammatical competence, or metalinguistic awareness). On the other hand in phonetic and language research pairs of sounds may be offered to be judged as the same or different: in some items they are actually different, in some identical. Here it is not clear that getting 'sames' correct is more at a premium than getting 'differents' correct, or vice versa, since both have to be identified in real life.

In instances like the first two, there are the same two ways in which cases can achieve either of the two scoring alternatives on any item. In the first example above, they may be right in identifying a real word as existing (*hit* or *true positive* response), or right in identifying an unreal word as non-existent. Similarly they can be wrong by claiming that a non-existent word exists (*false positive* or *false alarm* response), or by saying that an existing word does not exist. However, false positives are in a way a worse sin than the other type of error. Testees have no justification for the former, since they are unlikely to encounter unreal words outside such tests: they must be guesses. However the second type of wrong response could be genuine lack of knowledge (e.g. the word has never been met). On this sort of reasoning, a correction formula originating in 'signal detection theory', may be used.

First take a case's total of true positive responses and divide by the total of true items offered in the test: call that A. For example if there were 50 real words in an 80 item test and 40 were correctly identified, A = 0.8. Then divide the total of false positive responses by the total of false items offered in the test: call that B. So, if of the 30 unreal words included five were judged to be real, then B = 0.17 for that person. Then use the formula:

$$\frac{\text{Adjusted total}}{\text{correct score}} = \frac{\text{Total true items}}{\text{in the test}} \times \frac{A - B}{1 - B}$$

In the example this comes out as $50 \times (0.8 - 0.17)/(1 - 0.17) = 38$. Total correct scores are here 'out of' the maximum of 'true' items only, and get reduced to take account of possible guessing the more false positive responses there are. They may even be negative (Meara & Buxton, 1987; Meara *et al.*, 1994).

13.3 Alternative Ways of Treating Sets of Dichotomous Items

The fact that measurements like those of this chapter come from the *same* list of items for all cases means that you can, of course, examine the results separately by item rather than by person for how many of each of the two relevant choices were made for each. And whereas *one* person's answers to *different* questions in a test or inventory are only questionably independent of each other, *different* people's answers to the *same* item clearly *are* independent. Hence the 'score' each item gets in this way is usually best treated as a binomial categorisation of the testees (Chap. 18): so many people fall in the 'correct' category, so many in the 'incorrect' category for each item (or 'accept' — 'not accept', 'remember' — 'not remember' the item, etc.). For the possible extension of this to an error analysis of different wrong answers, or simply all the types of answer given to each item in certain types of test, see also Chapter 18.

As an example Quigley (1973), in a 73 item test of vocabulary used on 50 children, not only reports scores for the children, but also proportions for the items (i.e. words): 29 items (e.g. *dog*) were known by 100% of the children, 3 by under 50% (e.g. *cap*), etc. The label 'item analysis' can be used for this way of examining data from dichotomous tests and attitude inventories generally either in R or T work. If the test is criterion-referenced, since the items are representative of the totality of the things being tested — the 'whole' variable — looking at which items a group, or individual, got most wrong gives a good idea of what they don't know. In a T context this could lead to remedial teaching — i.e. such an analysis would serve the diagnostic purpose (2.2.2).

If the test is norm-referenced, however, you don't get this value from item analysis because the items are not chosen on this representative basis. Rather it is often done more specifically during the piloting of a test, where some consequent revision of the items would be envisaged. In fact items that most cases got wrong would be rejected, along with those that most got right, as being poor discriminators (10.4.2).

Item analysis in the more general sense may sometimes be more of interest than the total scores of the testees. This would be so if the purpose of the test just cited was to establish a set of words relatively unknown to children of the age group tested, for use in some other test as part of a learning experiment, where the familiarity of the words was to be controlled. However, if the prime interest is in the items, that *may* be an indication that they do not *collectively* constitute a unitary test at all, and that each item is best thought of as a separate variable. Thus unitary total scores over items for cases would not be meaningful — see 13.4.

13.4 The Single Variable and Equal Interval Assumptions

As has been mentioned, the normal assumption is that any set of items you choose and score collectively should measure one variable, not a mixture of two or more unconnected things (to the limit of one separate thing per item) or only *part* of something. Thus a higher score is taken as systematically representing the presence of more of the variable being measured. Checking on this *unidimensionality* assumption is largely up to the measurer's personal judgment plus item analysis, and can be uncertain (cf. Oscarson in de Bot *et al.*, 1991).

If a test of language ability contains some questions involving vocabulary and some involving grammar this might seem to violate this assumption — you could argue that two different variables are being measured and the total score reflects a bit of each, but in such a way that you can never tell from the total how much of the score is made up of success on vocabulary and how much from grammar.

On the other hand we might be more inclined to argue that this is in fact all right, since we suppose that there exists a single overall variable of language ability which we are measuring from its contributory elements (cf. the dimensions discussed at 10.4.2). Whether overall scores in such a test are legitimate turns on whether you believe vocabulary knowledge and grammatical knowledge are connected and (with other things) make up a unitary construct of language ability or are entirely separate variables — largely a matter of theoretical stance (though statistical techniques like factor analysis can also shed light). In the latter instance you should treat each subset of items separately as a separate 'subtest' measuring a separate variable and yielding its own total score, which you may *then* choose to combine — see Chapter 15 (cf. also the discussion of validity in 22.3).

A consequence of what has just been said is that you cannot glibly treat *any* set of questions presented to people for some quantification purposes as involving the present sort of scoring. You have to look closely to see if there are really distinct subsets of items measuring different variables, or indeed if *every* question is not really measuring a different variable, as is often the case with a 'questionnaire' of a sociolinguistic or dialectological nature. In that event often the answers to each question have to be dealt with *separately* as nominal categorisations, and it would make no sense to add up a total (q.v. Chap. 18).

Finally there is the usual interval assumption that larger scores reflect proportionately larger degrees of presence of the variable involved. So in our language ability example you have to assume that the difference between a score of 40 and a score of 45, say, represents an equivalent amount of difference in language ability to the difference between a score of 15 and 20, 20 and 25 etc. And, indeed, that the difference between the ability of Fred and George, who scored 40 and 45 respectively, is the same as that between Henry and Peter, who had the same two marks but got different items right. This is hard to prove and usually assumed as an act of faith, though test items do normally vary in the degree of the target variable they probably indicate. In graded tests like those described in 13.2, the items are *systematically* of increasing difficulty, and the strict administration and scoring regime is designed to deal with this. Thus one case cannot get the same score as another by getting right a set of items of a very different mixture of difficulties.

Elsewhere, there may be more of a problem if questions, even palpably measuring *one* variable, are of widely differing difficulty in a language proficiency test, or if, say, in the bilingual dominance inventory mentioned above you feel that some items are more important markers of dominance than others. 'Item analysis' and revision of the set of items may sort this out, or you can give differently weighted scores to different items (14.2). But if you feel there is *grave* doubt — e.g. if you feel a difference of 5 marks actually reflects more difference where high and low scores are involved than in the middle of the scale — you could treat your measurement as really ordinal. So you simply put those tested in rank order on the basis of the marks they get and forget the actual numerical scores. However, authorities vary in how important they regard the equal interval requirement anyway (cf. 16.4 and Hatch & Farhady, 1982: 40f).

Further reading

Oller (1979).
Valette (1967: Chap. 4).

On the tricky issue of whether different responses of the same person can be viewed as independent of each other, necessary for some statistical purposes, see Scholfield (forthcoming c).

14 Scoring on Interval Scales: Scores Involving Rating and Weighting

14.1 Scores on Overall Rating Scales

A rather different source of quasi-interval numerical scores is the rating scale. Here scores are derived from someone's direct summary judgment of a variable, leading to this sort of approach being characterised as 'subjective'. The variable being measured is usually regarded as having a very limited number of possible alternative scores or degrees — often much fewer than arises from the scoring systems in Chap. 11–13. Five or seven are probably the best to work with (Miller, 1956) — more than this presents problems of reliable discrimination for the 'rater' and may create a spurious impression of precision (11.4). However, examiners are sometimes expected by direct judgment to award a percentage score to compositions. Also, continuous scales are sometimes used, where a judge places a mark on a line between two extreme points, and its distance from the end is subsequently measured with a ruler to provide a score (similar is the last example in 11.4). Contrast *ranking* (Chap. 16) and *ordered categorisation* (Chap. 17).

14.1.1 Rating by measurer

Such scales are often applied direct by the measurer. For instance, rating language learners on a five-point scale for spoken ability in English, in effect he/she gives each case a score of, say, 1, 2, 3, 4 or 5. Alternatively 0, 1, 2, 3, 4, or -2, -1, 0, +1, +2 scales could be used — the exact range of figures makes no difference. These would be interpreted as corresponding to something like:

very weak	poor	moderate	good	excellent

Thus, there is a fixed maximum to the possible score of each case measured which is the same for all. The difference from what we have seen before is that the scores are not decided by adding up any 'discrete' scored items or occurrences, but in 'one blow' as it were. Examples:

> Rating by one speech therapist of parents of several speech handi-capped children for 'supportiveness' and the children for 'severity of disorder' based on his/her experience of them over some weeks. Or, less satisfactorily, each child and set of parents is rated by their own different therapist.

> Overall 'impression' marks for quality, out of 20, given by an examiner to some English essays.

> Rating by a teacher of each of a set of classroom activities, e.g. reading aloud, group discussion of a text, on a four point scale for how relevant they think it is to developing learners' socio-cultural knowledge, or fluency, etc. (Faerch *et al.*, 1984: 241f).

Many variables of the more global and less tangible variety are quantified this way, using data either observed non-reactively or elicited in a more or less structured way in quasi-natural interaction, both for R and T purposes. However, rating is also often an alternative to counting things up using some piecemeal scoring system on the same data (Chap. 12). So instead of marking essays impressionistically for quality of the language used, you can count up errors per 100 words, or use a regime such as Oller's (1979: 385ff), or count occurrences of key structures taken as evidence of advanced writing proficiency etc. Instead of a 'global rating' approach to measuring Spanish fluency, you could use counts of suitable items in recorded speech samples (e.g. hesitations, errors), combined in some way (cf. 15.2), or indeed administer standard 'discrete' tests of various aspects of competence, again with scores combined in some way.

The 'discrete' approach to quantifying variables along the lines of Chapter 12 and 13 is clearly more time-consuming than a swift rating, and, superficially at least, requires more expertise from the measurer, but it yields much more detailed information, and so would be of much more use for diagnostic purposes in a T context. However a rating (or a ranking — Chap. 16) would be adequate for many placement/screening type func-tions.

It should be noted that in discussions of testing, especially T communi-cative testing, there is sometimes a confusion involving the term 'discrete', often in the phrase 'discrete point'. This can be used to refer to aspects of either (i) of the construction of the items, or (ii) of the variable(s) involved, or (iii) of the scoring (the present concern).

(i) The term is perhaps most often used to refer to the lack of connected-ness between the items of a typical multi-item test, where they do not form a continuous linguistically coherent single text as they would in a cloze passage or dictation test, or language elicited in quasi-natural communication — Chapter 8. You can even have discrete items of this sort constructed on pragmatic communicative points (Rivera, 1984). Normally such tests will be scored discretely (iii), by adding up scores (13.1), rather than by an overall rating.

(ii) 'Discrete (point)' also often refers to the strictly separate matter of the test focusing just on one language subskill, one subpart of a level of language, etc. (e.g. the meanings of prepositions, in the reading comprehension mode) or, if it covers more, consisting of distinct subtests which do this. That is, fairly specific variables are attacked by each set of items. It must be noted, however, that a discrete test in sense (i) is not discrete in sense (ii) if items actually require many skills to be brought to bear to the extent that they are all tested. Conversely, you could imagine a cloze passage that was focused just on one specific kind of language point. All the same, *scoring* of a level or skill will usually be discrete (iii) again.

Finally, less controlled data, such as speech elicited in interview, is clearly not 'discrete' in either sense (i) or (ii). However, it can be *scored* discretely (iii), as we have seen in the discussion above of Spanish fluency or essay marking, by choosing specific variables to focus on, and counting things up, rather than relying on overall rating. Opinions vary currently about whether communicative competence, for example, is best scored from such data by global ratings or a discrete method. The former is used e.g. for the *FSI Oral Interview*, the latter by Hart *et al.* (1987). An obvious advantage of the rating approach to such a broad variable is that it bypasses the difficult problem of deciding adequately what precise specific variables make it up, or would be indicators of it (Chap. 22, 23), so it is likely to be more 'valid'. But rating is often felt to be less 'reliable' (19.3.2).

14.1.2 Rating by cases

Commonly overall rating of a variable also arises in a different way from above. Instead of the investigator or measurer doing the rating, he/she gets informants in a survey or subjects in an experiment etc. (the cases) to rate themselves, or some aspect of language etc., usually obtaining measures of opinion about language in an R context (Chap. 7). The scores obtained are then in effect measures of the judgments of the raters as much as of what is rated. Examples:

Self-rating by Spanish Americans for the extent to which they use Spanish. This can be done for use in particular 'domains' too, e.g. how much Spanish is used addressing workmates, as part of measures of bilingual dominance.

Measuring foreign learners' attitude to learning English by getting them to respond on a five or seven point scale from 'strongly agree' to 'strongly disagree' to the statement 'Learning English is very important'. This sort of agreement attitude scale is sometimes referred to as a *Likert scale*.

Often a series of such ratings is obtained from cases as they are asked to rate a whole set of words, sentences, voices etc. where each is of separate interest. That is, the ratings of separate words or whatever relate to separate conditions or variables to be compared in some R study. This must be distinguished of course from a series of ratings designed collectively to measure one thing (see 14.2). Examples:

Rating by native speakers of a word such as *beggar* on a seven-point adjectival scale like *strong — weak*. A way of quantifying connotative meaning, known as the *semantic differential* technique, used in experiments comparing large numbers of words and scales (Osgood *et al.*, 1957).

Self-ratings by subjects of the frequency with which a specific word was met — often/sometimes/never — quantifying 'word familiarity' (Carroll, 1971).

Rating by native speakers of a learner speaking with a foreign accent on tape on a five-point scale for 'intelligence'. Similar is rating a native speaker speaking in different regional accents, in research using the 'matched guise' technique.

Rating by learners or native speakers of a sentence for acceptability as normal English (cf. Prideaux, 1984: 219ff). Done by learners it is more a measure of learners' competence, done by native speakers it is more a measure of the sentence.

Rating by young children of their interest in a topic by asking them to ring one of five faces, which show differing degrees of frown and smile, in response to questions like 'How would you feel about reading a story all about dolls?' (Hare & Devine, 1983).

Cases are asked to sort attitude statements written on cards into 9 ordered heaps on the basis of how much they agree with them (or sort words on some criterion such as degree of acceptability etc.). Items in each heap score the same rating figure. So-called *Q-sort* procedure (Cohen, 1976: 133ff).

A special instance arises where cases are asked to rate difference/similarity between the members of *all possible* pairs of things, e.g. all possible pairs of words from a set of 8 (e.g. *robin, hawk, penguin* etc.) on a scale of 1 to 9 for 'similarity of meaning' (Prideaux, 1984 :273ff; Clark & Clark, 1977: 434). Similarly, pairs of sentences can be rated for similarity of naturalness, etc. Here the total pairs to rate is the number of words or whatever times that number less one, all divided by two: in this example: $(8 \times 7)/2 = 28$.

These are often most clearly presented not as a conventional list of 28 questions, but in a triangular 'matrix' where each slot has to be filled by each subject with a rating number for the pair of that column and row. One corner of this for the example would look like this:

	penguin	robin	monkey	...
hawk	—	—	—	...
penguin		—	—	...
robin			—	...

etc.

Ratings by cases could be involved in creating EVs as well as measuring DVs. So if in a psycholinguistic experiment you wished to measure ease of memory for concrete versus abstract words, lists of suitable words to be memorised could be obtained by getting speakers of English to rate words for 'concreteness' on a scale of 0 to 6 (Taylor, 1976: 60), and choosing from these a high scoring group and a low scoring group to make up a two-valued EV. Also less clearly linguistic variables can be approached this way: it may be more realistic to expect subjects to answer a question like 'How much time per week do you watch Welsh language TV?' on a rating scale than with an exact number of hours (as per 12.2.1).

14.1.3 Interval versus ordered category interpretation

As usual, for rating scales to be acceptable as proper interval scores, we have to be reasonably sure that *one* variable is being consistently measured, and that people are interpreting the intervals in the scale uniformly. Unidimensionality is helped if everyone has the same unambiguous definition of the scale and its points (19.3.2). However, a problem arises sometimes with rating scales that have a neutral middle value, since informants may choose this for more than one reason. For instance, asked to place the word *fruit* on a scale of one to seven reflecting how far it is rated as 'active' or 'passive' in a test to measure the 'semantic differential' of certain words, informants may choose the middle slot as much to register their feeling that this scale 'doesn't apply' or they 'can't decide' as to record a genuine 'middle opinion'. Thus what might better be treated as *missing* responses get included in the scores (cf. 13.2, 17.2).

To help with the equal interval interpretation, the raters should perhaps be presented with the scale in number form as well as glosses of how each level is defined. Prideaux (1984) has examples of this form of presentation: after 'anchoring' the scale (10.5) cases then go through responding purely by ringing one of the set of numbers offered beside each sentence. Alternatively a visual presentation of the scale may prompt the equal interval interpretation. So in semantic differential work often the rating scales are presented in the following form to subjects, who have to place a cross in one of the seven equal sized slots to record their rating of a particular word supplied:

hot   __ : __ : __ : __ : __ : __ : __   cold

But suppose we are asking a teacher to assess the fluency of learners of English in a class on a 5 point scale and we feel the teacher is thinking of a score of 3 for fluency as better than 2 but requiring a much greater competence to give 4 rather than 3. Then, strictly, we should think of the results as ordered categorisations rather than interval scores, and present them accordingly (Chap. 17) — we would regard the scores 0, 1, 2, 3, 4 simply as five ordered categories into one of which each pupil is placed.

Equally if ten people are rating a word on a five-point scale of 'concreteness', can we be sure that one person's 4 represents the same degree of concreteness as another's? (cf. 19.3.2). Are all measuring the same thing? However, in practice researchers don't seem to worry too much about this and interpret and analyse almost any rating results as interval without further thought, even when the scale has only three points — motivated perhaps by the fact that more familiar and powerful inferential statistical techniques are available for dealing with numerical results than with ordinal category ones! The limiting case of a rating scale with only two alternatives is not usually treated as interval however — see Chapter 17.

14.2 Counts and Totals with Weighted or Rated Items

14.2.1 Uniform sets of items

A more complex way of using rating scales is in combination with any of the techniques of Chapters 12 and 13. Instead of scoring each of a set of occurrences or items effectively as just 1 or 0 you, or your subjects, can record a score for each separate item on a scale, say 3, 2, 1, 0 or 1, 0.5, 0, to indicate *degrees* of correctness, agreement or whatever. You then total or average *these* scores to give the overall score for each case on some variable — and for each item, if desired, where a uniform set of items is used (13.3). In a sense the yes/no, right/wrong, agree/disagree etc. decisions on each occurrence or item in Chapters 12 and 13 are simply the extreme limit of a rating scale — one with only two alternatives. We first look at examples with uniform sets of items:

Scoring a cloze test on the basis that each word suggested by the testee to fill a gap is given 2 points for the exact word the tester deleted from the original text, 1 for an acceptable filler or near synonym, 0 for a word which doesn't fit at all, or perhaps with totally the wrong meaning. These marks are then totalled for each case (cf. 13.2). Alternatively you could award each response a figure related to the precise probability with which a native speaker would offer that response, as decided from pilot trials of the passage ('clozentropy' method, Brown, 1980).

Quantifying 'attitude to school' by totalling the agreement (Likert) scores recorded by subjects on five point scales for each statement in an inventory (cf. latter part of 13.1, and distinguish 14.1.2 above).

Measuring learners' 'self-concept' by asking them to rate *myself* on a series of seven point semantic differential-type scales like *muddled-or-derly*, and totalling the ratings (with due attention to the polarity of each scale, since the 'favourable' self-concept end should vary randomly between the left and the right). Cf.14.1.2.

Having cases rate each of four sentences with a particular kind of structure for 'naturalness' and taking the total as a measure of each case's judgment of the structure's naturalness. Typically the four items would be presented randomly mixed with other items representing other structures (Prideaux, 1984).

Many language performance and attitude variables and psychological variables related to personality are quantifiable this way, either with cases or measurers providing the ratings, particularly in research. In some circumstances the term 'weighting' rather than 'rating' is used of the values other than 0 and 1 used in such score calculations. Though there is some overlap, this is particularly so when it is the measurer or researcher rather than the subject who decides what figure is appropriate, and where some objective means has been used to arrive at the figures, beyond someone's direct subjective judgment. Thus the cloze example above would typically be said to involve a *weighted* scoring system, the others to involve *rating* by subjects.

The examples so far have been of rating or weighting applied to responses. However, in tests and inventories with a uniform set of items (Chap. 13), *either* the item stimuli *or* the responses or indeed *both* can have weightings/ratings attached. The cloze test example above is a case in point. In addition to/instead of having a scale for scoring responses to each gap, some gaps could be weighted as worth more than others, e.g. on the basis of how hard teachers regarded them.

Language attitudes are often quantified in a more sophisticated way than we have seen in examples so far in 13.1, 14.1.2, or above, in that each *stimulus* statement in the inventory may have an associated weighting assigned on some basis by the developer of the instrument. For instance, an instrument that could be used to measure attitude to a language teacher (Shaw & Wright, 1967: 497) consists of 45 statements which the informants simply have to agree or disagree with dichotomously. However, each statement has, unknown to respondents, a weighting related to how markedly it indicates a favourable or negative attitude to a teacher. E.g.

	weighting
Uses good English	10.0
Does nothing to interest the student	1.5
Makes vague assignments	2.1
Uses meaningful gestures	7.8

The attitude score of any informant is then not just a total of pro-teacher items agreed with and anti-teacher items disagreed with (13.1), but the average of the weightings of the items agreed with. If responses had been on a rating scale rather than dichotomous, the calculation would be more elaborate still.

Many sophisticated ways have been used to arrive at such attitude item weightings, which is normally done during the piloting and development stages of an instrument. An old and well-tried method, due to Thurstone, is to derive the weights from a group of judges, often of the same sort as potential respondents, who in effect rate a pool of statements for the degree to which they consider each represents a positive or negative attitude of the target sort. In the above example judges placed statements on a scale 1–11, by sorting them into eleven physical heaps which they were instructed to think of as representing evenly spaced degrees of attitude to a teacher (cf. Q-sort 14.1.2). The average rating of the judges of any item then became its weighting or 'scale value' when the inventory is used for real. Items on which judges vary considerably in their rating are rejected as not being clear and simple reflections of any degree of the target attitude 'construct'. Also, if relative discrimination properties were to be heightened (cf. NR – 10.2), only extreme weighted items would be retained.

Finally, one special form of weighting can be mentioned — that where item scores are weighted by scores of the same cases on another response variable. This can be found used for example where subjects take an 80 item test, and for each item indicate not only their response but also their confidence in it on a scale 1–4, from 'pure guess' to 'very sure'. Thus each case ends up with a score correct, which would in the normal way be out of 80, and a total rating, out of 320, reflecting his/her overall confidence. These can of course be examined as separate variables, but it is also legitimate to combine them to yield a 'confidence weighted accuracy' score for each case, if one was interested in measuring a combination of objective and subjective accuracy. In this instance this would typically be done on an item by item basis thus. Each item would be scored +1 for correct and -1 for wrong for each case (unlike the usual 1, 0) and this figure multiplied by the confidence rating, yielding a score between -4 and +4 for each case for each item. A case's total weighted score could then be calculated, to fall between - 320 and +320.

14.2.2 Counts

In count studies (Chap. 12) there is often the opportunity for the measurer to weight/rate either different linguistic subtypes of some unit counted or different qualities of rendition of an item. Thus in the calculation of an overall error score potentially different kinds of error can be weighted differently whenever they occur — e.g., rather crudely, grammatical errors rated more severe than lexical ones. Or each error can be rated by the measurer on a scale for how far away it seems to be from the apparent target item. Actual examples of the use of weighting in count studies are:

Measuring foreign learners' mastery of the plural of nouns in English from recorded material by giving 0 for no plural where there should be, e.g. *foot*, for *feet*, 1 for wrong plural forms, e.g. *foots*, and 2 for the correct form *feet*. These figures are then treated along the lines of 12.2.2 (Dulay *et al.*, 1982: 219, 253).

Every time it occurs in a sample of child speech, *you* is scored as 1, *he* as 2, on the grounds that the latter is developmentally more advanced in Lee & Canter's *Developmental Syntax Score* (Lee & Canter, 1971; Dale, 1972: 303) (cf. 12.1).

In a study where politeness is to be quantified, occurrences in free speech of *please* are scored 1, *excuse me* 2, *thank you* 3 (Crosby & Nyquist, 1977).

Watson (1988) scored spelling errors as:

0   Letters are inappropriate for the word spelled (e.g. *made* = ELD)

1   Beginning letter (or blend/digraph) only is represented correctly (e.g. *twirl* = T or TW or TWORK)

2   (a) Beginning and ending consonants are represented correctly (e.g. *made* = MD or MUD)

_   (b) Beginning consonant and an appropriate vowel are given (e.g. *bold* = BOW)

...and so on, up to 5 for fully correct.

Clearly much of what was said in Chapter 12 applies just as much to quantification in the present form. The main reason for using the more complicated scoring system is that it can overcome some problems noted there to do with uneven importance or difficulty of individual items, and accommodate degrees of approximation to some model in what is said or written. However, it can create some problems of other sorts.

Take the example of Winford (1978) who used such *weighted index* scores in a sociolinguistic investigation of the varying pronunciation of the *th* in *thing, through* etc. in Trinidad as [θ], [tθ] and [t] (cf. 12.2.2). Instead of simply adding up the 'correct' [θ]'s out of the total possible, and disregarding the complexity among the 'wrong' variants, or indeed regarding the three possible pronunciations as three categories and simply counting up the number of occasions when a given informant used each alternative (Chap. 18), he used a rating scale approach. So he scored his informants 0 for a [θ], 1 for a [tθ] and 2 for a [t] on each occasion where one or other had to occur. [tθ] is a sort of halfway pronunciation — saying, as it were, *t-thing* rather than *thing* or *ting*, so this can be regarded as a legitimate rating/weighting on phonetic grounds, and more refined than say just giving [θ] 1 and anything else 0.

Of course, as seen in 12.2.2 generally, the possible maximum scores of Winford's informants were different, depending on how many occasions when [θ] could have been used arose in the sample of the speech of each. Thus 15 possible occasions for [θ] would give a maximum possible score for that person of 30. Various methods, similar to those already described, can be used to even out such scores. So you can calculate:

(Actual total score)/(Possible maximum score) x 100

to get % (cf. Chambers & Trudgill, 1980). The possible maximum here would be twice the number of loci, of course, so the percentage maximum is 200% not 100%. You could readily convert these scores so as to be out of a 100% maximum, but despite the oddness of a maximum greater than 100%, this sort of scoring is quite often seen.

The main problem that can arise is as follows, and concerns the matter of measuring *one* variable only, with *uniform* intervals between the possible outcome scores. The example of [θ] - [tθ] - [t] is straightforward since phonetically this can reasonably be regarded as three alternatives on one dimension: [θ] is a fricative sound pronounced with the tongue on the upper teeth, [t] (in the example we are considering) is pronounced with the tongue in roughly the same place but is a plosive not a fricative, [tθ] is a combination of both, so naturally 'in between'. So it is not too controversial to quantify this as a single interval scale quantifying a variable you might call 'degree of replacement of [θ] by [t]' and so capture the extra information.

But what if [f] also occurs as a pronunciation where [θ] is standard (i.e. *fing* etc.)? [f] really differs from the [θ] along a different dimension from [t] and [tθ]. It is a fricative sound, but pronounced in a different place in the mouth, with lower lip and upper teeth, not tongue — in a sense as far away from [θ] as [t] is, but in a different direction. How then could we rate [f]? We *could* say that it differs from [θ] phonetically as much as [t] does, though in a different way, so give it 2. Even that is a problem because though [t] and [f] both differ from [θ] in one phonetic respect, [f] is closer to [θ] perceptually than [t] is. Also this really conflates two phonetic dimensions — the variables of 'place of articulation' — [θ] versus [f] — and 'manner of articulation' — [θ] versus [t] — so is of dubious suitability. A score of two becomes totally ambiguous, and derived totals or percentages even harder to interpret: a total of 2 from three possible occasions for [θ] could represent

Two [θ]'s and a [f]
Two [θ]'s and a [t]
One [θ] and two [tθ]'s.

But are these really 'the same'? In fact I think for certain purposes this *is* justifiable — but we must recognise that the variable quantified is now undifferentiated 'degree of phonetic divergence from [θ]' (contrast end of last paragraph). The other phonetic solution is to set up two variables instead of one of course — 'place divergence from [θ]' and 'manner divergence from [θ]'.

For a discussion of a more complex vowel example, where more dimensions and degrees of distance are involved, see Anshen (1978).

Alternatively you could resort to a different rationale, and decide to make the scale not reflect degrees of purely phonetic difference so much as degrees of social stigma attached to the variants. In this instance [f], as arguably the most stigmatised variant, might be given a score of 3 while the others would remain as scored above. But this sort of solution has to be carefully supported by prior research on what attitudes to the different variants involved really are, and quantifies in effect a different variable — 'degree of divergence in prestige from [θ]'. You might expect such a scale to vary from speech community to speech community, depending on the 'prestige' of particular variants in each community, in a way that a purely phonetic scale would not. And, as J. Milroy (1982: 39f) points out, degrees of prestige of variants may not always coincide with degrees of phonetic difference as closely as in the present example.

Any such approach also has to assume a standard 'norm' pronunciation, usually taken to score zero, as here for [θ] from which departures are quantified. But what variant this is is not always obvious — you could argue, for instance, that British standard [θ] is not really the local norm at all in some varieties of English. There is a problem in Edinburgh in that high prestige speech may be marked either by not sounding r in words like *heart*, similar to educated southern Received Pronunciation, or by sounding the r, as per the local educated Scottish accent. Also there may be problems with deciding what the norm is for particular lexical items and so where the relevant loci occur in a speech sample (J. Milroy (1982) on Northern Ireland and Jones-Sargent (1983) on Tyneside).

Problems like these lead us to conclude that, even if for convenient manipulation you follow existing practice and use such a rating approach, yielding quasi-interval data, it would be wise also to present and think about the results for each variant separately, e.g. as if values of a single polynomial variable (Chap. 18, and see Milroy 1987: 126).

Further reading

On rating scales generally: Henerson (1987); Frankfort-Nachmias & Nachmias (1992: Chap. 11); Sommer & Sommer (1991: Chap. 10); Pedhazur & Schmelkin (1991: 118ff).
On the sociolinguistic index score problem: J. Milroy (1982); L. Milroy (1987: Chap. 6); Anshen (1978: 12).

15 Scoring on Interval Scales: Combined Scores of Various Sorts

15.1 Interval Scores Derived from Combining Several Scores for the Same Variable

Another kind of numerical score you might be interested in obtaining for each case measured is one that is simply an average or total of several separate interval scores on the same variable for each case. Series of scores of any one of the types in Chapters 11–14 can be combined in this way, and though such a total or average score is in many ways only as good as the constituent measurements, it is in one important respect better — the combined score is a more reliable measure of the variable than any of its component scores (Chap. 19, 20).

In fact we have already seen many examples of essentially the same idea *within* various scoring systems reviewed in Chapters 12–14. For instance, one item in a multi-item test (Chap. 13) can be regarded as a measure of the variable the test as a whole measures. It's just that we don't usually feel one item on its own gives an accurate enough score, so we administer 50 'equivalent' items, and derive a total score instead. Some variables you can accurately quantify from a 'sample' of just one bit of behaviour from each case, but others you need a larger sample for.

A simple example is measuring MLU, the mean length of utterance in morphemes, of children or foreign learners, often done for R and T purposes as an indicator of linguistic maturity (23.2). Similarly the mean sentence or T-unit length in words is sometimes used. Here obviously if you want to measure the length of utterances people produce, you will not get an accurate indication by measuring the length of just one utterance from each person. Utterance length, unlike, say, their age, is just too inherently variable 'within a person'. So measurers use the average length of 50 or more utterances as a score for each *person* to be measured (= the cases of interest), each separate length measurement being of the type covered in 11.3 for each *utterance* (not of interest as separate cases here).

More elaborate instances where scores on several samples from each case are fruitfully combined:

> Measuring the average frequency of *however* in 10 different page-long samples of an author's work as a measure of his/her fondness for this word, rather than using the frequency from one sample only (cf. 12.1). This could be used in research on a work of disputed authorship.

> Using the average of four teachers' ratings of learners' fluencies rather than just one teacher's rating for each (cf. 14.1.1).

> Using the average of weighted [θ] articulation scores from 10 samples of a person's speech as that person's score (cf. 14.2.2).

> In a psycholinguistic experiment, subjects are shown various types of existing and non-existing word of English. It is desired to measure how quickly people are able to indicate whether a word exists or not — this sort of information for different types of word being able to throw light on how words are mentally stored and accessed. Typically you would not use the response time from just one word of a given type, but the total from, say, ten of each type as an indication of this. Or you might use only the average response time on items of a given sort to which the *correct* response was made (cf. 11.3).

> Using the mean length obtained by phonetic instruments from ten repetitions of a word by a person as a measure of the length of the vowel (cf. 11.3).

> Using testees' scores on two equivalent reading tests totalled as their scores for that variable (cf. 13.1).

Two points need to be made about using such combined scores as scores for individual cases. First, I have tacitly assumed that the everyday average — the *arithmetic mean* technically — is the one you would calculate to represent the set of scores for each case. Incidentally, just totalling the repeated measures is equivalent to averaging, with one less computation, assuming every case has the same number of repeated measures to be combined. However, in some circumstances it is better to take the commonest score of each case to represent the set — the *mode* as it is called. (Other summary measures such as the 'geometric mean' and 'median' might also be more relevant in certain circumstances — see Langley, 1979 or any basic statistics text for further explanation).

Take for example the work of Warren-Leubecker & Bohannon (1984), who wished to measure the frequency level (pitch) of the intonation of adults talking to children, to see if it was higher than when talking to adults. Obviously the frequency level measured at one instant for each subject would be an inadequate basis, so twenty declarative utterances from each subject were recorded and processed by a frequency analyser which sampled all the speech from one case every 250 milliseconds. At each of these many sampling points the machine automatically picked out the frequency level at which there was the most intensity, as this is known to carry the intonation. Then a display was constructed for each case showing how often among the sample points particular frequencies (0–2000 hertz) occurred.

If each person had used a range of pitch frequencies, with the commonest more or less in the middle of the range and less popular ones tailing off above and below symmetrically, the average would have been the best choice to summarise the pitches sampled from each. However, it turned out that people typically used a large number of relatively high pitches, with a range tailing off downwards into the lower ones (but not upwards). This sort of 'skewed' distribution is not well summarised by the familiar average. Hence the researcher felt it more suitable to use the mode — the commonest/most frequent frequency — as a pitch frequency score to represent the whole lot for a given case (though other solutions could also have been adopted).

Second, in instances like this where you have several measurements for each case measured, it may be profitable to look at how well the different scores being combined are agreeing with each other before blithely averaging and proceeding to use a single score alone as each case's score, thereby wasting the information in the original component scores. Thus if the measurement is supposed to have some absolute value — criterion referenced — you may have greater confidence in using the average or total of a set of repeated scores for one person on the same variable if these scores are reasonably close to each other in absolute level of score. With norm-referenced measures, you may be more convinced if it can be shown that there is high agreement of the *correlation* type between the general orders in which the cases are placed by the different sets of repeated scores. For instance you might not be so keen to lump together four teachers' ratings of ten learners for relative fluency if it could be shown that the four teachers were not agreeing very much with each other in who was relatively better than who, and by how much. These matters are essentially ones of 'reliability' (Chap. 19, 20).

The actual calculation of measures of (absolute) closeness and (relative) correlation of repeated measures of the same cases cannot be pursued here:

the latter is described in any basic statistics book (e.g. Robson 1983, Hatch & Farhady 1982) and both are overviewed in Scholfield (forthcoming b).

15.2 Interval Scores Derived from Combining Scores for Different Variables

Superficially similar to the preceding is obtaining overall scores for cases by combining measurements made of each case on several different variables, and maybe involving figures obtained in a variety of ways covered in Chapters 12–14. This is much less straightforward than what we looked at in 15.1, generally involving considerations of 'validity' (Chapters 21–23) rather than 'reliability', and must be carefully distinguished. For one thing, the combined scores here are usually quantifying a separate variable from any of the components. Furthermore, whereas normally only some kind of adding or averaging the scores of each case was involved in 15.1, here a wider range of operations, including subtraction and multiplication as well as addition may be relevant.

15.2.1 Subtractive combination

Subtractive combination arises commonly in one of two ways. Either you are interested in a variable that is really the *difference* between two other variables, or you are interested in what might be thought of as a *change* — improvement or the opposite — on what is in some sense the 'same' variable measured under different conditions, except that of course the different conditions make it strictly a different variable the second time.

The first situation can be illustrated from the work of Local (1982) on the frequency of different nuclear tones in the speech of Tyneside children (cf. 12.2). Around eight nuclear tones are commonly distinguished in English, these being, roughly, the major changes of pitch which occur at the most prominently stressed points in utterances — rises, falls, rise-falls, etc. But, as well as quantifying each type of tone as a percentage of all tones observed in declarative sentences of each case, there was some expectation from other work that the *difference* between certain tone frequencies might be of interest, e.g. distinguish sexes. So he also measured for each child variables such as '% difference between falls and rises' — i.e. % of falls minus % of rises. Such a score can range in theory from +100 to -100.

Again Winograd *et al.* (1984) played voices on tape to informants and then asked them to rate each of another set of voices on tape on a scale 1–4 for whether they had been heard before or not. In fact half had, half hadn't. A separate score (as per 14.2.1) was obtained for each case separately from responses to the items in the 'actually heard before' and the 'not actually heard before' conditions. Each case then obtained a 'discrimination' score calculated by subtracting the former from the latter. In this way a single positive or negative score was obtained for each case showing how far his/her rating was different, in a particular direction, for voices heard before from that for those not heard before. This was taken as quantifying his/her ability to distinguish voices heard before from those not heard before.

The second type of subtractive combination is commonly seen in work on learning in psycholinguistics and language learning research, as well as of course used to assess progress for T purposes (2.2.2). Often cases are tested, e.g. for reading speed, before following some special learning/ teaching regime, and then tested again with an equivalent test after. In research, commonly different groups would follow different regimes so comparisons could ·be made between the effectiveness of different teaching/learning techniques or the like. Or there is a desire simply to track developmental changes in proficiency from successive counts of things in naturalistic data. Now the variable of interest here is really the amount of improvement, or lack of it, as a result of the intervening instruction or developmental experience. This can most simply be quantified by subtracting the *pre-test* or *base-line* score of each case from his/her *post-test* score to yield a single *improvement* score for further analysis in the research results. In research in areas like foreign language vocabulary retention after cessation of instruction or contact with native speakers, these scores tend to be negative *attrition* scores.

Change scores like these need to be distinguished from ordinary quantification of achievement just at one point in time (1.2.3). That cannot in itself distinguish between knowledge of the content of the syllabus of a completed course of instruction that was derived from actually taking that course, as against knowledge that the person in fact already had before taking the course. In a T context it may require some thought to decide whether it is simple level of achievement/attainment or proficiency that one really wishes to assess and perhaps reward, or genuine *change* thereof.

Of course change scores have a rather different interpretation depending on whether the source measurements are criterion- or norm-referenced (Chap. 10). In the former instance, assuming parallel tests are used which randomly sample the same domain on both occasions, the difference scores reflect individual increases/decreases in the variable as a whole. It may even be possible by examination of change on individual test items or objectives to detect precisely what skills, bits of knowledge or whatever have been acquired/lost (cf. taking the driving test twice). However, discrimination may be poor between high improvers and low improvers.

In the norm-referenced instance, assuming equivalent parallel tests or whatever have been properly constructed for the two occasions, *amount* of change, and individual differences in that amount, will be highlighted more. For many R purposes this is what is required. However, you will not get the same information about what specifically has been learnt/lost.

For the assessment of individual progress in T contexts, e.g. in self-paced learning, or one-to-one language therapy, some have suggested that a third kind of 'referencing' is needed — viz. *self-referencing*, also called 'ipsative' referencing (Rowntree, 1977; Wiliam, 1992). This resembles criterion referencing except that the criterion is not some case-neutral domain of abilities, but rather the previously observed abilities of each individual. An individual case's performance is interpreted in relation to that particular person's ability or performance earlier, often purely qualitatively.

An element of quantitative 'self-referencing' in a different way seems to be obtained by the following. Where you want to give extra credit or 'weight' to improvements on low original (pre-test) scores in comparison with the same improvement on a high original score, the % *change score* seems more relevant than a simple subtractive improvement score. This is obtained simply by expressing the raw improvement/attrition score as a percentage of the pretest score, for each case:

$$\% \text{ change score} = \frac{\text{post–test score} - \text{pre–test score}}{\text{pre–test score}} \times 100$$

For example, based on data on words per minute improvement in reading (Hill, 1981):

	Pre-test	Post-test	Improvement	% Change
Case 1	160	226	66	41.26
Case 2	138	221	83	60.14
Case 3	160	243	83	51.88

Finally it should be noted that you will not always want to summarise improvement as a single score for each case without first analysing the improvement statistically. In R studies, often the crux is whether there has *been* any marked improvement, and whether it *really* differs for one group of cases as against another. The techniques for analysing such improvement start from the original 'before' and 'after' scores and cannot be pursued here. They are to be found in statistics texts such as Hatch & Farhady (1982: 28ff), Cohen & Holliday (1982: Chap. 14, 15, 19).

15.2.2 Additive combination

Most combination of separate variables is essentially of the additive type. One way in which this arises is where you wish to combine scores on two or more 'indicator' measures of supposedly the same hidden variable. Indicators are variables which are known only to reflect what you are really trying to quantify indirectly, and any one will only be partly valid. However, several indicators together may approximate closely the true variable, so-called 'construct', you wish to quantify. Thus to get the best possible measure of some texts' reading ease you might combine scores from two different measures of readability. Here the concurrent validity of the measures might also be measured as a check, since you would expect the two sets of scores to correlate (agree) well with each other in this sort of instance (see Chap. 23).

Often in such instances you think of yourself as using two or more different means to quantify 'the same' variable, and it is a moot point whether combining such 'duplicatory' measures is more like combining quantification of *two* variables overlapping in content (the view here) or more like adding scores on alternative forms of the same instrument measuring *one* variable (15.1). In the UK T context it arises in relation to assessment of the National Curriculum, where pupils' attainment of the same criterion-referenced 'statements of attainment' in English is quanti-fied both by informal 'Teacher Assessment' (TA) and 'Standard Assessment Tasks' (SATs). The combination of the two sets of grades is coming to be referred to as *reconciliation* in contrast to the type discussed next which is called *aggregation* (Wiliam, 1992). Some contention arose because it was originally proposed to achieve reconciliation in fact not so much by adding the two grades for any case on each SoA, as by simply choosing to go exclusively by the SAT result and only using the TA where a SAT result was unavailable.

The other common situation where you wish to combine variables additively is where they are more obviously complementary rather than duplicatory, and together measure some large scale variable or a large part of it at least. For instance many standard T purpose tests and exams are really test 'batteries', that is they consist not of one homogeneous set of items but of a set of more or less clearly distinct subtests, each in itself often a set of dichotomous items (13.1). Each of these yields a score which is then added to the others in some way to yield an overall score for the intended variable for each case. Examples:

The old *Modern Language Aptitude Test* (*MLAT*, Carroll & Sapon, 1959) consists of several distinct subtests, each supposedly measuring a different aspect of language learning aptitude.

You might measure the overall proficiency in English of several learners by giving them (i) a reading test, (ii) a grammar test, and (iii) rating their pronunciation on a seven point scale. The scores are then added for each case.

The standard measure of a person's school achievement in the USA — the *Grade Point Average* — is derived additively from marks obtained on a range of separate school subjects, of all sorts, including language.

In the assessment of English in the UK National Curriculum for certain purposes a pupil's three separate summary scores for criterion-referenced attainment in the 'attainment target' areas of writing, spelling and handwriting are combined to give one 'profile component' score. This then has to be combined with two other profile component scores, for speaking/listening and reading, which are averaged to give a 'whole subject' assessment (DES, 1989 and 10.4.2).

In these instances you would expect the separate measures for a number of cases to agree (correlate) reasonably with the combined measure, but not necessarily with each other. Individuals might well do relatively well on one separate measure, but worse on another.

There are a number of issues associated particularly with the types of complementary combination just illustrated. The first is that of the legitimacy and usefulness of combining scores on separate variables at all into one set of overall scores, pursued here. The other is the issue of how best to combine the scores, when desired, for which see 15.2.3.

One thread of the argument focuses more on legitimacy. If the individual measures are accurate in themselves, the result will be accurate in the sense of being reliable (Chap. 19), but not necessarily in the sense of being valid (Chap. 22), since nothing stops you combining any set of variables in this way, whether the output is meaningful or not. You *could* add together a person's age, speed of utterance in words per minute, and score correct in identifying the parts of speech, but would these add up to a measure of any sensible single variable — in the jargon, a 'meaningful unitary construct' (Gardner, 1974)?

The answer to this often goes back to matters of your personal theoretical persuasion which leads you to suppose that such and such a linguistic capability, e.g. communicative competence, is made up of this or that set of specific capabilities or dimensions (10.4.2) and so justifies you in combining measures of those separate capabilities. The more complex statistical procedures related to construct validity testing (22.4.2), such as factor analysis, may also help decide which, if any, of a set of variables can meaningfully be combined (Seliger & Shohamy, 1989: 228; Woods *et al.*, 1986: Chap. 15).

The measure of overall 'language ability' is a good example. In some areas of language study, especially child language and language pathology, there is disagreement as to whether measures of separate areas of language competence such as grammar, vocabulary, and pronunciation *can* meaningfully be combined in any overall measure, and they are often kept separate. Is 'language ability' a meaningful unitary construct? In other fields, e.g. foreign language learning, there is more of a tendency to combine and the argument has been the reverse — more about whether language ability can be meaningfully fragmented into separate constituent capabilities. So here some would hold that it is the *specific* variables like 'grammatical proficiency', 'vocabulary competence' etc. which lack meaningfulness, as they are held to be simply manifestations of the single 'language ability' variable (cf. Oller, 1979). But views on this issue have varied over the years, being more in favour of separation when 'discrete' testing was more in favour.

Another argument turns more on usefulness. Whether or not it is legitimate to combine separate measures, it may be more useful to take them separately for some purposes. So for diagnostic use in T situations it is clearly far more informative to see how a case scores on a range of measures of separate abilities, so you can pick out which he/she is weakest on for remedial work. In other words you can make comparisons within a person as well as between them. This information gets hidden in any aggregation process.

Similarly, two learners who come out moderately good on combined scores, may be quite different if you examine their scores on the constituent variables separately. One might be moderate on all of them, the other very good on some and very bad on others. Rowntree (1977) is particularly scathing about the lack of information in what he calls the 'all-talking, all-singing, all-dancing' unitary score which encapsulates everything, but tells nothing in detail. On the other hand, for some 'summative' T purposes (2.2.2) administrators and parents may find information on a range of variables too complicated and prefer to be given one summary grade. The UK national curriculum assessment for English allows for various levels of reporting of scores, from a profile of levels of attainment on numerous specific statements of attainment up to a three score profile and a single whole subject score (see above and DES, 1989: 14.31). In R work it may often be a lot easier for presentation and statistical handling of data to be able to deal with a single set of DV scores, one for each case, rather than a series.

In any of these situations where combining scores on separate variables is felt *not* legitimate/useful, you are left with a series of individual scores for each case. This constitutes what is often called a *profile*, which can be displayed in a variety of ways — most simply as a table with the cases, or one case on different occasions, down the side and columns of scores successively across the page for each specific variable in turn. For examples see Brown & Yule's spoken performance assessment profile (1983: 104), the *Edinburgh Reading Tests* profile (in Spooncer, 1983: 31) and the *Informal Reading Inventory* (Pumfrey, 1985). Crystal's *LARSP* (1982) is not laid out this way, but essentially also records a large number of scores on specific grammatical variables in speech for each case observed, without calculating any overall combined 'grammatical competence' score. Similar are his *PROPH* profiling chart for sounds and *PRISM* for meaning. Graphic presentations of profiles are also possible (e.g. Noll *et al.*, 1979: 72).

In general there is a lot to be said for avoiding the doubts that often arise about whether and how to combine scores on different variables, and the consequent loss of detailed information, by leaving data as a profile, which can readily be constructed for any kinds of scores, whether norm- or criterion-referenced. The 'referencing' status of a whole profile may be somewhat mixed, however (cf. 10.4.1). For instance the variables chosen for inclusion in *LARSP* mostly each separately admit of some absolute interpretation. However, every possible grammatical variable is not included, and according to Crystal the choice was of those that discriminate usefully between cases (1982: 6). Hence the profile as a whole has more norm-referenced interpretation.

15.2.3 Weighting and the role of multiplication

Another general issue to do with combining scores of the above sort, where it is done, is exactly how to deal with scores on different scales and of different types (Chap. 12–15) to ensure equal 'weight' for each variable — or, if desired, some other weighting. The notion of weight has already been met on the smaller scale in 14.2, in relation to the possibility of attaching different weightings to specific items in a multi-item test or inventory and taking these into account when totalling response scores.

Unlike in 14.2 (or 15.1) the scores you may wish to combine in the present instance are often on quite different numerical scales. This in itself introduces differential weighting and properly needs to be ironed out before any actually desired weighting is imposed. For instance if a test score out of 100 may has to be combined with a rating on a 1 to 7 scale obviously just adding or averaging the two scores for each case is unlikely to weight each equally. If you are combining scores from two tests with the same number of items, say 50, or scores which have all been turned into %, it might seem that there is no problem. However, in fact differences in the *spread* of scores play as much of a role as scale length.

If scores are more bunched on one variable scale than another, then the effectively *used* scale is shorter, and this variable gets less weight in straight addition. This can be seen from the following. Three imaginary cases score as follows on two variables:

	V1	V2
case 1	10	80
case 2	20	75
case 3	30	70

Regardless of whether the first variable in fact was scored out of 100 like the second one, or only out of 40, when the scores are added or averaged for each case, it is the first variable, with the smaller figures, that dictates who comes out best in the end. This is due to the greater spread or *variance* of the scores on V1.

In deciding what to do about this, a lot then depends on whether the measures are regarded as criterion- or norm-referenced. In the former instance, if the scores *have* to be combined, the best policy is just to use the scores as they are for each case, with or without conversion of each to percent (Rowntree, 1977: 225). Anything else destroys the criterion-referenced information in the scores (Chap. 20). This is in effect done by Thelander in arriving at his 'language index' — really a measure of how standard, as against regionally marked, the speech of an individual is (1982: 78).

In the norm-referenced instance, however, since the absolute score means nothing, only its distance from the average, the best plan is to transform the scores in a way that reflects this, and evens out the differences of spread too. The two common methods of converting interval scores to overcome these differences of scale length, average and spread are conversion to *standard scores*, also known as z *scores*, or some close derivative thereof, or to ordinal *percentiles*. Many basic statistics books describe how to do this (e.g. Cohen & Holliday, 1982: Chap. 7). This converts scores on each variable to a form with identical scale length, average, and spread. Standard scores, for example, are all on a scale from approximately -3 to +3, with an average of zero. For example, suppose Alfonso scores 19 out of 50 in an imaginary dictation, where the average score is 21, and 18 out of 30 for cloze, where the average is 12. Treating both as norm-referenced, and taking into account the spreads of the scores, these might come out as standard scores of -0.7 for dictation and +1.1 for cloze, since such scores have a sign reflecting whether they are above or below the average. If these are to be equally weighted, the combined average is +0.2.

If weighting other than equal is desired, the usual procedure is first to get the scores on all the variables to be combined into equal weighted form, then to multiply the scores on each variable with a constant figure appropriate to the desired weighting before adding and dividing by the total of the weighting figures to get an average. So in the above example cloze test results are to be weighted three times the dictation results, then Alfonso's standard score of -0.7 would be multiplied by 1 (i.e. stay the same) and his 1.1 by 3 to give 3.3. These added and divided by 4 give him a combined weighted score of +0.65. The weightings themselves may be decided in a variety of ways such as those mentioned in 14.2.1. Weighting by multiplication is also a part of the proposed National Curriculum English assessment procedure. For instance at one point in the procedure of combining scores, a child's speaking/listening, reading and writing scores (which are in principle criterion-referenced) are combined weighted respectively 20% 40% 40% to give the 'whole subject' score.

The complex approach to combining variables that uses 'principal components analysis' or 'factor analysis' and inevitably is done on computer should be at least mentioned here. It was attempted by McEntegart & Le Page (1982: 108) as a way of combining a range of social variables measured in a survey. It is also a standard feature of Osgood's 'semantic differential' measurement, where subjects rate words on a large number of seven point adjective scales and you are often then interested in judiciously combining the results across groups of scales to make the data more manageable. For simple accounts see Seliger & Shohamy (1989: 228); Woods *et al.* (1986: Chap. 15); and Oller (1979: 423ff).

15.2.4 Combination by established formulae

In both T and R contexts, combination of variables is often in practice done simply following some more or less established formula for a particular complex variable. The exact formula, with any weightings built in, is often the result of quite ad hoc decisions that have proved to yield useful overall scores as much as any reasoned theoretical basis. However, for comparability and continuity it is often better to use an established formula than invent one of your own. Such formulae may involve mixtures of all the basic mathematical operations applied to a set of scores of each case on different variables.

Numerous studies have endeavoured to quantify 'communicative competence' by various combinations of scores from various more specific variables. One such is that of Fischer (1984) who, in order to measure written communicative competence, gave learners a quasi-natural task of writing a job application. This was then scored for three variables: (i) marks 0–6 (a rating) for 'pertinence and communicative value' of the content, (ii) marks 0–6 similarly for 'clarity of expression and level of syntactic complexity' of the form, (iii) 'structural accuracy' measured by a count of the number of errors in vocabulary and structures that had been studied in class divided by the total number of finite clauses in the piece of writing. He chose then to combine the three measures by the simple formula (i) + (ii) - (iii) to yield each person's 'communicative competence' score. This unsophisticated formula, with no special standardisation or weightings, was no doubt useful for the purpose at hand, but there is obviously a danger if every teacher and researcher independently develops a different combinatory measure of this sort for the 'same' variable.

Many standard tests designed especially for T purposes provide formulae or tables which make the combination of variables purely mechanical and identical for all users of the instrument. An example (described in Oller, 1979: 320ff) is the scoring and weighting procedure to obtain the overall score on the *FSI Oral Interview*. In this learners of English are rated on five six-point scales for accent, grammar, vocabulary, fluency and comprehension. The rating anyone receives on any of these variables has to be weighted before adding to the others, but this is done simply by reference to a table of equivalences supplied with the test, avoiding the need for the teacher to multiply component scores by formula, but having the same effect. So if a case is rated 2 for fluency — 'speech is very slow and uneven except for short or routine sentences' — this converts to 4. But a rating of 2 for grammar — 'constant errors showing control of very few major patterns and frequently preventing communication' — converts to 12, since the test constructors feel grammar should have more weight in the overall score.

The *Syntactic Density Score* (Simms & Richgels, 1986) takes ten counts of various sorts from a language sample, adds them with various weightings, and divides by the number of T-units. For instance number of modal verbs is multiplied by 0.65 before adding, and words per T-unit by 0.95. The weights were derived on the basis of a multivariate statistical analysis of the sort mentioned in the last section. However, the measure has been justly criticised for its curious mixture of types of component measure and the way T-units figure twice in the calculation for some of them. Like the type token ratio it is susceptible to variation just depending on the size of the language sample used (12.2.3).

A standard measure with a set of formula of a different sort is the Flesch measure of 'reading ease' of a book or text. You take a hundred word sample and measure A the total number of syllables, and B the average words per sentence. So in effect word length in syllables and sentence length in words are the variables used. Only those parts of incomplete sentences that are within the 100 words are counted, so if 6.66 sentences, measured in words, fall in the 100 word sample, the mean number of words per sentence = 100/6.66 = 15. Then you simply insert your two figures in this formula and calculate the answer:

Reading ease = 206.835 - (0.846 x A) - (1.015 x B)

Scores on this scale *could* theoretically range from minus quantities up to 121.22 but the figures have been chosen in part so that in practice scores usually fall between 0 and 100. The higher the figure, the greater the ease (though there is some doubt over the equal interval nature of the derived scale: a difference of 10 between two texts seems to mark a greater difference of readability near the bottom of the scale than the top).

Finally here are some brief examples of formulae from further afield in language study. For instance:

> The variables of population size, distance, and linguistic similarity rated on a scale 0–4, are combined in the dialectological *Linguistic Influence Index* for pairs of cities. This quantifies for each city the likelihood of it adopting a new linguistic feature from the other (Chambers & Trudgill, 1980: 197ff).

> Proportions of monolingual and bilingual speakers of all the languages in a multilingual community are used to calculate an *Index of Communication* for each community, which quantifies the likelihood of any two speakers from that community being able to communicate in some language or other (Fasold, 1984: 124ff).

> Efficiency of instruction in language teaching has been defined as: the mean % improvement score of a group (15.2.1) divided by time in hours of instruction (Wigzell, 1992).

> The 'verb-noun ratio' — i.e. the number of verbs in a text sample

divided by the number of nouns — has been used in stylistics as a measure of more spoken or written style (Bruno, 1974).

It should be noted that what are called *ratios*, like the last example above, *generally* consist of counts/scores for mutually exclusive variables divided by each other, or expressed in words like 'Nouns outnumbered verbs by 5 to 3'. So also one can have ratios of off-task time to on-task time, of incorrect to correct responses etc. This is in contrast with *proportion* scores, often expressed as percentages (as seen in Chap. 12), which normally are based on division of a count or score for a variable by a figure for some larger category of which it forms a subtype or part, e.g. verbs as a % of all words, proportion of time spent off-task. The 'type-token ratio' (described at 12.2.1) is therefore a departure from the commoner use of the term 'ratio'.

16 Individual Rank Ordering

16.1 Quantification by Rank Ordering Cases Individually: Introduction

Here the cases we are measuring are simply placed in order depending on which have more or less of some single measured property than the others. So the scale basically consists of as many ordered, numbered slots as there are cases measured, and each person/thing 'scores' a rank number 1 or 2 or 3… (or 1st, 2nd, 3rd…).

Thus if a learner is assigned rank 3 for fluency by a researcher or teacher, this simply indicates that he/she has less of the measured property than the person ranked 2 and more than one ranked 4. But the *amount* by which she/he differs from these two need not be the same. In other words 'intervals' are *not* assumed to be equal, as they are with interval numerical measurement. This is particularly important to be clear on, since the numbers 1, 2, 3 etc. appearing in a table of figures, or in a file of figures stored on computer, are usually initially interpreted by any reader, or computer, as having fully numerical, interval values, unless it is made explicit that this is not so.

In such quantification you can rank by giving rank 1 to the case with the most of whatever variable is being measured, or the least: it doesn't matter. In T purpose work the former is common practice, in R work the latter is quite often done. In either instance the scale of figures involved for any group ranges from 1 to the total number of cases measured (often labelled N or n). Thus the maximum rank is entirely dependent on the size of the group measured, quite unlike a maximum score in interval measurement. To turn a ranking from the top down into one from the bottom up, simply apply the formula:

rank position counting from bottom = n + 1 - rank position counting from top

A technical point that arises in all this has to do with ties. If often happens that two or more cases are given the *same* rank because there is no perceptible difference between them in the amount of the variable being quantified. Here the normal convention in statistical work is for the people or things with 'tied' rank to be given the average of the ranks they would have been given had they all been of different rank. For example, if an informant is asked to rank words in order of what he/she judges to be their frequency of occurrence and if *and* was given rank 1, and *put* and *call* equal next rank, followed by *handsome*, the ranks of *put* and *call* would not be 'second equal' as in everyday parlance (and the way the informant might most naturally respond) but the average of ranks 2 and 3, i.e. 2.5:

	Rank	Everyday rank
and	1	1
put	2.5	2=
call	2.5	2=
handsome	4	3

The effect of this is that the sum of the rank numbers remains the same, however many ties there are, for a given number of cases. If n cases are ranked, the sum of the ranks will always be: number of cases ranked times one more than that number, divided by two. So for n = 4, however many ties there are, the total is always $(4 \times 5)/2 = 10$.

This fact can be used to check you have not got mixed up in assigning ranks correctly to a large group, with several ties: you simply add all the rank numbers you have given, and see if it equals $(n \times (n+1))/2$.

16.2 Simple Rank Ordering of Cases by Some Judge

The most straightforward source of ranked data is where someone uses their direct global judgment of a variable to put a set of people or things in rank order in terms of how much of the variable they have: there is no counting up of any separate items, as is involved in so much interval measurement, in order to arrive at this. In many ways this is close to 'global' rating (14.1), and is open to similar labelling as 'subjective', though there are a number of differences.

For instance, being definitely only ordinal, ranking has the advantage of not raising the questions rating did about whether intervals really are equal. But of course if further statistical processing of results is required, there are certain implications. You can't use the more sophisticated so-called 'parametric' tests on purely ranked data, because they assume interval level scoring, amongst other things (see e.g. Langley, 1979).

Then ranking pushes the measurer into discriminating more, since ideally everything ranked gets put in a separate rank position: when things are rated, normally many will be rated the same, as rating scales often have few points. To avoid too much artificiality, ranking should normally be done under the instruction that ties *are* permitted, though.

Finally, it is hard to conceive of ranking as ever being other than a norm-referenced activity, since the essence of it is that it is done relative to a group. Hughes, for example, got six teachers to *rank* classes of ten in a language centre for oral comprehension of English and the like because 'it was not thought that the teachers could assign absolute values to this ability' (1981). Rating, however, can be conceived of as either norm- or criterion-referenced, depending on the exact instructions, but is most often the latter (10.5).

16.2.1 Ranking by measurer

In one form of ranking it is the measurer who uses his/her judgment to put some cases in order on some well defined basis, for example:

Ranking by a therapist of seven patients for severity of language disorder.

Ranking by a researcher of ten texts in order of 'formality' of style.

Ranking of 5 informants by a sociolinguist in order of 'cooperativeness' from his/her experience of them in quasi-natural interview.

This is often used in T purpose quantification, since it may often be easier, and sufficient for the purpose in hand, to judge the rank order of pupils in a class than to administer a test or whatever to obtain actual numerical scores for each pupil. See again the discussion of 'discrete' and 'global' scoring in 14.1.1. In R purpose work certain global or hidden variables may be more approachable this way. In general this sort of ranking can be based on data gathered across the full range of techniques of Chapters 4–9.

16.2.2 Ranking by cases

Perhaps more commonly than the preceding, it is the person investigated who is asked to put something in order, so the rankers are the cases of interest, as much as whatever is ranked. Examples:

Ranking by children of 10 bird names in order of 'typicality' as birds. For instance out of *owl*, *parrot*, *robin*, *ostrich*, etc., which is the most 'birdy', which the next most 'birdy', and so on? This is common in psycholinguistic research on 'prototypes' (Aitchison, 1987).

Ordering by native speakers of taped material spoken by an actor in different accents of English for how they would judge the trustworthiness of the speaker.

Ranking of some learners' errors in order of 'gravity' (i.e. seriousness) by language teachers.

Ordering by native speakers of the words *table, leg, furniture, house* in terms of closeness of meaning to the word *chair*. In an experiment, subjects might be asked to do this for several different sets of words (i.e. different variables cf.14.1.2).

Rank ordering by native speakers of 8 samples from different books in order of 'readability'.

Clearly this particularly arises when you are measuring via speakers' opinions of various things in R work (Chap. 7). This sort of ranking may also feature as part of the procedure of setting up the EV in an experiment in, say, psycholinguistics. The investigator may get a number of native speakers to rank order a sample of twenty words for apparent 'concreteness', derive a combined ranking (16.5), and then use the top and bottom five as stimuli in an experiment into how easily people recall concrete versus abstract vocabulary.

16.2.3 Problems with simple ranking

Simple rank ordering of these sorts is not seen used all that commonly, the main reason being that it turns out to be quite difficult either for a measurer or subjects to keep more than about 10–15 things in their minds at once, and so be able to rank them accurately: i.e. there are problems of reliability (19.3). The Rokeach value survey (1973), as Johnson & Giles comment (1982), is unusual in requiring subjects to rank separately two sets of 18 things — such as equality, salvation, and the world at peace — for how highly they value them. Alternatives are doing the ranking in pairs (16.3 below), or using a series of ratings of each thing separately rather than one overall ranking (14.1).

Examples of ranking used in the literature often exhibit instances of what might be called 'selective ranking', which reduces the burden of ranking a lot of things, but often makes further (esp. inferential statistical) handling of the results difficult. For instance Groebel (1981) gave people a list of fifteen activities such as 'read the title', 'look for key words', which they were required to rank by the order in which they carried them out when reading, *omitting* any activities they did not do at all. Clearly it would be unrealistic to get people to rank activities they did not use at all. Here you can collect up an overall rank order for the activities (16.5), but do little more because of the gaps in the data. Similarly Sikiotis (1981) gave Greek learners labels of fourteen kinds of reading material (e.g. adventure, crime), but they were each asked only to pick their top three and rank them for interest.

16.3 Individual Ranking Derived from a Number of Ordered Pairings

Instead of rank ordering, say, samples of utterances from five stutterers for comprehensibility, or getting a normal adult native speaker to do so, you can consider the samples in pairs. You take each stutterer in turn and compare his/her performance with each other stutterer's repeatedly judging which of each pair is the more comprehensible. You can then derive an overall rank order from all these ordered pairings. Since it is easier to make clear judgments about who/which of *two* cases has more of some property than the other than to judge sets of three or more at one go, this technique is generally more reliable than ranking a whole set of people/things at once. Any of the examples of 16.2 could be done this way in principle, and often the stimuli could be laid out in matrix form as described for *ratings* of pairs in 14.1.2.

However this approach suffers from the disadvantage that properly you have to judge *every* possible pair and there will often be a large number of these. To rank 5 people by this method you would have to judge 10 pairs. In general to rank n things by this method you will have to judge $\{n \times (n-1)\}/2$ pairs (i.e. $(5 \times 4)/2 = 10$ in the example).

To work out one overall rank order from someone's ranking judgments within all the pairs, in essence you add up for each case ranked the number of pairs in which it was preferred, giving a figure that can range between n-1 and 0. The rank order of these totals gives the overall rank order of whatever was ranked. It is also possible to tabulate the pairings and to check on how 'consistent' the person doing the pairing was — i.e. were there many instances where, say, Mary was judged more comprehensible than Joan, Joan more than David, but then also David more comprehensible than Mary? Too many 'vicious triangles' like this and you would doubt whether it was worth giving any credence to the resulting overall rank order (see e.g. Chambers, 1964: 116–19 for details).

An example of the pair-based approach is Politzer's study (1978), in which primarily he wanted to find out the overall rank order of 'seriousness' in which 146 native speakers of German placed six categories of error produced by learners of German, e.g. vocabulary errors, word order errors, gender errors. Using the approach described, and one example sentence for each kind of error, each informant would have had to deal with 15 pairs of sentences, with the same six sentences recurring over and over again in different pairs. However, since it was clearly unrealistic to represent whole categories of error-type by just one erroneous sentence each, Politzer's scheme was in fact more elaborate. He used twenty *different* sentences containing each kind of error (120 in all), and these were deployed so that (i) none occurred in more than one pair of sentences judged and (ii) four pairs of sentences had to be judged for every one pair of error categories. Thus four pairs of sentences exhibited the comparison 'word order error — gender error', and any one sentence with a gender error in was not reused within these pairs or elsewhere.

Thus the informants actually each judged 60 pairs of sentences, all different. An overall rank order of the types of error was obtained as follows, pooling results for all informants. A total was made of the number of times sentences of each error type were judged the more serious in pairs where they occurred, as per the usual procedure. These totals could then be rank ordered. For instance vocabulary errors came out the most serious, being judged worse in 2234 pairs, out of a possible 2920 (= (6-1) × 4 × 146), verb morphology next most serious (1600), then word order (1562), etc.

16.4 Individual Ranking Derived from Interval Scores

In practice the greatest sources of rank ordered data are not those just described, but rather instances where measurements on some *other* kind of scale have been made and, for some reason or other, these are *converted* or 'transformed' into a rank ordering. Here far and away the commonest source is interval data, of any of the ultimate sources described earlier (Chap. 11–15).

There are various reasons why such scores have to be converted to rank order data, with consequent loss of information in any ensuing calculations, of course. For instance, if you want to combine measurements, some of which are rankings and some of which are interval, you have to turn the interval ones into rankings so that they are all of the same sort and can be easily combined (as per 16.5). Also if there is grave doubt about the equal interval nature of a numerical scale, you might wish to convert, so there is no misunderstanding of the implications of the scores in a T context. This might arise if, say, a multi-item test contains items of a very disparate nature and uneven difficulty.

But most often it is the following situation, typically an R one, that leads to interval-to-rank conversion: the desire to use inferential statistical tests on results which are in interval form, but do not meet the full requirements for the tests to be applied. The crux is that there are no simple inferential statistical techniques which use the full information of interval data but *don't* assume a further characteristic known as the 'normality of population distribution' of interval scores, and indeed often other things as well. This is what is meant by the term 'parametric' applied to the usual tests that allow you to generalise results from samples of cases to wider groups sampled. If data scored on interval scales does not meet such requirements, typically it should be treated as rank ordered instead, and weaker 'non-parametric' statistical procedures used. This cannot be pursued here: for a proper account of all this see elementary statistics books such as Robson (1983), Langley (1979) and Rowntree (1981).

16.5 Individual Ranking Derived from Combining Several Rankings

In 15.1 and 15.2 we saw two general situations in which interval scores could be combined. Rather similarly you may wish to combine several measurements of the same cases where all are in form of rank orders (or have been converted into this form) and proceed to use the combined ranking for some purpose forgetting about the separate rankings. Much of what was said for the interval instance applies again here, e.g. about the difference between combining repeated rankings for the same variable and combining rankings on different variables, and in the latter instance, the choice between combining rankings, on equal terms or not, and working with profiles. Again, too, there are further checks you might perform before combining scores in either situation. So if several 'judges' have ranked the same twenty speech retarded subjects for severity of speech impairment you would probably view the combined overall ranking for each subject in a different light if the judges agreed substantially from that if they didn't (again measures of correlation could be used to assess this — Scholfield, forthcoming b).

In order to actually combine several rankings additively, provided equal weight is being given to all the rankings, you need do no more than add or average the different rankings of each thing ranked, and re-rank the totals. For instance two judges have ranked four people for speech impairment:

	1st judge	2nd judge	Rank Total	Combined Ranking
Case A	1	1	2	1
Case B	4	3	7	4
Case C	2	4	6	3
Case D	3	2	5	2

Strictly speaking, if there are ties in any of the sets of rankings, the rankings will not be getting perfectly equal weighting, but for most purposes this is unimportant: ties in a column have the effect of slightly increasing the weight of that column in the overall result. Any desired weighting can as usual be achieved by multiplying the ranks in a given column by a constant before adding.

An alternative presentation to the above that is often seen, usually where there are a lot of 'judges', not just two as here, collects up the rankings of the judges and displays them thus:

	Number of judges (out of 2) choosing the case as:					
	Rank 1	*Rank 2*	*Rank 3*	*Rank 4*	*Rank Total*	Comb. Rank
Case A	2	0	0	0	2	1
Case B	0	0	1	1	7	4
Case C	0	1	0	1	6	3
Case D	0	1	1	0	5	2

Note that the simple total of each row here = the number of judges; the unweighted *rank* total for each thing ranked is obtained by multiplying each figure in the main table by the rank number at the head of the column before adding.

This can all be done similarly in the event of the rankings being 'selective' (16.2.3 above), provided ranking is numbered from the bottom up for computation purposes. For instance in the Sikiotis (1981) study above, all the rankers had to select just three types of reading material and rank them from most to least favourite. Thus if we record a first choice as rank 3, a second as 2, a third as 1 and a non-selection as -, we would get a table of this sort (fictitious), showing that overall Adventure is top favourite, then Crime, etc. (see Table overleaf).

Finally there may be a problem if you wish to combine individuals' rankings when each case was ranked out of a different sized group for different occasions or variables. For example, how do you combine Alfonso's 5th place out of 20 students for reading with his 9th place out of 35 for writing so as to give it equal weight (reckoned from rank one as the top in both instances)? To cope with this eventuality you have to express the rankings as percentage rankings, known as *percentiles*, and combine them in that form. That is, you turn all the rankings into ranks as if out of

Topic	Learner						Total	Comb. Ranking
	1	2	3	4	5	6		
Crime	3	2	1	1	2	2	11	5
History	1	–	–	–	–	–	1	2
Sport	–	3	–	3	3	–	9	4
Adventure	2	1	3	2	1	3	12	6
Politics	–	–	2	–	–	1	3	3
Card	–	–	–	–	–	–	0	1

100 people/things. Conventionally higher percentile figures reflect higher ability. To achieve this, first convert rank positions into ones calculated from the bottom up. So Alfonso's ranks become 16 and 27 respectively (cf. 16.1). Then apply this formula:

$$\text{percentile rank} = \frac{\text{raw rank position counting bottom} - 0.5}{n} \times 100$$

So Alfonso's reading ranking becomes 77.5 and his writing one 75.7, showing that in both abilities three quarters or so of the cases did worse than him. These percentiles could now be added, if required, or presented in a profile as genuinely on level terms (see Cohen & Holliday, 1982: Chap. 7 for more detailed computation where scores were originally interval).

Similarly, the 'selective ranking' data of the Groebel (1981) study mentioned in 16.2.3 above differs from that of the Sikiotis (1981) one in that judges were free to pick out and rank a *varying number* of things. Here again the rankings in each column, as well as being reversed, would usefully be re-expressed as percentiles in relation to the total number of things that person chose to rank, before adding rows.

17 Ranking in Ordered Categories

17.1 Quantification by Placing Cases in Ordered Categories: Introduction

Here the cases measured are each placed in one or other of a set of two or more categories or 'levels' which have an intrinsic order. The categories, though primarily labelled with names, could be coded 1, 2, etc. for reference, e.g. on computer. The numbers would just reflect the fact that cases falling in successive categories have more of some property than those in the one before. Unlike with individual rank ordering, the number of categories, and so the maximum ordered category number any case can be assigned, is decided a priori, not by the number of cases categorised (n). Typically, then, a number of cases fall in each category and, since there is no more detailed ordering, in rank order terms you have a series of tied groups of cases.

An example of this would arise for instance where members of a group of 25 learners are classified as having either 'native-speaker-like fluency', 'good non-native fluency', or 'halting or non-fluency' in English. Note that with this sort of wording there is no implication that the *size* of fluency difference between all those in the 'native-speaker-like' category and those in the 'good non-native' category is necessarily the same, or identical to the difference between those in the 'good non-native' category and those in the 'halting/non-fluent' category. In fact the third category probably covers a rather wider span of fluency ability than either of the others.

Of course if you think there *is* reasonable equidistance, and there are more than two categories, treatment as a quasi-interval rating scale (14.1) could be better. You could reword the scale so that it encourages an equal interval rating-type interpretation more clearly, and overtly administer a number scale as well as verbal labels. If the variable is a DV in a research design and inferential statistics are to be used in analysis, in fact, this might be a good move. The reason is the relative lack of well-known inferential statistical tests specifically for ordered category DVs. Such data often has to be treated rather unsatisfactorily as rank ordered with a lot of ties, or nominal, for such further processing of results. However, ordered categories are prominent as EVs and in certain descriptive techniques (see further 17.2.1 and 17.3.2). In any event the first requirement is to be clear about which sort of scale one is claiming to be working with, and act accordingly.

Two other features of categorisations in general also apply here. One is that categorisations often interlock in hierarchies, but what are really separate variables connected in this way should not normally be conflated in one categorisation. This is illustrated more fully in 18.1 for the nominal instances. The other is that categorisations normally should be exhaustive, with no categories left out of a set that logically should be there, and so no cases omitted. This is taken up below, where some exceptions to the rule are noted.

17.2 Simple Ordered Categorisation by Some Judge

Like ranking (Chap. 16) and rating (14.1), this involves someone's global, subjective, judgment of how cases are placed on a variable. However, the fine discrimination of rank ordering is not required, nor the equal interval assumption of rating, though like rating the activity can be effectively either norm- or criterion-referenced, depending on the exact instructions for doing the categorisation (10.5).

17.2.1 Ordered categorisation by measurer

Linguistic variables are often directly assessed by measurers in categories that can be regarded as at least ordered. Examples:

Classifying several reading texts into 'Easy', or 'Advanced'.

Judging the gravity of some learners' errors as 'Howler', 'Bad Error', 'Error not worth correcting'. (But see discussion at 18.2.3 of situations like this, where the cases are several observations from each of several people).

Judging the overall English pronunciation competence of each of a class of learners, from memory of hearing them speaking in class, as up to a certain standard, or not (i.e. Pass, Fail).

Classification by a sociolinguistic investigator of each of a sample of Puerto Ricans in Jersey City from tapes as nonspeakers of Spanish, Spanish speakers to some extent, or fluent speakers.

In both T and R work, especially based on information obtained relatively non-reactively, this is often felt as an easier method than ranking or rating, let alone more 'discrete' approaches that would yield clearly interval scores (14.1). For instance you might choose to categorise sentences in a sample of text as Simple (1 clause) or Complex (2 or more clauses). Though this could be perfectly well done numerically, by giving each sentence a score for the number of clauses it contains, for many purposes the speed of getting this less detailed information makes the category approach better. Standard published instruments requiring the award of global scores on different levels usually involve quasi-interval rating (14.1). However, it is reported that the *Interagency Language Roundtable Oral Interview*, where samples of oral language have to be placed on a scale with six defined levels, has a bigger gap between level two and three than between level one and two (Bachman, 1990: 45), so has to be considered really only an ordinal categorisation.

Commonly in R work it is EVs rather than DVs that are quantified on this sort of scale. A good example is where a sociolinguist categorises each of fifteen informants for their social class in order to then compare them in performance on some other variable (DV) such as /h/ dropping, which would be quantified by counting (Chap. 12). Many standard statistical tests work well on data of this sort, where the EV is in categories and the DV interval. One common UK social class classification is the Registrar General's (1966, 1971), which consists essentially of five categories defined using 'occupation of the head of the family' as an 'indicator': Professional, Intermediate, Skilled, Partly skilled, Unskilled (cf. Hall & Jones, 1950).

Note that often only a *selection* of the levels of an EV ordered category variable are in fact used in an R investigation. For example you might choose only to compare the linguistic behaviour of informants from three of the five social classes of the above classification. You might choose to get some native speakers to rate for annoyingness some sentences containing what you judged as a teacher to contain severe errors as compared with ones with mild errors, leaving out ones you judged to contain moderate errors. This is normal practice, and depends in effect on how you formulate your R hypothesis.

However, you must be aware all the time of the difference in what you can conclude from work where comparison is based on an EV made up of *all* relevant values as against a selection of values only. Certain choices may lead to dramatic-looking differences in DV scores for the different groups/stimulus types or whatever being compared, especially if extreme, non-adjacent, categories are chosen.

Thus you must always be aware of the limitations of this selective approach, in your own work or others', and look carefully at EV's to see if *all* appropriate levels have been included or not. If not you may then consider the basis on which the choice was made — random, or deliberate. Indeed for the purpose of some statistical tests it is of some importance whether the EV levels chosen are a deliberate selection on some basis from the possible ones — a 'fixed effect' — or a random selection — 'random effect' (see Woods *et al.*, 1986: 212ff).

Categorisations are also, less obviously, very important as CV's (3.1.4). For example often a sociolinguistic or psycholinguistic study will be deliberately limited to informants/subjects of a homogeneous background e.g. one social class category, one educational level, and so on. So again ordered categorisation of cases occurs prior to the study, as part of a screening procedure, and cases from selected categories only are used.

17.2.2 Ordered categorisation by cases

Researchers need not themselves categorise, they may get informants/subjects to. Examples:

Getting 20 informants to put a sentence into one of the categories 'Acceptable', 'Doubtful/Unacceptable'. Often a whole set of sentences would be judged this way, each with a distinct error. Treatment as a series of ratings is often a close competitor (14.1.2).

Getting informants to indicate whether they are English Monoglot, Speak some Welsh, or are Fully Bilingual Welsh and English (cf. the examples at 14.1.2).

Getting informants to indicate that they agree or disagree with the statement 'I like learning English'. (Note: *multiple* items of this sort used to quantify a single variable would be dealt with as an inventory — Chap. 13).

Welsh speaking children respond as to whether they address their uncle a familiar *ti*, polite *chi*, or 'depends' (G. Jones, 1984).

Clearly much data arising from measurement via opinion, of both self and others, often obtained by questionnaire, can be of this sort, just as rating and ranking data is (14.1.2, 16.2.2).

It is worth noting that there are some instances where you may overlook a category in sets like these, and hence those cases that fell in it. This arises particularly where there is a third, neutral or ambivalent, category with two opposing ones. Thus in the last example above your interest is probably only in the difference between cases using *ti* and cases using *chi*, not in the matter of how many people vary. However, considerations of reliability and validity force you to include a neutral third option so as not to artificially bully informants into choices they don't really feel able to make.

In such an instance you would state the figures for all three categories in your descriptive account of the results. But for inferential purposes, it is often regarded as legitimate to overlook the neutral category and use the appropriate statistical test just on 'those that expressed a preference' as the pollsters say. It might seem in this procedure that there was no point in having a neutral category if you are not going to include it in the statistics afterwards. However, the neutral category does exert an influence even when apparently left out of account. The more people or whatever in a sample of cases fall in the neutral category, the fewer are available to fall in the two 'marked' categories and the harder it gets for a noticeable difference to appear between the two categories you are interested in (Langley, 1979: 256).

Incidentally, in this example don't confuse cases falling in a neutral category (expressing no clear *preference*) with those who don't answer at all (express no *opinion*) e.g. because they refuse to participate, are out when you call, or write something undecipherable on the questionnaire sheet. They get left out unavoidably but are in principle different. They do not represent a category on the same logical level at all but rather a value of the variable 'responding' versus 'not responding'/'missing'. Separate also are those for whom a particular variable is not *applicable*, e.g. because they have no uncle: an option should have been offered for them to be able to record this.

17.3 Ordered Categories Derived from Data where Cases were Originally Recorded on other Types of Scale

There are quite a few possible indirect sources of data in ordered categories. One arises simply where a more elaborate ordered category scale is condensed by lumping together some of the ordered categories into one. For instance a scale of five social classes is boiled down to three. See further 18.4.2 on this. However, the most prolific sources are all conversions from some *other* type of scale, which we review here.

17.3.1 Ranking and rating scores

(i) Results ranked individually. Where there are a lot of ties in a ranking of this sort, the results might preferably be grouped and treated as an ordered categorisation instead. What constitutes *too many* ties is a matter of measurer judgment. As an example, let us suppose a Moroccan informant in a sociolinguistic investigation is asked to rank nine potential interlocutors on the basis of how likely he/she is to speak Colloquial Arabic to such a person, rather than French, but he/she is unable to differentiate them more satisfactorily than this:

Interlocutor	Informant's Ranking	Statistician's Ranking
Wife	1=	2.5
Boss	2=	5.5
Friend	1=	2.5
Parents	1=	2.5
Bank Clerk	2=	5.5
Teacher	3=	7.5
Doctor	4	9
Brother or Sister	1=	2.5
Civil Servant	3=	7.5

Clearly what we have here is rather poor as a rank order. Our informant has really done only a little more than discriminate three ordered groups. In such an instance it could well be better, using the ties as a guide, to think of his/her results as really being a categorisation of the nine interlocutors into three classes 1, 2 and 3 — representing relatively High, Mid and Low frequency of address in Arabic, putting doctor in with teacher and civil servant in the lowest category. And another time you might use an ordered category scale from the start (or perhaps a rating scale) — e.g. ask your informant to place each of the interlocutors in one of the three groups labelled as just stated. An alternative is to persist with rank ordering but not to allow the informant the option of giving any ties in future, but that might distort the facts and lead to unreliability if the informant would naturally choose ties in some instances.

(ii) Rating scales. As already seen, if there is doubt over the equality of intervals between numbers on a rating scale you can think of the results as ordered categories instead of quasi-interval 'scores' (14.1.3). So if a word is being rated by 50 people on a 7 point scale you may then treat the 7 points as 7 ordered categories rather than a score and count how many people pick each (i.e. fall in each category) for that word.

17.3.2 Interval scale sources generally

Interval scores of any sort can be treated as ordered categories, if desired, though much information is wasted in the process. For instance, as part of a questionnaire you may have gathered age information from a group of informants as a precise number of years. This you may for some purpose later group into ordered categories: 10–12, 13–17, 18–25, over 25. Though rarely discussed, this sort of reduction is commonly done as there are many occasions when it may be desirable.

In all such reduction the crucial question is *where* exactly to divide the interval scale — i.e. what *cutting scores* to choose — and often also *how many* cuts to make (one being the minimum), in order to derive a suitable set of categories into which the cases will then fall. Obviously the number of categories produced is always one more than the number of cuts. Quite a range of principles have been suggested, only some of which will be suited to a particular purpose, and it is quite a complicated matter to decide on the best way of doing it in a particular instance. In general we should follow the policy of not categorising at all unless definitely necessary, unlike what happens in some T circles, where there can be a love of A, B etc. grades for their own sake. And where possible we should choose to divide into more rather than fewer categories, so there is less loss of information.

Usually the principles used are different if the scores have some absolute versus only relative interpretation. In the former instance there is often appeal to measurer judgment based on some criterion: here cutting scores can often be decided in actual score or test item terms *before* you actually make any measurements at all, and remain the same every time you measure different people. In the latter instance there is often reliance on the results actually obtained for some group of cases, and so the actual scores at which the scale is cut are not so constant (for a fuller account see Scholfield, forthcoming a).

(i) Scores may be reduced to categories just because the interval status, normality of distribution, or the like of the numerical scores is in doubt (cf. 16.4). However, you would normally convert to individually ranked data by preference as less information is lost, and, if required, better well-known statistical tests are available for further handling of results, *unless* the original scores had absolute, criterion-referenced value that you wished to retain. If no better method presents itself, it is probably best here just to cut the scale into a number of equal parts to form the categories.

(ii) In R purpose work there may simply be an interest for its own sake in *discovering* a categorisation of some sort from data basically measured on a more continuous numerical scale. For instance measuring the amount of omission of the past tense morpheme among Creole speakers, you will typically be using a numerical scale, e.g. recording % omission of this morpheme out of the possible occasions when it could have been used by each case. You may then be interested in seeing if there is any basis for identifying natural divisions of the scale at particular points of % use which might mark off, say, a high range of omission scores, a mid range, and a low range, corresponding to the sociolinguistic notions of 'basilect', 'mesolect' and 'acrolect' (cf. Escure, 1982).

The best guide to cutting here comes from examining the results obtained when relevant cases are measured on the interval scale. If it turns out that they fall into, say, a high scoring group and a not so high scoring group, then whatever point on the scale is clearly in between the scores of the two groups — a score which hardly any case scores — is the natural score at which to divide the scale. Similarly if three groups or *clusters* of cases (as they are technically called) emerge, then two intermediate cutting points, and hence three categories, may present themselves.

(iii) A common R occasion where conversion to categories is seen is where an EV is concerned, as many research questions/hypotheses, and attendant inferential statistical techniques, require the EV to be treated as in categories, even if not originally recorded in this way (cf. 17.2.1 and see also nominal scales Chap. 18). Thus suppose you are studying the behaviour of children who speak both Navaho and English, wishing to see if those for whom Navaho is the dominant language sort blocks of various shapes and colours differently from those for whom English is dominant. The nature of the Navaho language might lead you to expect that the Navaho dominant group would choose to sort blocks into groups by identity of shape more than the English dominant group, who would go by identity of colour.

Now in reality any test of bilingual dominance is likely to show a cline of dominance from those dominant in one language through those more or less equal to those dominant in the other. But for the purpose of this research you will typically have to find some way of cutting the numerical scale so as to yield two groups of subjects for comparison, or perhaps three groups, to include a middle group — more or less balanced Navaho-English. Given a norm-referenced test of bilingual dominance, such as the spew test (8.1), two groups would be obtained by putting the cases in rank order from those with highest dominance in one language to those with highest dominance in the other and picking the middle person's score as the cutting score (this being technically the *median* score). Three categories could be obtained similarly by using as cutting scores the scores of the cases one third and two thirds way down the rank order list.

This sort of situation arises very widely in any form of screening/ selection of subjects in order to make groups of people to be compared, that is, to become EV categories or levels. It also arises to eliminate some types of people, i.e. to provide CV categories to choose from, where the natural measure is interval.

All this also arises for stimulus materials in more reactive measurement. For example if memory for sentences of different lengths (in words, clauses, or whatever) is to be compared, you will typically have to establish two, three, or whatever distinct *spans* of length to use as stimuli (i.e. ordered categories). Or indeed you may choose just two or three *specific* lengths, and leave all the rest out. You may measure the readability of a variety of texts with Flesch (15.2.4), wishing to extract a set of clearly 'difficult' ones and a set of clearly 'easy' ones for use in a psycholinguistic experiment, or just a set of easy ones for use in a T purpose reading test, and so on. Again you must on some basis choose to carve up the interval scale emerging from Flesch. Again the median method, or the like, may be the best.

In phonetic research you can synthesise innumerable subtly different [u:] sounds by varying at least three component pitch levels ('formants') in exact frequency and intensity (approx. loudness). But if you wish to test informants on whether they hear an [u:] or an [o:] etc. as you vary these different parameters, in practice you have to carve up your interval scales of frequency and intensity and choose only a small selection of levels to try out as an EV. Being more absolute in nature, these scales could be cut into equal scale lengths, or simply in accordance with previous practice in the research field.

Finally, much research involves time as an EV, and again very often you have to carve up the continuum on some basis and select certain spans or points to compare. This arises for instance if you get a group of people to learn 50 words in an unfamiliar language and test the number they can recall on three occasions — after 1 hour, 2 days and 1 week: on some basis you have chosen these cutting points. Here again there might be expectations from previous work on memory that suggest what, possibly unequal, periods of time it is likely to be interesting to allow to elapse after some sentences have been learnt before you test subjects on them. Or you may deliberately want to try different periods from those used before.

(iv) In T measurement there may be a need for a categorisation conversion for the purpose of making some *decision* about the promotion, selection or whatever of individuals (cf. Chap. 2), as against just assessing them. Thus after a test of English irregular verb forms, you may need to turn the interval score of each learner into a 'pass' or 'fail' categorisation, or for some standard examinations such as the *GCSE* in the UK, you may have to produce a more elaborate classification such as 'A', 'B', 'C', 'D', 'E', 'unclassified'. Such categories are in T contexts usually called 'grades'.

In criterion-referenced quantification, cutting scores will typically be decided by expert judgment of what percent correct indicates what degree of mastery of an objective (cf. Subkoviak & Baker, 1977: 282ff; Hambleton *et al*, 1978). If the source scores are norm-referenced, on the other hand, the average score of some norm group is often used as the basis. For instance a passmark, or one of a series of grade threshold marks, may be set to be such and such a distance above the mean. Or it may be desirable to set the passmark such that just 20% of cases fail, etc. If further divisions are required, commonly this is done so as to ensure that certain percentages of cases fall in each grade/category to reflect roughly the distribution of a 'normal curve' (Rowntree, 1977: 212ff). Example:

A	B	C	D	E	F
10%	15%	25%	25%	15%	10%

On the other hand, the UK *GCE 'A' Level examination*, essentially norm-referenced, worked on the following percentages in the period 1963–1987 (CNAA, 1987):

A	B	C	D	E	O	F
10%	15%	10%	15%	20%	20%	10%

A corresponding need arises in some R work, less for an evaluative purpose, more for technical statistical ones. For example, to apply further procedures like 'variable rule analysis' (Cedergren & Sankoff, 1974) or 'scalogram analysis' (Hatch & Farhady, 1982; Chambers & Trudgill, 1980), usually data initially in interval numerical form, either from tests or counts in recorded material from each person, has to be reduced to binary categories.

Thus speakers of English who, as on so many variables, vary widely in their speech between saying [in] or [iŋ] for *-ing*, would have to be categorised e.g. as '[in] users' or not: but where do you cut the scale? It seems 'unfair' to classify a speaker as non-standard on the basis of just *one* use of [in] for *-ing* out of a possible 19 recorded in a sample, i.e. to set the cutting score at 100% (though that is the most obvious cutting score on an absolute scale), but opinions vary about whether 90%, 80%, or even 50% is the best cutting score.

Similarly, children or foreign learners have to be categorised as having mastered/not having mastered each of a set of linguistic features (variables) like noun plurals or -*ing* verb inflections. Here again there has been some arbitrary variation in choice of cutting scores. In child language work the range of cutting scores at which 'acquisition' is judged to have occurred is particularly wide — e.g. 90% (Brown, 1973), 5 occurrences of a structure in 5 hours of observation (Bloom & Lahey, 1978: 328), one occurrence plus increasing ones later (Wells, 1985: 3.8).

17.4 Ordered Categories Derived from Combining Several Ordered Categorisations

Similar general points could be made as above Chapter 15. For repeated categorisations on the *same* variable, where it has some criterion-referenced value, you can choose the 'modal', i.e. most commonly chosen, categorisation, as the single one to represent the set of gradings for each case.

It is quite difficult sensibly to combine several ordinal categorisations of the same cases on *different* variables if they have any criterion-referenced significance (see 18.5 for methods that yield a single categorisation that is often not ordered).

A norm-referenced combinatory procedure is to convert the categorisation of each variable, or repeated measures on the same variable, separately to what is the standardised form for ordered data — percentiles. The median percentile of each ordered category of a particular variable is assigned to cases falling in that category. That is, each categorisation is treated as an individual rank ordering with a lot of ties which are then expressed as percentiles (see 16.5 for percentile formula and cf. the example at 17.3.1). These can then be added or averaged across variables to give each case a combined percentile. But leaving the information as an uncombined profile is often better, especially for T purposes (Nisbet, 1974).

18 Nominal Categorisation

18.1 Nominal Scales: Introduction

Here the cases are simply placed in distinct categories, which are not assumed to be in any sense logically 'ordered'. They do not reflect greater or less presence of some property, just *difference* in some respect — in itself a qualitative rather than quantitative matter. That is, the scale consists of two or more specific categories, which may be labelled with words or numbers, but in the latter instance the numbers are not understood to be anything more than labels of distinct classes. When a case 'scores' a number of this sort, by being placed in a given category, that is nothing like scoring a number on an interval scale. If our results are to be analysed by computer, probably all nominal scales will have to have their component categories coded as numbers for the purposes of the computer program. So we shall have to convert the often required scale

> gender: male, female

into

> gender: 1, 2

or

> gender: 0, 1

by arbitrarily assigning numbers to genders. But we could equally well number the other way round provided we were consistent: no ordering is implied.

The smallest nominal scale, containing the minimum of information, has just two categories into which the cases are placed. Such scales may be referred to as 'binomial' or 'binary' and are said to have two 'values'/ 'conditions' (other words for the two alternative categories). Nominal scales with 3 or more values are referred to as 'polynomial' or sometimes 'polylog'. There is no need to discuss these types separately in this chapter as most of what is said here applies to both. But in a fuller work on statistical methods used in R work, they would have to be distinguished since many inferential statistical techniques apply only to one type (see for example the guide to inferential tests at the end of Langley, 1979).

Terms like 'binomial' are also often applied to two category scales that are strictly speaking ordered, and indeed the distinction between ordered and unordered tends to become blurred anyway where there are only two categories. Statistically the two are usually handled the same way also, so the distinction is not worth agonising over. As a rough guide, opposites that are in linguistic terms 'non-gradable' are likely to label unordered category scales (one cannot normally be *more* or *less* male), while 'gradable' opposites will label ordered ones (one *can* be more or less fluent). However, linguistically there is considerable scope for reconceptualisation of non-gradable scales as gradable and vice versa (Lyons, 1977: 9.1). As a result, some of the discussion earlier of *ordered* categories (Chap. 17) applies here, and vice versa.

The general principles of good categorisation, alias 'classification' or 'taxonomy', need consideration. These include the 'exhaustiveness' requirement, with provisos (already talked about in Chap. 17), and the principle that one categorisation scale should normally record one variable, not a mixture of several, and hence that any one case should not be able to be placed in more than one category on a given scale — the categories being mutually exclusive. It is not just that departures from this are likely to lead to unreliability when the scales are used, but any further statistical processing normally just cannot cope with categorisation not made in this way.

The principles often apply also to the categorisation that underlies many scoring methods that yield quasi-interval data (Chap. 11–14). For instance counting occurrences of particular types of word or construction in speech samples, to yield a summary score for each case, assumes measurer ability to classify words or constructions appropriately so as to know what to count. The following illustrates some of the principles for an example discussed in nominal classification terms, but which could result in count scores (12.2.2), depending on your assumptions (18.2.3).

In error analysis studies one often meets classifications of the following type. All the errors in a piece of written work by a foreign learner of English are entered on the 4 category scale:

> Spelling errors
> Grammatical errors
> Vocabulary errors
> L1 induced errors.

There is an *exhaustiveness* problem — does a discourse-structure error fall clearly in *any* of these categories? There is also an *exclusiveness* problem, in that many spelling, grammar and vocabulary errors may *also* be L1 induced (i.e. due to transfer from mother tongue). Prima facie, an error can fall in more than one category at once — a sure sign of a faulty scale. The real solution here is to recognise that we really need *two* scales because there are *two* relevant variables. The fourth category is really of a different sort — to do with the *cause* of the error, not what *kind* of thing has been got wrong. A better system would then be to record each error on two scales (variables) such as:

Kind of error: Spelling — Grammar — Vocabulary — Discourse
Cause of error: L1 — Target Language — some other cause.

Any given error will then figure twice — being classified in *one* category of each scale.

In the above example, the two variables involved essentially *cross-classificatory* categorisations: in principle some errors of all of the four *kinds* could arise from each of the specified causes. However, you also encounter categorisations connected rather by one being *nested* in the other. That is, one nominal scale containing a certain number of categories as levels or values is *itself* a value in a broader scale. For instance we could categorise some errors also as involving either putting in extra letters, omitting letters, reversing letters or substituting the wrong letters. But these categories only apply to spelling, of course, so this variable does not cross-classify the 'kind of error' scale above. Rather the variable 'kind of spelling alteration' really subclassifies only *one* value of the 'kind of error' variable. In this way categorisations can form hierarchies of categories and subcategories.

The precise definition of such categories, their values, and how they interlock is ultimately a matter of linguistic 'content', so may be the subject of theoretical disagreement (cf. validity Chap. 22). For instance, some would argue that the notions of omission, addition, reversal and substitution can be extended and generalised across *all* error types — so for instance grammatical errors can involve *omission* of essential grammatical words or inflections, wrong word *order* and so forth. If so, then these four 'alteration types' do crossclassify the other scales mentioned above after all.

Then what about a classification of errors into 'verb inflection errors', 'noun inflection errors', 'other'? This appears at first to be a rough subclassification only of grammatical errors. But it could be argued that the errors in *I walk home yesterday* and *She buyed an apple*, though both involving verb inflection, differ in that the first, involving a regular verb, is genuinely grammatical, the second, involving an irregular verb, is at least partly a vocabulary matter. To make the first error, the learner simply fails to apply a general grammatical rule, to make the second he/she applies the general grammatical rule but shows ignorance that the specific vocabulary item *buy* is an exception to the rule. Thus 'verb inflection error' versus others could be argued to cross-classify the 'grammatical error' — 'vocabulary error' distinction. Clearly if pursued further, the interlocking of error category scales becomes even more complicated. For a notation and framework (based on 'systemic linguistics') in which to explore and express networks of categories and subcategories see Bliss *et al.* (1983).

18.2 Simple Nominal Categorisation by Some Judge

18.2.1 Nominal categorisation by measurer/researcher

A great deal of linguistic work can involve the researcher categorising people/sentences/etc., by global judgment, following some definition, for properties which either are there in one form or another, but do not lend themselves to being viewed as *more* or *less* there. Examples:

Categorising some dictionaries as either monolingual or bilingual.

Categorising the palate (roof of the mouth) of each of a group of subjects as: palate too high, too low, cleft, normal.

Categorising the languages of the world into those that place the adjective primarily before the noun and those that have it after.

Classifying language learners as either self-taught, taught in a private school or taught in a state school.

Data obtained both reactively and non-reactively lends itself to such categorisation, and usually you would think of the classification having some absolute rather than just relative interpretation.

Normally the categories for the scale will be decided before any cases are actually classified, though it is common to discover as you go along that you missed a relevant category. For instance you might set out to categorise some Belize informants as either Creole speakers or Standard English speakers, but realise as you go along that this scale is a straightjacket into which some cases cannot readily be forced. You might well need a category for speakers of both varieties, and even speakers of neither. Indeed you could well 'binarise' the scale into two binomial ones (see 18.4.2). It can greatly distort research results if missing categories go unnoticed, and either when categorising yourself or getting subjects to do it (18.2.2), it is often as well to have an 'other: please specify' category in any set just in case there is an eventuality that you overlooked.

In some instances of very exploratory R work you might develop suitable categories into which to divide the nominal scale *entirely* on the basis of the results themselves. So in the instance of the word association test, if you had no prior idea how to classify the responses, you might wait and see what words occur as responses, before deciding how best to classify them into categories. This arises most commonly with *open* questions in opinion measurement, such as you may include in a questionnaire along with ones with preset alternative answers which the informant ticks or circles, and which can relatively easily be reduced to figures after.

For example an open questionnaire item to a foreign learner like 'How do you go about trying to learn vocabulary items?' would elicit a great variety of responses, long and short. From these you might, usually with difficulty, be able to distil one or more classifications of learning strategies into which the informants can then be placed. Though ad hoc categorisations of this sort are very useful initially in previously under-studied areas, e.g. in pilot studies, they can lead to confusion if standard classifications are not soon agreed on and offered in questionnaires, with an 'other' alternative, to allow for the eventuality of a previously undetected alternative cropping up.

In the study of learning strategies, for example, where not only questionnaires but also quasi-natural observation of the learner learning, and elicitation of 'think aloud' protocols are used to gain information, there is still a tendency for every researcher to 'find' a slightly different classification. Even where the same category *is* identified, it may be called something different, making it very difficult to compare findings.

Genuine nominal categorisations are most often met in R work with two or more variables, where one of them, the EV, if not ordered categories, will often be polynomial or binomial. So if you are comparing the amount of Welsh spoken in four districts of the city of Bangor — Maesgeirchen, Hirael, Penrhosgarnedd, Upper Bangor — these four districts are a polynomial EV. If you record the gender of your subjects in a comparison of girls' and boys' reading ability at age 5 you are in effect categorising the children on a binomial EV scale, classifying them as male or female.

A slightly different situation arises if, in a psycholinguistic experiment, you divide your subjects into three groups each of which has the task of trying to learn the same list of words but by three different techniques. Then you are in effect placing each subject on a nominal scale of three IV categories — techniques 1, 2, 3. It is particularly obvious here that there is no inherent sense of 'increase' implied by the numbers: any of the techniques could be labelled 1, provided you were consistent. Only after the research you might be able to order the methods by their discovered 'effectiveness'. Notice that in these examples it does not matter that in the last paragraph the category into which an informant falls was intrinsic to him/herself, whereas in the last instance it is imposed by the researcher in an experimental design: all are nominal.

Finally a great amount of nominal categorisation in language research is associated with linguistic categorisations used as the basis for EV *stimuli*. Many psycholinguistic experiments require responses from subjects to a set of stimuli which actually contain two or more types of thing mixed up (the IV), the responses to which (the DV) are to be compared. Hence a categorisation of the stimuli is presupposed — e.g. into concrete and abstract words, active and passive sentences, passages of text spoken in three different accents, or the like.

As seen earlier (17.2.1) the exhaustiveness requirement is often not adhered to where EV's are concerned. Thus it is common to compare the effectiveness of just two methods of memorising vocabulary — say, your special new method and a standard procedure like 'repetition' which serves as the so-called 'control condition' — though there is really an indefinite number of other methods you could also include in the comparison. The scale of the variable 'methods of memorisation' has an indefinitely large number of values. The comments at 17.2.1 hold again about how the selection of categories is made.

In many ways special instances of the preceding are the variables of the means of quantification itself — the so-called 'facets of observation' (4.2). These mostly constitute nominal scales — e.g. 'structured' versus 'unstructured' interview, 'open choice' versus 'multiple choice' test item, 'internal' versus 'external' examiner, observation in 'school' — 'home' — 'street' — 'laboratory'. Selected values of selected facets are used to make EVs in research on measurement itself (see 21.2.3).

18.2.2 Nominal classification by cases

In many R and T situations you get your subjects or informants in effect to categorise something, or themselves. Examples:

After hearing a story, subjects in a psycholinguistic experiment are asked to judge if a given sentence occurred/didn't occur in the story.

After reading a passage, learners of English are asked to judge if a given statement about something discussed in the passage is true/false.

Hearing the sentence *The dog is being chased by the cat*, children are asked to pick out which of two pictures the statement describes — picture A, showing a dog chasing a cat, or picture B, showing a cat chasing a dog.

People each supply one word association response to a given stimulus word, e.g. *hot*. Thus they effectively place themselves in categories depending on which response word they choose. For example some will probably reply with *cold*, some with *dog*, some with *sun* etc. The best set of categories could well be determined by the investigator after the event.

You play a synthesised sound: do they say they hear it as an /s/ or a /θ/ or a /f/?

Given the sentence *John inferred that there had been an accident* speakers of English are asked to say which of three alternatives is closest to the meaning of *inferred*: *stated / concluded / implied / denied*. Individual items from multiple choice tests generally can be looked at this way as well as just in right/wrong terms, as part of 'item analysis'.

In a survey Moroccans are asked which of three languages — Moroccan Arabic, Standard Arabic, French — they use at home. Here the cases categorise themselves.

Sometimes the subject is expected to find the categories, rather than being given them. For instance when a child is set to sort three blocks differing in shape and colour into two groups of his/her choice to see if he/she chooses to sort by colour or shape (a 'sorting task' or 'classification test'). Also in 'concept formation' studies cases are given examples and model categorisations so they can induce a rule and then asked to categorise new examples as evidence of what classificatory rule they have in fact formulated (Ohala & Jaeger, 1986: Chap. 12).

Categorisation of these sorts arises in more reactive measurement, in questionnaires or tests, in instances where each item is perceived as a separate variable. Often, of course, a series of binary categorisations made in a parallel way by the same person is what is counted up to give them a unitary interval score for one variable (see Chap. 13), rather than treated as separate categorisations. This must be clearly distinguished.

Similar to 17.2.2, a 'missing' category may arise where cases omit items in a questionnaire, or where ambiguous questions are interpreted in an unintended way. For instance:

How is your study financed?

in a questionnaire to language teachers taking overseas courses yielded some perfectly natural responses such as 'well' and 'monthly' which were actually irrelevant to the targeted variable 'source of funding', and so had to be omitted (British Council, 1987; cf. 'escapes' 6.3, 20.5 v).

18.2.3 Problematical independence of cases categorised

The above were intended as clear instances of nominal categorisation.

However, there are many situations where superficially you seem to be categorising things, and indeed for many purposes it is satisfactory to think of what you are doing as this, *but* for the purposes of any ensuing inferential statistics you may have to conceptualise what you are doing differently. This arises especially where the cases you are classifying don't approximate one observation each from a *different* person or the like, as in 18.2, but rather approximate a lot of observations from one or a few only. Hence it is doubtful if each observation is *independent* of the others. Examples:

Counting numbers of occurrences of *while* verses *whilst* in an essay of disputed authorship.

Counting frequencies of eight different types of sentence in someone's speech/writing. (Or the same for types of illocutionary act, or alternative renditions of [θ], types of error or the like).

The cases/observations counted here are not uncontentiously independent of each other as they would be if each were from a different person. It can be argued that a speaker's use of a word in one sentence is not entirely unaffected by his/her choice of that word a sentence or two before, for example. Hence it would be better to think of counts 'within people' as unitary scores for each person separately, as per Chapter 12. On the other hand some argue that if occurrences are far away enough from each other in time or space (i.e. distance in text), such dependence of choice is unlikely. That is certainly the view of many stylisticians (e.g. Kenny, 1982). If the observations were in *disconnected* samples of speech or writing, albeit from the same person, this could certainly be more strongly argued. But, as indicated, this is not something worth agonising over unless you propose to use inferential statistical tests on your data, as those for quasi-interval scores are different from those for genuine nominal categorisations. However, the following are more generally unsatisfactory, since the categorisations are of a *mixture* of observations from 'within' people and 'between' different people.

Classifying all the hesitation phenomena of two speakers in a recorded conversation into types such as filled pause, unfilled pause, repetition, other.

Determining proportions of the different parts of speech in samples of language from children of a given age: i.e. pooling all the words from several children into one classification as nouns, verbs, adjectives, adverbs or function words. A common approach in some older taxonomic studies (Bloom & Lahey, 1978: 324).

Getting n subjects to judge several sets of four pairs of sentences, saying which they prefer in each pair. In each set of four the same point is at issue. What are taken as the relevant 'cases' to compare judgments of one point with another in an ensuing statistical test are the $4 \times n$ judgments of pairs relevant to the same point (Prideaux, 1984: 256).

For instance the last example would arguably be better treated by calculating a score out of four on each point, for each person as case (Chap. 13); the score for a group of cases would be the average of these. On the other hand some would argue that if pairs of sentences from the different sets of four are presented in randomly intermingled order, independence of judgment from one pair to another *is* achieved. Even if that is accepted, Prideaux's nominal treatment of the data definitely loses information that might be of interest about the amount of variation in judgment between people in the group, because variation within and between people is conflated (cf. Milroy, 1987: 6.8.3). At least you need to be clear in your mind about what you are claiming if you do decide to treat this sort of data on a par with clearly nominal data. For further discussion see Scholfield (forthcoming c).

18.3 Nominal Categorisation Derived from Application of a Series of Binary Criteria

We saw at 16.3 that rank ordering can sometimes be made a simpler and more reliable, if longer, activity by fragmenting it into a task of ranking a lot of pairs. Thus each person/thing ranked gets considered several times rather than just once. So also categorisation (including ordered categorisation — Chap. 17) is sometimes operationalised not as a global decision about each case classified, but as the result of application of a series of specific criteria. Each *criterion* or specific *attribute* checked for resembles a mini binomial categorisation in itself, but its only purpose is to contribute to determining what category each case belongs in on some ulterior scale. Each can often alternatively be conceptualised as a 'test' for category membership.

Stewart's classification of languages into seven types (reported in Fasold, 1984) is a good example. To determine the classification of any language the researcher has to decide whether or not it has each of four attributes (standardisation, autonomy, historicity and vitality). Different patterns of 'yes' and 'no' decisions correspond to particular types on the overall categorisation. For example a Standard language has all four attributes, a Classical language all but the last, a Pidgin none. In fact four binomial attributes could define a scale with $2^4 = 16$ values, but apparently only seven combinations occur naturally. Thus the output seven categories are empirically but not logically 'exhaustive'.

In this example there was a category on the output scale for several combinations of specific attributes that cropped up. Alternatively, in some approaches of this sort, you keep the output scale binomial by adopting a rule that puts a case in category A only if it passes *all* the criteria (or the majority, or at least certain specified ones), in category B otherwise. For instance Ferguson's classification of a language as 'major' or 'minor' in a given country is decided from these three criteria on the rule that it is major if it meets *at least one* of the criteria:

It is spoken as a native language by more than 25% of the population or more than one million people

It is an official language of the country

It is the language of education of over 50% of those completing secondary school (Fasold, 1984).

Alternatively you can change the way you are quantifying more drastically. You could decide to regard the criteria as variables in their own right and not try to summarise them — i.e. keep them as a profile of categorisations of each case (cf. end of 18.5 and Fasold's view, 1984: Chap. 3). Or you could add up criteria passed for each case and award interval scores for 'number of relevant attributes present' (13.1).

Pure linguistic categorisations are often decided in a similar way, with decisions on the criteria usually made by the linguist's own introspection (7.4) about the 'ideal speaker-hearer' of a language regardless of any variation in actual language use. For example he/she will typically identify a number of characteristics as relevant to deciding if a verb is modal or non-modal in English, e.g. (simplified):

(a) allows negation with *n't* attached

(b) takes the following verb as an infinitive without *to*

(c) lacks -*s* in the third person singular present form

(d) inverts with the subject in yes/no questions.

Thus *must* passes all these and is modal, *like* fails them all and is non-modal: *You mustn't answer, must you? He must* is acceptable but *You liken't drive, like you? He like* is not (it should be *You don't like to drive, do you? He likes to*).

In more theoretical discussions, classifications of linguistic units are often expressed in a quasi-algebraic *feature* or *componential* notation. Thus *must* might be designated +M, *like* -M. In this example the situation is complicated by the fact that there are some verbs which can be used either in accordance with these criteria or not on different occasions, like *need* and *dare*. These could be made a third category of 'semi-modals', ±M. Or, to avoid the exclusiveness problem, you could decide that there are really two categorisations relevant: +M versus -M, and +V versus -V (where V stands for 'full verb'). Then

> *must* would be +M, -V
> *like* would be -M, +V
> *need* would be +M, +V

and of course a word like *red* would be -M, -V. Similar notations are used to classify sounds in phonology and word meaning in semantics. For instance the sounds [n] and [m] are +nas (i.e. nasal), [p] [d] and [b] -nas; the word *man* is +ADULT +MALE in meaning, *woman* is +ADULT -MALE etc. Such notations tend to be heavily embedded in particular linguistic theories, where they are usually conceived as forms of linguistic 'analysis' rather than 'classification', and cannot be pursued further here (see e.g. Radford, 1988; Leech, 1981).

18.4 Nominal Categories Derived from Data Originally Recorded on Some Other Scale

Apart from the above examples it is possible to get nominal data by conversion of data originally of some other form.

18.4.1 Ordered categories as a source

Since inferential statistical techniques specifically for ordered categories are few and less well known, it is common to treat counts of things in ordered categories as if the categories were unordered nominal ones (see further e.g. Cohen & Holliday, 1982). In particular many popular statistical tests used to compare, say, the language performance of groups belonging to different social classes, actually compare the groups representing the EV without taking into account their ordering. Furthermore, there are some occasions where ordered categorisations need to be 'binarised' in a similar way to that described below (18.4.2). See further Jones-Sargent (1983).

18.4.2 Nominal scales condensed or converted as a source

Another common source of nominal scales is simply by conversion of more elaborate nominal scales. For instance a five category polynomial scale may be reduced to three categories or even two by lumping together some of the categories. For certain inferential statistical procedures (especially the chi squared test) this has to be done in certain circumstances where the number of cases falling in some categories is very small (see e.g. Robson, 1983; Langley, 1979). Often this yields a dustbin 'other' category, but is normally preferable to *leaving out* the unpopular categories. Or it may be done just to simplify matters for some purpose. A variety of L1's might be recorded by informants in answer to a questionnaire question, but for a particular research purpose you might only be interested in 'English' versus 'non-English'.

In some instances it is desirable to *binarise* a polynomial scale, by 'exploding' each value/category into a separate binomial variable. Thus you might initially set up this three valued scale for what you think of as one variable in a dialect survey of Wales, expecting each case (informant site) would fall in one category or another:

> Word used for 'gate'   1: *llidiart*
> 2: *clwyd*
> 3: *gât*

If it emerged that some sites/informants reported using *more* than one of the words for 'gate', 'binarising' would be a good idea to overcome the exclusiveness problem (18.1). The original scale would convert to three binomial scales:

> Using *llidiart*   1: Yes
> 2: No
> Using *clwyd*   1: Yes
> 2: No
> Using *gât*   1: Yes
> 2: No

Here a location where for example *clwyd* was the word reported would be classified 2 on the first new scale, 1 on the second, 2 on the third. This binarisation is also required in order to apply some advanced statistical techniques like cluster analysis, and was used on the Tyneside Survey (Jones-Sargent, 1983).

18.5 Nominal Categorisations Derived from Combining Series of Categorisations or Scores

Where repeated polynomial categorisations on the *same* variable are involved, you can take the modal (commonest) categorisation of a case as a single representative categorisation (cf. Scholfield (forthcoming b) for further agreement checks you might wish to do). If the categorisation is binary, then you would probably add up the total of one alternative for each case and treat it as a quasi-interval score (cf. Chap. 13).

Where only two or so *different* (cf. discussion at 15.2) categorisations are to be combined, especially if they have some absolute interpretation, this is sometimes done by creating a 'hybrid' scale that has categories for all possible combinations of the separate categorisations. Thus you could combine the two scales suggested for errors above (18.1) into one scale with values: grammatical L1 based error, grammatical target language based error, vocabulary L1 based error, and so on. The 'Creole' — 'Standard English' — 'both' — 'neither' example in 18.2.1 is also really a hybrid of two binomial scales, as would be a +M, -M, ±M classification of verbs (18.3). Such a scale appears to violate the rule that one scale must correspond to *one* variable, of course, and must be supported by an argument that the composite of the two variables combined is a valid new variable (cf. discussion at 15.2.2).

This is also seen done for ordinal category scales, including ones that have been converted from interval (Chap. 17). For instance in psycholinguistic work you often measure subjects on two variables on a set of items. You score them for response time on each item, so each subject gets an overall average response time score. You also record how many items they respond correctly to, so each subject also gets a 'score correct'. One method of combining these would be to first combine the scores in interval form, e.g. weight one by the other (14.2.1), and *then* divide into ordered categories (17.3.2). The present way is to *first* categorise each scale separately, e.g. divide into two at the middle scoring person's score (the 'median'). Thus one scale becomes 'relatively fast' versus 'relatively slow', the other 'relatively accurate' versus 'relatively inaccurate'. You can then combine these as a hybrid four category scale with values: 'fast and accurate', 'slow and accurate', 'fast and inaccurate', 'slow and inaccurate'.

However, the most sophisticated solution, useful for larger sets of variables, involves *cluster analysis*, which in principle can be performed on any set of variables, provided they are all of one scale type, especially all interval, or all binomial. The output is 'natural' groupings of cases into categories based on the collective evidence of the overall profiles of cases across all the variables. There is a whole variety of cluster analysis methods and the technicalities cannot be gone into here (see Scholfield, 1991 for a review). For example Baker & Hinde (1984) got a number of informants in Wales to rate each of 26 possible addressees on five point scales for how much they would speak Welsh with them — always English, English more than Welsh, equal, etc. From these 26 variables, using one version of cluster analysis, it was possible to derive a grouping of the subjects into three categories with distinct profiles of language use across addressees.

Similarly Ahmed (1988) binarised a number of polynomial classifications of learners in terms of what vocabulary learning strategies they used to a series of around 50 binomial ones (18.4.2 above). That is, all strategies became recorded as either used or not used by each case. Cluster analysis over these variables yielded evidence of five reasonably distinct categories of learner marked off by their use and non-use of distinct combinations of strategies.

As usual, for many purposes, especially T, it may be more profitable to examine the *un*combined profile of each case — how he/she figures in each separate categorisation.

Further Reading

Fasold (1984: Chap. 3).
Bennett-Kastor (1988: 75ff).

19 Overview of Quality Issues and Reliability Measurer and Cases as Sources of Unreliability

19.1 Quality Assurance and Quality Control

19.1.1 Quality in quantification

Whatever quantification technique you are using, for whatever variable, recorded on whatever scale, you want your measurement to be 'good'. In general there are two approaches to ensuring this — by 'quality assurance' and 'quality control'. Following the former, you pay the closest possible attention to avoiding sources of error during the 'process' itself of constructing instruments, gathering data and reducing it to figures. Following the latter approach you rely more on mechanical checking on the 'product' afterwards, especially when it is used in *pilot trials, quantifying* quality itself and rejecting what is unsatisfactory — a bit like sampling and testing a batch of components off a factory production line to determine the percentage of defectives. This book is designed more to help with quality assurance, and many things relevant to good quantification have been mentioned already. For instance in Chapter 9 I highlighted how to ensure naturalism in balance with control-like features. In 11–18 a lot of attention was paid to how to ensure figures come out on scales with suitable properties.

By contrast, in the literature, especially that on 'testing' for T purposes, it is commonly quality *control* that is focused on, in the form of various formal tests and procedures that can be carried out to check on and measure measurement. This may in part be because of the popularity of norm-referenced multi-item tests, which, as we saw (10.4), have to rely rather more on this by their nature, or because it seems more objective. But commonly in everyday T contexts, where quick teacher-made assessments are needed, and in many small R projects, it is simply not feasible or cost-effective to pilot every test, questionnaire, or other data gathering and scoring procedure and submit it to formal checking procedures and revision before real life use. As Bachman (1990: 56f) remarks, the costs of possible wrong decisions due to error in quantification have to be weighed against the cost of elaborate checking on reliability and validity.

'Testing the tests' is commonly discussed under the twin heads of *reliability* and *validity* corresponding to the two major kinds of error that can arise, the term *dependability* being preferred for the former by some for criterion-referenced measurement. Though I shall adopt this conventional distinction, I shall in this last section of this book continue to look more at the detailed features that may *cause* unreliability or invalidity, gathering together things either overlooked or only mentioned in passing earlier in the book, from various stages of the quantification sequence of events. Formal methods of reliability and validity checking, some of which are statistically technical, will just be introduced briefly at appropriate points.

19.1.2 Reliability and validity: Introduction

Offhand, we would probably say the prime feature of good quantification is that it should be 'accurate'. This is sometimes equated with how 'precise' it is, though, with Wiliam (1992), I have distinguished that as pertaining rather to the level of detail attempted (11.4), which may be achieved with greater or less accuracy. In particular, trying to be too precise might lead to inaccuracy. We might also want measurement to be 'practical' — i.e. quick and cheap to perform, not requiring complicated equipment, and easy to score, but obviously that should be a secondary consideration in the end. Apart from that, most of the detailed accuracy criteria you might think up will turn out to come under one of the twin heads of 'reliability' and 'validity'.

Put simply, if quantification is *reliable*, in this technical sense, that means it gives virtually the same scores or categorisations if done repeatedly in the same way, i.e. with the same choice of values for facets of observation (4.2), in the same conditions on the same cases by the same or a different measurer. Thus you can be confident it is recording more or less the 'true' score/categorisation of each individual measured on any occasion for whatever variable it measures. So-called 'random errors' or *measurement errors* are minimal — there is relatively little misclassification, or awarding slightly higher or lower marks than should be on any occasion. But note that what constitutes 'the same score' differs a bit depending on whether quantification is in the absolute or relative sense (see Chapter 10).

If quantification is reasonably reliable, then it is measuring *something* and you can consider if it is *valid*. If so, that means it measures the variable you claim it to measure, not one a bit different, which would introduce a 'constant error' or 'bias' whenever measurements were made. (Note, in everyday use, *reliable* is often used in the sense of *valid*.) In fact we have already indirectly discussed two broad sources of invalidity — claiming to measure natural language use but not achieving this, e.g. using a highly artificial test, and failing to apply controls, as in non-elicitation observation, and so perhaps not measuring quite the variable wanted (Chap. 5–10).

Clearly quantification can be reliable without being valid, but not really the reverse. Ideally it is both, whether for T purposes, where individual cases are often being assessed, or for R purposes, where further inferential statistical work may be based on it. The following is a simple illustration of the difference.

Age of informants might seem easy to quantify accurately, just by asking (Chap. 7). But consider informants who don't know their age, as there will be in some parts of the world. You could estimate age intuitively by looking at each case, but clearly reliability will suffer as other researchers, and yourself a week later, might well disagree on the likely ages. Some people's ages will be overestimated on one occasion and underestimated on another, or by a different observer, and others' vice versa. Thus the ages recorded by any one observer on one occasion will differ more or less randomly from the actual ages. Labov (1972) in fact estimated age in this way in his department store survey to keep it non-reactive.

More subtly, what about informants who know their age but don't like to admit it, so consistently give a different age from their actual one in answer to questions? For instance a teenager may add a few years, a person over 50 deduct some. Here there would be apparent reliability, if the informants were totally consistent, but the results would be invalid — we would be measuring not 'chronological age of informant' but 'age informant would like to be thought of as being'. There would be a constant distortion of any individual's age up or down. Of course, if cases *in*consistently misreported ages on different occasions, that would be rather another source of unreliability. This demonstrates the difficulty in the end in making a *watertight* distinction between factors which cause unreliability and those that cause invalidity. This must be borne in mind in what follows.

In fact all language quantification involves human participation at some point, and most has a considerable socio- or psycho-element in the cases and data gathering technique as well as the measurer. There is heavy use of unstandardised approaches in many areas, and many language variables are not available to be quantified very directly. Hence it is very common for there to be unwanted variation of both types in your measurement. We look at reliability in Chapters 19 and 20, validity in Chapters 21–23.

19.2 Good and Bad Reliability: Introduction

It is normal and unavoidable for there to be some degree of unreliability in any kind of measurement, hence the use of the expression 'gives virtually the same scores' in the original characterisation of reliable measurement. The main aim is to reduce the random errors that may make measurement unreliable to a minimum, so that something close to cases' *true scores*, or true categorisations, rankings etc., get recorded. Note that the 'true scores' often referred to in reliability discussion are true scores on whatever the measure quantifies, which may not be 'true' in the sense of 'valid'.

The importance of reliability differs somewhat depending on the purpose of your measurement. In R work you are often interested in average scores for *groups* on a variable, and comparing groups in some way, rather than in the scores of individual cases, hence *some* lack of reliability can be tolerated. If the scores you obtain in, say, a test of twenty people on any occasion all differ a bit from those people's true scores, for whatever the test measures, and if that variation is random, then some score a bit higher than they should, or would on another occasion, others a bit lower. But in a sense, looked at together, this variation cancels itself out. You would be likely to get very much the same *mean* (average) score from this group on different occasions if you measured it repeatedly even though you got a different score on each occasion for each individual *case*, due to random variation.

Thus even if a memory test has some unreliability, it may yield true evidence of the difference between two methods of memorising vocabulary, if there is one, when you test the group that has memorised by one method and the other by another. However, typically the more unwanted variation there is in DV results, the more differences between groups may get clouded, so the difference between memorisation techniques is made harder to prove to be substantial enough to bother about. In other words unreliability of measurement would be one factor in making it harder to reject the null hypothesis that there is no difference between the two methods. The more 'noise' of this sort there is, the larger the group difference has to be to show through clearly. Unreliable measurement will *obscure* real differences between observations, whereas invalid measurement will systematically *bias* observations (Robson, 1983: Chap. 3).

If, as in much T work, you are interested in *individuals'* scores and pass/fail classifications and decisions are to be made from them, unreliability is certainly serious. In the long run if you kept remeasuring, the overestimates and underestimates of an individual's true score would cancel each other out. However, in practice you usually don't remeasure cases, e.g. in school exams or speech therapy clinics, several times with the same technique to make an assessment at any given point in a person's development: there is no time, apart from other problems. Remeasuring after an interval of time to check progress is a different matter of course. Since you assume the case's true score may have changed, this can't be averaged with the original measurement to get a more reliable idea of the original true measurement. Hence reliability needs to be pretty high for any quantification techniques used primarily to evaluate individuals for T purposes. It receives particular attention in the areas of language study that involve language teaching and is relatively neglected for example in psycholinguistics. As Christensen (1980: 85) says, 'This is a matter in which experimental psychologists have been extremely lax'.

Reliability should always be examined informally, whether in one's own or others' work, simply by looking for possible sources of it that may have arisen, such as those to be discussed in the rest of Chapter 19 and Chapter 20. If you perform formal reliability checks, you will find that with the more accessible methods you can put a figure on how unreliable particular aspects of a way of quantifying a variable are, but not really *overall* reliability — i.e. you have to choose what is most relevant to check on. The figure is derived from data gathered either in special pilot trials or, in some instances, as an adjunct to 'real' data gathering and measurement (Appendix 2).

The relevant statistical measures usually yield a coefficient of reliability which, if perfect, would be +1 (or in some instances 100%), but in practice is of course somewhat less. Opinions vary as to what levels of reliability are desirable: a typical view would suggest aiming for 0.6 in exploratory research, 0.75 for hypothesis testing research, and 0.9 for T purposes (cf. Pedhazur & Schmelkin, 1991). Note, however, that with some, lesser known, reliability measures for criterion-referenced scores, zero corresponds to perfect reliability and figures substantially greater than one may be obtained, reflecting poor reliability of some sort (Scholfield, forthcoming b).

With due attention to which aspect of reliability you have quantified, you can use a reliability coefficient in a number of ways. It will help you decide how much confidence to place in the results when you measure, and can in some instances provide an estimate of the span above and below a case's recorded score within which their true score is likely to be (the 'standard error of measurement', see e.g. Cohen *et al.*, 1988: 117ff). This is important in T uses where there is an interest in individual cases' scores: the greater the unreliability of quantification, the larger the distance between one person's score and the next has to be for one to be confident that one really has done better than the other. Reliability information may also suggest that specific cases' scores/categorisations are particularly unreliable. Especially, it may prompt you to improve some aspect of data gathering, scoring or whatever in future.

As we shall see, ways of improving reliability often involve increased 'control' in the sense of elimination of unwanted factors, which may be at the cost of naturalism. Another general principle is 'The more the better'. That is, larger or repeated samples of behaviour from each case, longer tests and inventories, more than one person scoring or categorising each case, and suchlike, all tend to improve the reliability of the overall resultant scores or categorisations obtained (cf. 15.1, 16.5, 17.4, 18.5 for how to make the combinations).

As we have already begun to see, there is really no such thing as *the* reliability of a means of quantifying some variable, though it is often spoken of this way. There are different *sources* of unreliability, varying in effect for different types of *case*. These are quantifiable with a variety of non-equivalent *coefficients*, behind which lie a variety of technical statistical models. When reading about and relying on reliability coefficients reported for standard published tests, for example, you have to remember this and try to spot what sort of reliability was quantified, on what cases, in what setting etc. and whether it applies, given your own proposed way of using the test.

For convenience I shall consider unreliability by sources, based on different elements of the 'measurement event' — the facets of observation and the cases themselves (Chap. 4), though in reality they all interact. These are taken as: the person doing the measuring, the cases being measured, the circumstances where the measurement takes place, and the data gathering technique itself.

19.3 Unreliability Arising Predominantly from the Measurer

19.3.1 Measurer slips

The measurer or his/her proxy can be a source of random error at all phases of the quantification activity reviewed in this book, but particularly the coding and scoring phase. One broad type is slips due to boredom, inattention, memory span and the like. Measurers, like cases (20.1) have 'off moments'. Examples:

Misrecording figures from indicators on an instrument, or misreading the display on a computer screen.

Inconsistently setting controls — e.g. sometimes setting the loudness wrong on a tape recorder when recording, so that some of the sounds turn out to be indistinguishable.

Failing to add up test marks correctly for all cases. Templates or computer administration help here.

Misclassifying some of the errors you are diligently going through 50 learners' work to code and collect, or allowing shifting criteria for what is an error to creep in.

Missing instances of a sound you are checking through a tape for. Producing a phonetic transcription of the tape as a (laborious) first step before counting up helps avoid this (cf. Faerch *et al.*, 1984: 301).

Relying on memory of what was said rather than taping it — for instance Labov (1972) in his department store survey could not tape his shop assistant informants without making the study 'reactive'. He relied on short term memory of how they answered and made notes about their pronunciation of *r* after he had moved away out of their sight.

Misrating cases through trying to rate them on several variables simultaneously, as might happen in the *FSI Oral Interview* in which examiners normally have to rate testees on the spot for several aspects of their language, without taping the proceedings and being able to recheck.

Grading pupils for their fluency over several weeks as they speak during normal classes, doing a few each week, and consequently allowing criteria to vary.

All these little things make your observations depart slightly from the 'true' ones and hence cloud the 'real' position of whoever or whatever you are measuring on the variable. At least these are potentially under your control and should be eliminated simply by using due care, and rechecking wherever possible. They can't usually be detected in the work of others, since you would have to be at their shoulder throughout their work to spot them.

Clearly some quantification techniques are in themselves particularly subjective, and so lend themselves to unpredictable variation by the measurer. Tests, being more controlled, are inherently least prone to this: indeed one characterisation of what tests are is 'devices interposed between examiner and subject to improve the reliability of observation' (Perkins,

1977). At least as far as the scoring procedure goes, an objective multiple choice test is likely to be reliable if the response to be counted as right is clearly specified. This is so even if there is underlying inconsistency in the decision of the test writer as to which alternative *is* right, see 20.5. Rees (1981) reports no slips in scoring whatever detected in 2400 objective test items he rechecked in Senegal!

19.3.2 Varying interpretations of vague definitions

Often in more naturalistic and subjective approaches there is some vagueness in what is to be coded as what, what exactly is being rated, what the definition is for classification and so on. This leaves it open to a single measurer to shift interpretation inadvertently. If *different* measurers/judges quantify different cases, as often in T contexts, for example, variation may be considerable.

Usually reliability can be improved by clearer and more practical specifications. An example would be specifying what is or is not a modal verb. Classifications of linguistic units like this are often needed either to count tokens in recorded language samples, or in specifications of test item domains, or to make the EV in a psycholinguistic experiment. Here a dictionary definition such as 'verb used to express the mood of another verb — i.e. an added idea of obligation, necessity, probability etc'. leaves a good deal of room for subjective interpretation by measurers, and doubt over what fits the definition. For example, are *should* and *require* both modal verbs?

To counteract subjectivity and improve reliability here you can alter the definition of what has to be observed so that it is more objective and easy to agree on. Particularly in psychology related work there is emphasis on *operational definitions* — ones which specify some objective steps to be taken to reach a measurement or classification, rather than specifying variables or their values by rather vague paraphrases. Linguists achieve this by referring to explicit observable criteria or attributes, like those described in 18.3, to define categories like 'modal verb'. On those, *should* definitely is modal and *require* is not. Trying words in criterial test frames such as 'Can it be made negative with *n't*' requires less force of thought than trying to apply the verbal definition above and will lead to less inconsistency both within and between measurers, even though a subjective decision still has to be made over each specific criterion. Also the operationalised definition could be more profitably used in a test submitted to native speaker informants in an empirical study to resolve the matter than the original version of the definition (but cf. Clark & Clark, 1977: 475).

Part and parcel of this often, as again in the modal example, is that a series of small decisions can be made to replace the original one big one in arriving at a score or categorisation. This, following the principle of 'the more the better', is usually more reliable. This is a general characteristic that differentiates scoring based on counts (Chap. 12 and 14.2.2) or multi-item tests and inventories (Chap. 13 and 14.2.1), ranking based on pairs (16.3) and categorisation based on specific attributes (18.3) on the one hand from global rating (14.1), ranking (16.2) and simple categorisation (17.2 and 18.2) on the other.

Many definitions of classes of linguistic items and so forth that are initially worded in 'notional' terms can be replaced similarly by more operational criteria of this sort provided by linguists. In some areas of investigation the operational definitions may have to come from other experts too — e.g. to define 'dyslexic' or 'bilingual' or 'major language' (18.3). One problem is that this approach may require you in effect to change the nature of the variable measured slightly and may therefore involve problems of validity if the two definitions don't actually specify quite the same thing. Making definitions *clearer* improves reliability but is separate from the matter of what is the *right* definition (see Chap. 22).

Clearly some variables can be more easily 'operationalised' than others. Increasingly researchers and teachers are interested in aspects of language that are not easy to define objectively. For instance they want to classify utterances not just by 'easy' things like their length, but by what speech act (illocutionary act) they perform. However when a child says *That doggie*, even when the circumstances are known, it is inevitably a matter of interpretation whether this is intended as a statement equivalent to 'I'm saying that that is a doggie', a question, effectively 'I'm asking you if that is a doggie', a request for action meaning 'I'm requesting you to give me that doggie', or what. It would be hard to operationalise this as it necessarily involves intuiting the child's intention: such variables are inherently prone to unreliability. The parent may well be a better judge than the researcher (cf. Bloom & Lahey, 1978: 47ff). Even with adult utterances there can be doubt if you can't ask them their intention.

Another big area for these problems is global rating, ranking and ordered categorisation by measurers. If teachers are expected to give an overall impressionistic mark for quality of writing to an essay, as in some traditional language exams, who knows what varying definition may be used — correctness of language? content? rhetorical organisation? or what? Without clear criteria established in advance, the marker may simply 'discover' a subconscious personal specification of what is being rated as he/she goes along, prompted by the protocols themselves, so cases marked early are really scored for different things from those scored later. Again, how unambiguous and stable are notions like 'intelligibility' of brain damaged patients, 'teaching ability' of language teachers, 'oral ability in English' of learners, or 'difficulty' of extracts from authors, all commonly globally rated by measurers? There may be considerable unsystematic variation between measurers, or within one measurer at different times, due to different conceptions of what is being measured (cf. Matthews, 1990).

In such instances again it is necessary to make the variable being rated, or in terms of which the ordering is being made or whatever, as specific and explicitly defined as possible. On the lines exemplified above you could break down global things like 'spoken ability in English' into more specific things easier to agree on the definition of, which collectively form a valid measure of the global thing, and rate each separately — e.g. fluency, grammatical correctness, vocabulary level. In effect you create an inventory or recognise it as really a complex variable composed of several others. However, see Oller (1979: 325) for a discussion of an instance where the breakdown does not appear to add to the reliability.

This is not all that is needed though. Judges may also vary in their interpretation of the levels or categories of ordered scales. One person's 'good' may be another's 'moderate'. The same person's 'moderate' may be inclined to vary — e.g. rise to 'good' if the last few protocols scored were all 'poor'. This is most serious when one measurer cannot assess *all* the cases personally, and where the scale is meant to record some absolute standard (10.5). Thus clearcut definition of the levels is needed too, particularly for standard measures to be used by relatively untrained measurers, such as teachers in a school all assessing the fluency of different children of different ages, supposedly on a common basis (cf. Spooncer, 1983: 63).

This is one area where 'more' is *not* 'better', in the sense that reliability is not helped but worsened by having more levels to be distinguished (14.1). Rather it may be achieved in a variety of ways, such as by giving actual model examples of bits of language that clearly fall in one grade/category or another. For instance the *Cambridge First Certificate* exam guide (L. Jones, 1984) offers, in addition to a verbal characterisation of each grade, examples of actual essays which typify each of the grades of the scale used. In effect they are samples from what is an ordered domain, in the jargon of criterion-referenced measurement (cf. Chap. 10 and Nitko, 1980). This is often better for relatively untrained markers than trying to characterise the levels in metalinguistic terminology — in terms of types of clauses, connectives, etc. used. (See also G. Hill, 1982).

Another answer to most of the problems of this section is prior training of measurers to a uniform standard. This can be checked by measuring agreement with an 'expert' — the prime researcher, chief examiner or whatever — in rating typical material (19.3.4). Cunningham (1985), for instance, in a study categorising mothers' utterances addressing children, accepted only coders who in pilot trials had reached a minimum of 80% agreement with someone directly trained by the researcher himself. Less formally, training takes the form of co-researchers discussing scoring problems with each other, and UK teachers meeting for 'agreement trialling' of sample ratings of pupils' English compositions *vis-à-vis* mastery of criterion-referenced National Curriculum objectives. Teachers have to get together in schools to hammer out among themselves what the 'statements of attainment' mean and what data from pupils does and doesn't evidence having attained them (10.4.2). This is 'moderated' by the local education authority which expects to see sample files of work from the schools.

Even where training is possible, some use *two* judges as standard for all cases, and, if they don't agree, a third to break the deadlock. Or, where the evidence on which the rating or whatever is based is on record in some form — always a good idea — a second measurer checks a random sample of the judgments of the person who did the whole job, and a full remark is only done if agreement is poor. In general, combining the scorings or categorisations of more than one judge, e.g. double marking exam papers, should always improve reliability (cf. 15.1). It is also a common experience for the *same* measurer going over protocols a second time to 'see more'.

A final policy sometimes used is 'If in doubt leave it out'. In other words, bits of data, or even whole cases, on which different measurers cannot agree, or which a single judge cannot make up his/her mind about, however often he/she reexamines the protocol, are treated as 'unanalysable' (and so on a par with 'missing responses'). This improves the reliability of scoring/categorising over the remaining data/cases. It is not too harmful in counts (Chap. 12), unless loci are in short supply, and was Local's solution in his count of tones (Local, 1982). However, it is more problematic if whole cases are omitted. In R contexts this may damage the randomness of sampling of cases as part of the design of an investigation. In a T situation it is hardly feasible at all to omit cases just because their protocols present too many problems to the rater or examiners!

19.3.3 Variation in the procedure of administration

Apart from introducing random errors into the scoring and recording aspect of measurement, the measurer may introduce an element of unreliability during the actual administration of a test or interview in more reactive work. There can be interactions, which are in detail unpredictable, between whoever administers the test or questionnaire and the person measured. In laboratory tests male researchers tend to look at female subjects more than male ones, for example, with consequent possibilities for some subjects to be more distracted than others in an unsystematic way. There clearly can be an effect of varying the interviewer in a socio-linguistic survey — or possibly of keeping him/her the *same* in a multi-ethnic society. McEntegart & Le Page (1982) discuss the problem of differing popularity.

In opinion surveys and tests generally it is known that the exact wording and tone of voice of a question or instructions spoken by the investigator can affect the results obtained. Equally if the time allowed to answer, amount of practice allowed, and so on is variable for different cases, unsystematic variation is introduced within one occasion of data gathering from cases that is never going to be duplicated on any other occasion. The only way out of this is to keep procedure strictly constant, and play the same tape of the instructions, verbal stimuli, e.g. sentences whose acceptability is to be judged, to everyone. However, there is some variation in practice here. American dialect surveys have typically left it to the individual fieldworker to formulate his/her own question to find out for instance what a particular informant's word for a cow house is, whereas British surveys typically prescribe a set form of question (Petyt, 1980).

In elicitation via natural communication of course you can't regulate in these ways without destroying the natural communication. It is down to the researcher to keep conversations with different people as standard as possible. For example with children you should be consistent in whether or not you have five minutes or so 'familiarisation' playing with the child before you start your interview/test, in whether or not you supply encouragement during a test, etc. Such things can affect, for example, the average length of utterance produced by the child. If parents are used as proxy data gatherers, again training is important to ensure some uniformity.

19.3.4 Checking on measurer unreliability

The main formal checking procedures for measurer reliability that are used focus on and quantify unwanted variation primarily of the sorts discussed in 19.3.1 and 19.3.2. In one approach you simply get more than one measurer/judge to score, rate or categorise the same data from the same cases. This is normally done from recorded, transcribed or written protocols, though it can also be done live, as when two observers sit in on a class and each make their own count or rating of some aspect of the teacher in charge or the language activity of different pupils. You then use an appropriate statistical measure of 'correlation' or 'agreement of judges' between the two or more sets of scores or categorisations to put a figure on the *interjudge reliability* detected. A superficially similar approach is to calculate agreement between each judge and a 'criterion' expert judge separately, though since the judges compared are then clearly 'different' in kind, this might be regarded as rather a matter of validity (23.7.1).

Alternatively you can get the *same* measurer (e.g. yourself) to remark the same essays, recalculate the total scores on some test protocols, listen to the same tapes of recorded interviews or whatever twice, in a different random order. The agreement measure then quantifies *intrajudge reliability*. However, there has to be some time lapse between the two measurements, long enough so the measurer does not simply remember what marks/category he gave each case last time, which would boost apparent reliability, but not so long that his/her true standards may have changed. There can anyway be a problem similar to that of 'practice effect' (20.3), especially with subjective marking. The experience of marking a set of essays or whatever once is prone to change a marker's personal frame of reference next time.

Since reliability is case-dependent, in either approach obviously the cases, and the judges, used in a reliability study should be typical of those generally involved in quantifying the particular variable you are interested in, for whatever R or T purpose. Also you must remember since only one gathering of data on one occasion from one set of cases is used, many sources of unreliability are not quantified in the resulting coefficient.

These include unsystematic effects on cases' behaviour of variation in administration or situation where measurement is done, random variation in cases' behaviour on different occasions, and inherent variation within a measuring instrument. In practice, inter- and intra-judge reliability are usually quantified for less reactive data gathering approaches, where a lot of weight rests on measurers to count or rate or categorise. With many tests and inventories on the other hand the more or less automatic scoring procedure is usually assumed to give rise to negligible unreliability from this source.

Thus McEntegart & Le Page (1982: 110) report considerable disagreement between experts in counting up how many children's vowels in taped conversations were nasalised — superficially a straightforward phonetic variable. Reliability for subjectively marked/rated essays, can be as low as 0.35 (Mitchelmore, 1981). Greenbaum (1977) reports 44.3% agreement, averaged over many informants/judges, for their consistency categorising the same structures twice for frequency (albeit the structures, when they recurred, were in sentences with different vocabulary like in an 'equivalent forms' reliability check, 20.3).

The actual statistical methods for quantifying reliability differ, as generally, depending on the scale type of the measurements involved, whether they have absolute or only relative value, and whether just two or more than two measurements of the same cases have to be examined for agreement.

Further Reading

On reliability generally, in this and the next chapter:

Frankfort-Nachmias & Nachmias (1992: Chap. 7)
Pedhazur & Schmelkin (1991: Chap. 5)
Nunnally (1978: Chap. 6 and 7)
Cohen *et al.* (1988: Chap. 5).

On statistical methods of quantifying reliability in this and the next chapter:

Overview: Scholfield (forthcoming b)
Partial, reasonably digestible, up-to-date account: Bachman (1990: Chap. 6).
More technical: Pedhazur & Schmelkin (1991: Chap. 5), Dunn (1989).

20 Cases, Circumstances and the Measuring Instrument Itself as Sources of Unreliability

20.1 Unreliability Arising Directly from the Cases Themselves

Where the cases are people there will always be some random variation in their performance. Their response times, opinions about acceptability of sentences, memory of past linguistic events, proneness to errors when speaking another language and so forth all are subject to 'good' and 'bad' times, depending on mood, health, biorhythms, tiredness and so on, however you quantify them.

Some kinds of people may be more variable than others — e.g. children versus adults — but you can't often alter the cases measured just to improve reliability. The only real solution is to take samples of the behaviour of cases repeatedly and combine the scores/categorisations. This is often more feasible in a T context than an R one — e.g. by time sampling a speech disabled person's speech at successive therapy sessions, or 'continuous assessment' of language learners in school.

Though the internal state of mind of subjects/informants/testees is largely beyond the researcher's control, *motivation* to pay attention and cooperate can be manipulated and made uniform, e.g. in R work by paying subjects or, if students, rewarding them with course credits for participating. It is usually guaranteed anyway in T purpose measurement if evaluation is to ensue.

Where cases are themselves expected to rate, rank or categorise things, training of subjects to apply a clear definition is important, as per 19.3.2 for measurers. Care not to overdo time pressure may alleviate anxiety and hence erratic behaviour. In fact, in general, dealing with the things covered in 19.3.3, 20.2, 20.4 and 20.5 will mostly improve reliability via their effect on cases' variability of behaviour during data gathering.

20.2 Unreliability Arising More From the Circumstances in Which the Cases are Measured

Something relevant that the measurer *can* have some influence on, provided he or she doesn't mind being more reactive, is the situation in which the measuring is done, of which, as we have already seen, he/she or a proxy is an important part, along with any other people present. This setting can have quite a direct effect on reliability. Thus McEntegart & Le Page (1982), striving to record children in St. Lucia in naturalistic settings (cf. Chap. 9) found their recordings harder to interpret reliably because of the literal 'noise' from *other* children when they were interviewing among friends in the open air. Allowing your informants to chew gum may also improve naturalism — but conceal the phonetic variable you're trying to get data on.

On the other hand too formal a setting, apart from reducing naturalness, as we saw earlier, may induce anxiety ('exam nerves') which in turn is likely to make some people do better, some worse than their 'true' performance. The usual recommendation to reduce this sort of thing is to choose a setting which is free from distractions but at the same time puts cases at their ease and keeps them interested. Too big a room, with a lot of people measured at once, might daunt people, and inhibit them from asking if they are not clear about what to do or the like.

As far as possible the setting, whatever it is, and addressees, should be the same (controlled) for all the cases. Or else sometimes differences can be coped with by lumping together repeated measurements as in 19.3.2. Local (1982: 87) was at pains to include in his analysis of children's intonation more or less equal samples of speech obtained from the full range of situations when the children were observed speaking: to peers as well as adults, in the sitting room and bedroom, etc. However, given differences in individual preferences, it is also possible to argue that settings which would be subjectively parallel in their effect on people's performance might be objectively *different* ones for different cases.

In opinion surveys and interviews where speech samples are recorded it is inevitable that the group of people you get observations from will not be measured simultaneously, and perhaps not by the same person either. It is quite common to test people for some types of phonetic or psycho-linguistic experiments in sequence as well, rather than all at once. If you send a questionnaire by post the times and circumstances when they are filled in will vary considerably. Clearly differences between individuals in the times and circumstances of their measurement will introduce some random variation in results which will not be repeated exactly if you were to remeasure them on another occasion. Children, for example, more than adults, may score very differently when tired at the end of the day from when fresh in the morning, or when uncooperative because they are missing school break as against motivated because anything is better than the maths lesson they have been taken out of.

Where there is a choice, it is a moot point whether more reliability is obtained through group administration of a test, or separate administration. The former is more anonymous, which may be less stressful for some, but more daunting for others, and the conditions are the same for all. The latter can usually be made more informal and the tester can appear more sympathetic, but there may be more variation in the setting and measurer's behaviour. Often practical considerations decide it: group administration is quicker but often harder to organise.

20.3 Checking on Unreliability Arising More From the Cases Measured and Factors Affecting Them

A long-standing formal reliability check consists of remeasuring the same cases twice with the same observer/measurer and setting. With more reactive data gathering, the same or an equivalent instrument is used and the same procedure of administration. Statistical measures of correlation and agreement between the two sets of scores/categorisations then quantify what is called *test–retest reliability*, reflecting the fact that this is most often seen used for more artificial measurement. In that instance, if the same task/test/inventory is used twice, then you have to try and ensure that cases don't simply remember their responses and repeat them. A gap of one or two weeks is usually used. In any event it is hard to avoid some 'practice effect' — that is, an improvement on the second occasion solely due to the experience of doing the task on the first occasion. On the other hand there may also be a 'motivation effect' — boredom at doing the same thing again so soon.

The 'equivalent forms' or 'parallel forms' version of this approach overcomes the memory effect problem for test items and so forth, but not the practice effect one (or the general motivation effect). Also it can be troublesome to produce parallel versions of tasks, tests or inventories, and very hard to be sure they really are equivalent. The correlation coefficient may quantify the equivalence of the instruments as much as the wider aspects of reliability. In the more sophisticated realms of standardised testing for T purposes 'item banks' are now established, on the principles of either norm- or criterion-referenced test construction (10.4), which can be sampled to produce parallel tests.

Of course in either approach if the gap between the two measurements is too long, then the cases' 'true' scores may have changed anyway, through the normal process of learning or development, or attrition, so you find the reliability investigation has become a piece of research with time as an EV — e.g. longitudinal studies of children. This is likely to arise more for young children, language learners and speech disabled cases than normal adult native speakers, many of whose attitudes and linguistic performance capabilities remain reasonably stable over long periods. However, remeasurement after a sizeable gap is often unsatisfactory for other reasons — e.g. the difficulty of getting hold of the same cases again.

The 'test–retest' approach, with the provisos above, enables you to quantify unreliability arising from a number of sources in an undifferentiated way. For the kind of cases sampled, it reflects a mixture of unsystematic variability either inherent in cases (20.1) or within the instrument (20.4, 20.5), or in administration (19.3.3) or intra-setting (20.2). If scored by the same person both times, it also reflects any intrajudge but not interjudge variability, though where tests are being assessed, unreliability from this source is often discounted as negligible anyway. It is also possible to combine quantification of test–retest and interjudge reliability by measuring on two occasions with a different measurer each time (e.g. Frick & Semmel, 1978).

The test–retest idea was used quite simply by Labov (1972), for example, when he re-interviewed some of his informants on Martha's Vineyard after a moderate interval of time, too short for the informants' true use of a particular pronunciation to have changed, to see how different the results were for certain vowels whose exact pronunciation in conversation he was recording. Another example is that of Hart, Lapkin & Swain (1987), who considered a test–retest approach to establishing the reliability of their communicative test of French but did not proceed when they found not only a strong practice effect, but also an unacceptable boredom effect on the cases, due to the length of the tasks being repeated.

Two further examples throw light on how far what is the appropriate length of time to wait can vary in different circumstances. It is reported (Fasold, 1984) how Lieberson used a ten year time lapse. The same census questionnaire item about mother tongue should get the same response from the same cases at any time in their lives, if they are reliable informants, since someone's mother tongue (= first language learnt as a child) cannot change. So it was quite legitimate to compare % of different mother tongues reported among 14 year olds with those of 24 year olds ten years later in the same country as a reliability check (though admittedly there would be some imperfection due to the fact that the cases would not be identical — some would have moved away, migrated in or died).

On the other hand, Greenbaum & Quirk (1970: 42ff.), eliciting manipulations of doubtfully acceptable sentences, e.g. asking for a tense change, in fact repeated some identical sentences and tasks as little as 18 minutes apart, in and out of other ones. They found the informants did not even recognise the sentences *consciously* as being repetitions at all. However that does not rule out the possibility of memory and practice effects being present as above. Nevertheless, it may be that some variables *are* inherently beyond even sub-conscious influence by such effects. Candidates would be purely phonetic ones like 'voice onset time' — the time between the initiation of a [b] sound as the lips part when someone begins saying a word like *bar*, and the point where the vocal cords start vibrating.

The statistical measures of test–retest reliability are similar to those for inter-judge reliability. However, there is nowadays a much more sophisticated approach to quantifying *all* kinds of reliability via analysis of variance known as 'Generalisability Theory'. This requires elaborate trials with different occasions and measurers but yields information on reliability *separately* for different facets of the quantification activity which otherwise get lumped together (Bachman, 1990).

20.4 Unreliability More Attributable to the Data Gathering Technique or Apparatus

Though it is not easy to disentangle them from aspects that stem from the setting or person gathering the data, we look here at unreliability arising more from the materials and task of the data gathering technique itself, and any apparatus involved.

Apparatus can be dealt with quickly. These days the machines and computers used for example in instrumental phonetics are likely to have high inbuilt reliability — once you get them to work properly in the first place! Indeed they may come with indications of the margin of random error you may expect (e.g. +/-1% for a timer) due to temperature and current fluctuations etc. Tape and cassette recorders, on the other hand, vary a good deal in quality. Cheap ones are likely to have an adverse effect on reliability in that the recordings may be of poor quality with a lot of hiss and make it hard to decipher what was said, or identify sounds consistently. The same result may arise from using a recorder hidden away, to secure more naturalism.

The naturalistic approaches to quantification of language are so fluid as hardly to be capable of *inherent* unreliability separate from that arising more from those areas already touched on. However, two features not already covered are worth a mention. One is, in elicitation via more or less natural interaction (Chap. 5, 6), the topic chosen to talk or write about. For maximum reliability this would usually be kept constant for all people interviewed, though again this may militate against naturalism, as it is found to affect the length of children's utterances, for example. It also affects their ability to 'avoid' (5.5). Brown & Yule (1993: 108) emphasise this under the rubric 'constancy of elicitation input' — making the point that the communicative task — e.g. description, evaluation, explanation — needs to be uniform, as well as the subject matter — e.g. a mincer. If several topics are covered, scores from each may best be treated as for separate variables — i.e. topics are different choices for a facet of observation, not variants of a single value (see also Bachman, 1990: 161).

The other factor is length of the interaction or text, or the number of different mini-essays, or short bits of speech elicited. This may have to be great if the item you are trying to count, or occasions when it might occur, come up only rarely, or if much is unanalysable (5.3). It is intuitively fairly obvious that small frequencies are unreliable, and less likely to yield closely parallel results if the cases were remeasured, than large frequencies. Researchers normally look for *at least* five potential occurrences of what they're counting to give a reliable indication of an individual's performance — otherwise the case is omitted. Milroy (1987) recommends a minimum of ten and ideally 30 for phonetic variables. Certainly anecdotal evidence of single occurrences in a child's speech, say, is no good. This can be difficult for many variables within the scope of the usual half-hour spoken interaction. Note that from this point of view, uniformity across cases in number of possible occurrences/loci is more important than uniformity in total time of interview/length of text.

Lack of topic consistency and insufficient length are two factors which particularly lead to unreliability in non-reactive word frequency counting work, in what in some quarters is known as 'quantitative linguistics'. Even if you diligently sort through 5 million words of books, newspapers, recorded radio material and so on, as some have done, or got computers to do, you will always end up with a lot of words that only crop up once or twice in all that material. In a sense your sample is too short for them. The actual frequency you obtain for these words is then highly unreliable (the term 'unstable' is also used). If you could count another 5 million words you might easily get no further instances, or several — and what you get appears to depend considerably on the topics that happen to be covered in your 5 million sample. Relatively rare words, like *schism*, tend to be highly topic-bound. If early church history is represented in a sample you might get a whole nest of recurrences of this word, otherwise none at all! By contrast frequent words are much more *uniformly* frequent in disparate samples of English.

In more reactive work — opinion measurement and some kinds of test — often the subjects/informants are asked to categorise sentences, or put words in order or rate things. These activities, dependent on global subjective knowledge, can yield unreliable results in just the same way as when the measurer/investigator performs them (see 19.3.2). For example a question like

> Do you speak Welsh (i) often, (ii) a middling amount of the time, (iii) rarely, if ever

is sufficiently vague to encourage a good deal of random variation in response. Will any two informants have the same idea of what speaking Welsh 'often' consists of? Milroy (1987: 187) reports studies of multilinguals who lack even a consistent set of names for the languages they speak. As suggested in 19.3.2, reliability may be helped by breaking up the one overall opinion required from informants into a series of items about which the informants' opinion is asked separately. For instance you ask separately about people's amount of Welsh speaking with workmates, with the boss at work, in shops, with their children. Or else clearer definitions of the levels of scale involved are needed, with examples, and training of cases.

In any such elicitation obviously the instructions have to be clear to the relevant cases. This can be hard to judge: contrary to what you might expect, Potts *et al.* (1979) report that quite young children *do* understand and comply consistently with completion-test requirements if worded appropriately. Questionnaires *seem* easy to construct, but it is easy to create confusion, e.g. by not being clear where more than one of the offered responses to an item may be ticked, as against only one, or where an item is a contingency question (i.e. only to be answered at all by an informant if they answered 'yes' to a previous question). Equally, some wordings of items may confuse — e.g. questions in the negative or really containing two questions rolled into one such as:

> There are not enough TV programs in Welsh   yes/no
> Is dyslexia diagnosed and treated effectively in your school? yes/no.

Technical terms the informant won't know, may yield inconsistent results. Leech (1968) wanted to ask questions like 'Does the proposition *John is my halfbrother* necessarily entail *John is my brother*?' but wisely recast this as:

Insert YES or NO as appropriate:
'Is he your brother?'
'...he's my halfbrother'.

since it is unlikely many of his informants would have had much idea of what the original question meant.

Again questions beyond the competence of informants to reply to accurately — perhaps asking about their own pronunciation or to self-report on their reading processes — are likely to yield erratic results (cf. 7.3). In any event an ordering from easy background and factual questions to more taxing linguistic and attitudinal ones is usually helpful. Also delicate questions that informants may refuse to answer should be last as they may disturb the frame of mind of informants and affect the reliability of what follows. Thus in the Tyneside Survey (Jones-Sargent, 1983) wisely the last of 38 social background items asked informants' individual voting preference.

Similarly, an informant who really can't decide if the sentence *Honestly, he replied to the question honestly* sounds acceptable English or not may plump for 'yes' or give 'no' haphazardly just to say something. In this connection note the value of allowing a 'don't know' option. Categorisations are likely to be unreliable, if not, indeed, invalid, if appropriate alternatives are not provided, or if the set of alternative categories offered is incomplete. Informants usually feel constrained to reply within the range of categories offered, even if they feel a bit uncomfortable with them. A 'doubtful' category, though from the point of view of the researcher a nuisance, is often essential to complete the set. Piloting, however informal, is essential to help spot many of these faults.

Finally, often many opinions about different things are elicited from informants in *one* long questionnaire, e.g. ones in dialectology with hundreds of items, each one often measuring a separate variable, which take several hours to go through. These may induce boredom and unreliable or missing responses by sheer length, which unfortunately is exacerbated if some of the questions are fragmented into mini-inventories, as suggested above. Questions should only be there if essential to the T or R purpose, or as necessary distractors.

20.5 Unreliability More Attributable to the Structure of a Multi-Item Test

Tests, especially multi-item ones, are often highly controlled and would seem to be inherently very reliable (Chap. 8), but in fact there are a number of ways they can fall short, particularly when not constructed by professional test-makers. Pilot trials, even haphazardly with a few acquaintances, are essential again to help spot problems. Some well-known sources of unreliability are:

(i) Insufficient number of items. Since such a test usually contains only a selection, random or not, of all the possible items, you need to be sure that enough are covered to give a reliable indication of a person's 'true' score. Short tests, like small frequencies, tend to be unreliable. If you ask testees to put two sentences into the passive that is obviously not as reliable a measure of their ability as trying them on 20 sentences. Standard tests in language learning have as many as 100 items — otherwise there is too much of a chance of a testee who should score low just happening to know the majority of the few items tested on some occasions and a good testee scoring lower than he/she should through 'bad luck'. But, of course, longer tests may become unreliable towards the end through boredom and inattention, especially where children are concerned, unless breaks are introduced. Yet, as Meara points out (1987), the vocabulary of even moderate speakers of a language is so big that it is hard to manage tests of vocabulary proficiency that are long enough to reflect more than a very small sample of it.

When constructing a test, you may be interested in the matter of the number of items the other way round — i.e. you may be prepared to make the test as long as is necessary to achieve a reasonable degree of reliability. In fact formulae are available to work this out. You would have to first pilot a test with the number of items chosen by you, then work out its reliability as a coefficient between 0 and 1 by one of the standard means. Then you can use a formula to see what the improvement in reliability would be for longer tests of the same sort. One such formula widely used is the Spearman-Brown 'prophecy formula' (rel = the reliability coefficient calculated form the pilot test):

$$\text{Reliability coefficient of a test with } n \times \text{ the items of the given ones} = \frac{n \times \text{rel}}{1 + ((n-1) \times \text{rel})}$$

(ii) Inadequate instructions and/or practice items built in. Tests, especially some psycholinguistic ones, often involve unfamiliar and unnatural tasks, as we have seen (Chap. 8). Hence clear instructions, in the native language of learners, some examples, and up to ten practice items are essential. Poor instructions may yield erratic responses throughout a set of tasks, and lack of *planned* practice items means that the first few items in the test proper serve as practice items by default, and may yield unreliable evidence.

(iii) Items too difficult. This encourages haphazard response, which reduces reliability. Of course item analysis in a norm-referenced test should eliminate such items anyway, and in a criterion-referenced test some may be unavoidable. Allowing insufficient time can have a similar effect of increasing difficulty, though we saw that for other reasons allowing *more* than sufficient time is also often undesirable (9.6). For example, presenting a picture stimulus for only one twentieth of a second is probably too fast.

(iv) Multiple choice items with too few alternatives. Although often regarded as more objective than open choice tests, and so superior, multiple choice tests carry with them the problem of blind guessing. If you guess on multiple choice items with only two alternatives supplied, obviously in the long run you will get about half of them right purely on a chance basis. This is likely to be a temptation especially in T contexts where something hangs on a case getting a high score. Example:

> An axe is for cutting wood
> > (a) True
> > (b) False
> (or) I _____ here since three o'clock
> > (a) am being
> > (b) have been.

Indeed the testee who liberally guesses will do better than the more cautious testee who omits questions he/she can't answer and is scored wrong on them — the usual practice (cf. 13.2). To even out the last element you would have to actually instruct *all* testees to guess if they don't know an item, rather than leave it out, though you then increase chance errors in your measurement! Formulae which adjust total scores for guessing, on the assumption that everyone does it were discussed at 13.2.

The best solution is to have more alternatives — at least four — so that the effect of guessing is diminished. But this is a subtle business. If some alternatives are very obviously irrelevant, they don't appreciably add to the choices. Example:

> I ____ here since three o'clock.
> > (a) am being
> > (b) have been
> > (c) a book

for all but absolute beginning learners of English will still be effectively a two-choice item, since (c) is so grossly a non-contender. Thus the number of *effective* alternatives in any set depends very much on who the test is for.

Various ways are documented in which distractors/foils can give themselves away to 'test-wise' cases as right or wrong — e.g. by their distinctive length or lack of fit in some elementary respect (see e.g. Heaton, 1975: 2.4; Oller, 1979). Some general kinds of distractor may be more effective than others (Goodrich, 1977). A good simple way to compile a set of genuinely competitive 'distractors' is to do a pilot trial of the test items, in open choice form, on some of the sort of people the test is intended for, and use the commonest incorrect fillers supplied as distractors in the multiple choice form. Additionally of course you can check on the effectiveness of distractors by extending item analysis after a pilot trial of the test itself to examine what proportions of testees of the targeted type who get a question wrong went for each competing wrong alternative (18.2.2). If nobody ever picks (c) in the item above, that is a clear indication of its inadequacy.

Thus there is a lot to be said for open-choice items where, as it were, there is an indefinitely large choice of possible alternatives, so getting the right answer by pure chance guesswork is a very remote possibility. Example:

I say, _____ you been here since three o'clock?

with no alternative supplied, leaves a choice of potentially all the words of English he/she knows for the haphazard guesser to choose between. Although we often speak of having to 'guess the right word' in such items, you cannot effectively ever guess the right answer in such items without some knowledge, so a person's score in such a test is in this respect likely to be close to their 'true' score.

(v) Items constructed so that there is doubt over what answer(s) count(s) as correct or whatever, and which not. To take multiple choice items first, it is surprisingly common in T purpose language tests, especially when constructed by non-native speakers of the language concerned, to find items where there is not one clearly right alternative and the rest clearly wrong, albeit 'close'. This is likely to lead to muddled marking if the 'right' answer is not spelt out for any user of the test with a key, and generally obscure the true score of an individual. For instance consider this item

As he came into the room he turned ____ the light
    (a) in
    (b) on
    (c) out
    (d) with

Certainly *on* is the first correct choice that probably comes to the native speaker's mind, but if you think hard enough and use a little imagination *all* the others are possible too if you supply the right scenario! How do you mark it? If you only count *on* right, you are gratuitously lowering the total score perhaps of some good candidate who chose *out* here. Or you are testing some variable quite different from the one you may think you are: one that includes a component of 'native speaker pragmatic expectancy' as well as 'language competence' (a validity issue). But if you count *all* the alternatives right, the item is useless. If you are making up your own test of course you could get a second opinion to try and spot such items and either exclude them or rescue them — e.g. here by accompanying it with a strip cartoon where a man is seen entering a room and turning on the light (cf. Oller, 1979: 240ff.).

This may arise with published tests too — such as a multiple choice item from the *Southgate Group Reading Test* (Spooncer, 1983: 78):

I bounce a *bell boat doll bun ball*

Though such tests may tell the scorer what answer to count as right, and so make the *scoring process* reliable (19.3.2), the evidence is still unsatisfactory as a measure of the cases.

In open test items there also needs to be care over the possible answers and what counts as 'correct'. Often here it is not possible to construct items so that only one right answer is available, so marking cannot be so mechanical as with multiple choice items. For instance take the following example (based on Potts *et al.*, 1979) designed to test children's mastery of the pseudo-cleft construction in English. After seeing pictures of a woman spilling something and then wiping it up with a rag they had to complete the following:

Carol got a rag and what she did next...

Combinations like ...*was wipe it up* or ...*was wash off the sink* have to be counted as correct, whereas ...*wiped it up* or ...*wipe all the paint up* are wrong. This is a good item since most of the answers you will get will be like those above and clearly right or wrong. However, it is quite difficult to exclude totally the possibility of 'loophole' or 'escape' answers — ones which are in a sense correct, but avoid what you are trying to test. In the above example a continuation like ...*didn't surprise me — she wiped it up* would be of this sort since it makes perfect sense but escapes using the pseudo-cleft construction (*what she did...was...*) which the tester was trying to force out. Potts *et al.* excluded items which evoked 5% or more such loophole responses in a pilot, since they create problems *vis-à-vis* reliable scoring.

Finally, and this applies to all kinds of measurement, there are some specific phenomena and means of testing them which are known from experience to be more reliable than others when you measure them. Thus it is reported (Oller, 1979) that listening tests tend to yield less reliable results than reading tests in the realm of foreign language learning, and that cloze tests with gaps after constant numbers of words (e.g. every 9th word) are more reliable than those with gaps selected on some other basis such as specific vocabulary items. In other words it would seem that some variables you may try to measure are perhaps *in nature* more reliable than others. But obviously if you need to quantify them you just have to live with this source of unreliability.

20.6 Checking on Internal Reliability of a Measuring Instrument

Wherever each case's score for a variable being quantified is based on a sample of several observations, it is possible to determine its *internal consistency*. This applies to scores based on counts, totalled opinion inventories and multi-item tests of all sorts, included ones with weighted/rated items (ch.12, 13, 14.2) though it is usually discussed just in relation to multi-item tests right/wrong. In the simplest version, you gather data from typical cases on a single occasion, divide the set of occurrences or items into two and calculate a score for each half separately for each case. From the correlation or agreement of two sets of scores for a group of cases you can then calculate the *split-half reliability* as it is called.

In this approach usually the halves are not the first half and the second half of a set of items. That would be open to 'practice effect' problems, and would not work for tests that get progressively harder. Also, if a test has subtests quantifying markedly different variables that are regarded as components of the overall variable quantified, or using different facet choices — e.g. part is open choice and part multiple choice — the procedure would be best done for those subtests separately. Then typically *alternate* occurrences/items are assigned to the two halves. This makes it like a virtually simultaneous test and retest. Technically an assumption has to be made that a case's response to an item is not affected by their response to the previous item, so the halves are deemed to give two 'independent' scores for each case. This may not actually be true, especially of more integrative or communicative tests, e.g. responses to successive cloze text gaps, or naturalistic data (cf. discussion at 18.2.3), and may boost apparent reliability.

However, splitting by using alternate items is usually taken as ensuring that any unsystematic variations in administration, setting, individual cases' mood, and scoring are likely to be the same, so what is primarily reflected is inherent variation in the items themselves in their focus on the same variable (i.e. sources of error in 20.4 and 20.5) — their 'consistency'. This is more true for items in a test or inventory, for which usually higher internal reliability coefficients emerge than test–retest ones. Clearly potential occurrences of variables counted in naturalistic data gathering may well be far enough apart for it to be quite possible for some of these other things to have changed and so be reflected in the scores and ensuing reliability coefficient — i.e. separate observations approximate more *different* 'occasions'.

As we saw (20.3), unsystematic variability stemming from the measuring instrument is also reflected in test–retest reliability coefficients. However, it is not so clearly possible there to see its contribution separately from that of various other sources, and there is no internal analysis of total scores for each case. In the present approach, intra-instrument error is quantified from inter-item/inter-observation variability. It is the easiest kind of reliability to quantify in practice because it can be done any time you use the instrument, without need for special extra measurement or scoring on a second occasion just for reliability checking purposes. Often it is worth assessing first, since if an instrument is not reliable in this way, it is not worth pursuing other sources of random error by the procedure of 19.3.4 or 20.3 (see Appendix 2).

Another use of this approach is that two norm-referenced tests designed to be 'equivalent forms' (20.3) can be checked for how equivalent they really are. The items from the two forms are combined alternately to make one big test. This is trialled as just described and if genuinely equivalent the split half reliability coefficient should be high.

The quantification of internal equivalence reliability is potentially very sophisticated nowadays in the realms of tests and inventories with a *uniform* set of items. For instance, there is an approach which effectively examines the sets of pairs of scores that would arise if you divided the set of items into half in *all* possible ways. The coefficient obtained is called *Cronbach's alpha* which, where the items are dichotomously scored, is also known as the *Kuder-Richardson 20* (see further Allen & Davies, 1977: 194ff.; Hatch & Farhady, 1982: 247ff.).

21 Overview of Validity: Measurer, Cases etc. as Sources of Invalidity

21.1 Good and Bad Validity: Introduction

The idea of invalidity was introduced in 19.1 as a matter of systematic error or *bias* in contrast with the unsystematic error that constitutes unreliability. It is clear that quantification can be reliable without being valid — we can measure something consistently but it can be always a bit 'off' what we claim/want to measure. The opposite is hardly possible, viz. that we can have quantification that is valid but not reliable. You really need to be measuring *some* variable with a good degree of consistency before you can ask whether what you are measuring is what you intended to measure, but in reality since neither quality is perfectly achievable you settle for a balance, in which the degree of reliability sets a limit on the achievable validity. Thus from here on we assume the techniques discussed are acceptably reliable. We saw that reliable techniques yield scores or categorisations close to cases' 'true' ones on whatever variable is being quantified. For such techniques we can now ask whether such scores are 'true' in the more fundamental sense of quantifying the *right* variable.

Though in simple instances validity seems achievable because we can quantify what we want very directly or by some well-known dependent manifestation, it is often a problem. What we are trying to measure is often intangible, such as communicative ability, and often a bone of contention in some branch of language study as to its definition. It is often not directly measurable, and furthermore, the process of measurement often has a big human element.

High validity is clearly vital for both R and T purposes. Lack of it will quite simply lead to faulty conclusions being drawn from data. In R studies, hypotheses about the effects of different types of case or different conditions on some language behaviour may seem to be supported when they should not be. Imagine a study to test the hypothesis that communicative competence increases with social class. If the categorisation of types of case into social classes (EV) was invalid, or the measure of communicative competence used (DV), you might find a significant relationship where none really existed between the variables intended, or the reverse. Perhaps what you *really* show is that cases with higher income parents are more fluent in standard speech in formal situations. It is worth noting also that if one's quantification of variables is invalid in the first place, no amount of statistical manipulation of the results later, e.g. in the framework of some elaborately designed investigation, will be of any use whatever.

In a T context, consider the consequences of a university needing to select for Forestry courses foreign students only with a good competence in 'English for academic purposes'. Suppose it relies on the scores obtained on a standard EAP test that is in fact invalid for quantifying this particular ability, focusing on ability to choose correct grammatical forms in multiple choice items rather than essay writing and lecture listening skills. Indeed where decisions radically affecting individuals' lives or with consequences for society generally are made on the results of language quantification, gross invalidity is clearly unethical and even illegal (cf. Labov, 1982). A distinct but confusable problem in T contexts, not pursued here, is inappropriacy of use of quantification in relation to the purposes sketched in Chapter 2. This would arise, for instance, if you chose to use for the above selection purpose a test that did not even *claim* to quantify EAP ability. (See further Bachman, 1990: 279ff.).

Systematic error may actually be either more group related or more individual in effect. It may take the form of *all* cases coming out, say, too high on a measure whenever it is used, as when certain kinds of test are used instead of observation of natural language use to quantify learner correctness in spontaneous use of the -s inflection. This is going to be particularly important for work where conclusions are reached from examining group scores, using measurement with some supposedly absolute interpretation — e.g. R work on the average frequency of use of certain constructions.

On the other hand bias may come as a persistent raising of some particular cases' scores and lowering of others' *within* a group of interest, i.e. the constant effect is not the same for all. The example of age reporting at 19.1 was of this sort. This *may*, as a fluke, cancel itself out over the group, but will obviously be unacceptable for measurement where individual cases are focused on for T purposes.

In reports of how variables are quantified, validity is less often reported on than reliability in respect of means used either to assure or control 'quality'. This does not mean it is unimportant. It rather reflects the fact that the ways of trying to ensure or check it are not so mechanical or foolproof as those for reliability. To try to build validity into a means of quantifying some variable, you often not only have to pay careful attention to unwanted effects of cases and choices in respect of facets of the means by which quantification is done, where these effects may be systematic rather than random (21.2), but also to questions concerning the real substance of what you are trying to quantify, in the context of current theories in a subdiscipline of linguistics (Chap. 22, 23). That is, it involves the more philosophical matters of stage (a) of quantification (1.3), not just the more practical matters of (b) and (c).

More formal checking of validity can take several forms, depending on where you think the main problem may lie. Objective reliability checking had a common theme of examining with some sort of statistical 'agreement' measure instances where 'identical' measurement was done more than once in some way (19.3.4, 20.3, 20.6). Formal validity checking is more disparate (see 21.2.3, 22.4, 23.7). Where it involves statistical measures, they may be of any sort, not just the range of correlation, proximity and suchlike measures relevant to reliability. And the formal procedures often leave you with the feeling that you have not so much *removed* subjective measurer judgment as to whether some quantification is valid or not as merely *attenuated* it by making reliance on it more indirect.

The benefits of examining validity are also often not so tangible. Rather than being able to put a figure on how valid quantification is, or actually do something to improve validity, often you only benefit by becoming more *aware* of shortcomings and so able to temper your interpretation of scores/categorisations accordingly. Exercising greater control may help with some validity problems, but may exacerbate others — e.g. by making measurement more artificial and non-natural. Combining data from repeating observations with the same approach or instrument will not improve validity as it does reliability since if an error is constant it will be repeated. Combining observations obtained by *different* means may do, though.

Validity is really about what you *claim* or *intend* for your measurement/categorisation, i.e. what variable in what cases or what situation it is supposed to quantify. Thus the same measuring technique may have to be decided *in*valid as a way of measuring variable x but *valid* as a way of measuring variable y. So a general way of making invalid measurement valid is simply by changing your claim about what you were wanting to quantify, allowing the tail to wag the dog, as it were. In order to do this, however, you do have to be *aware* of what you are really measuring.

Though essentially a unitary concept, validity, like reliability, has many forms and possible sources. For one thing, the lack of match between variable actually quantified and target variable or 'construct' — the 'validity gap' as it were — can be thought of as taking one of several forms. We may measure something slightly less than what we intend, e.g. language ability in Standard English when we want to measure communicative ability in English generally. Or we may quantify what we intend *plus* something else, e.g. reading ability *and* prior knowledge of oil refining when we want to measure reading ability alone (using a text about oil). Or we measure something a bit *different*, e.g. ability to do multiple choice vocabulary tests as against ability to use vocabulary items correctly, or opinion about use rather than actual use.

The possible sources of invalidity or reduced validity are very varied and not a totally distinct set from those that lead instead to unreliability. I shall review sources of invalidity under three roughly distinct heads (Chap. 21–23). To be able to make fair claims about what some means of quantification *is* actually measuring, you need to ensure or check for (a) constant effects cases and facets of the means of quantification may exert on what is actually quantified (in some ways an extension of the reliability discussion Chap. 19, 20); and (b) whether the specification of the target variable is an appropriate one, and the measure does measure it closely either directly or (c) indirectly.

21.2 Invalidity Due More to Measurer, Cases, Circumstances and Facets of the Instrument Used

The sources of error considered here are of the same general type as those described in Chapters 19 and 20 as leading to unreliability. We focus here on ways in which they may generate more systematic error. However, there is considerable overlap in that in appropriate circumstances some errors covered in Chapters 19 and 20 could lead to invalidity rather than unreliability, and some to be discussed below the reverse. For instance, sociolinguistic fieldworkers might haphazardly misclassify some vowel sounds they hear, thus reducing reliability, or might consistently overestimate their length, thus reducing validity. Gender of measurer may in some circumstances have a constant effect — e.g. young children may perform better for females. Unclear instructions on a test could bias results consistently one way rather than just increase random inaccuracy. 'Giveaway' distractors in multiple choice items (20.5: iv) may be a source of constant bias if some cases *consistently* exhibit an ability of 'test-wiseness' that enables them to exploit them (Allen, 1992). In general, if you decide to counter a possible source of unreliability by holding something constant, you have to be careful you do not then create a source of bias. Because of this ambiguity, some extend the term 'measurement error' to include errors of the sort to be discussed here as well as those that involve reliability (cf. Bachman, 1990: 222ff.).

We have already seen a number of examples of this sort of 'systematic measurement error'. For instance in Chapter 9 several of the ways of improving naturalism can be looked on as effects people, circumstances, materials used etc. can have that make your observations more valid if you are claiming to be observing variables in natural language behaviour, or which, if disregarded, may make such observations invalid by tending to reduce the genuine naturalism. I shall here focus more on examples of possible bias not directly connected with the matter of naturalism and which indeed might be *made worse* rather than better by those precautions that were suggested as aids to the valid observation of natural language behaviour. The problem is that the sort of control which is often *counter to* naturalism often *promotes* other aspects of validity (and reliability). This is a pervasive conflict in language quantification.

21.2.1 Measurer effects

One well-known bias of the measurer arises particularly in T contexts and where more subjective measurement is involved, such as rating English essays, ranking learners for conversational ability. Often co-operative pupils, or those with good handwriting, those known to be good in other subjects, etc., are inclined to get judged better than they are by a teacher or therapist — a phenomenon known as the *halo effect*. In effect, a strictly irrelevant variable is quantified along with the one meant to be measured.

The best antidote to the halo effect is to score protocols blind — i.e. anonymously — and/or use a different kind of measurer — one who is unfamiliar with the cases (in T terms, 'external assessment' rather than 'internal'). Technically you change the value chosen for the measurer facet of quantification. This will eliminate the influence of variables that a measurer only has information about from long-term familiarity with the cases. However, variables inevitably reflected in the work assessed, along with the intended one, such as handwriting of a composition, may still have an influence. All the same, this can be an argument against continuous assessment of pupils by their teacher and in favour of exams marked by an outsider, though the sample of data so obtained may be less representative (cf. Rowntree, 1977: 141).

Alternatively, measures that help reliability may help here too, such as talking with raters to get them to externalise their criteria, or, in criterion-referenced jargon, characterise the dimensions of the domain of linguistic or other behaviour they are really sampling to arrive at a rating. Instructions to raters may then be revised in the light of this (10.5, 19.3.2, and Black & Dockrell, 1984).

In R work terms like *investigator effect* can be used to label similar problems. A gross investigator effect would occur if errors in transcribing or coding and counting things in speech samples were not random but always biassed one way — by the researcher in effect editing dialect material or whatever (Prideaux, 1984: 8). In child language research it takes the form of data being interpreted in adult terms, for example (cf. 5.2). This sort of thing normally happens quite unconsciously — the bias usually being in favour of making scores/numbers in different categories etc. suit the prior expectation of the researcher, which is therefore in effect getting measured too (cf. Plutchik, 1974: 195ff.). As Beer says (cited in Bloom & Lahey, 1978: 33) 'There can be no such thing as pure observation'. One solution suggested in T contexts is to somehow combine the observations of different *kinds* of observer — e.g. so-called *triangulation*. This would exploit the viewpoints of teacher, pupil *and* external observer about language behaviour in a class, for example (Hopkins, 1985; Matsumoto, 1994).

Further, when gathering observations personally, measurers by their tone of voice or the way in which they cast questions may build in a permanent *suggestion* of a particular response to the testees — e.g. 'leading questions' with a built in presupposition. In an investigation of the effectiveness of two ways of memorising words, if the subjects know or can pick up from the investigator which one has in the past proved effective, or which one the investigator expects or *hopes* will come out on top, that one has a good chance of coming out with higher recall scores just from this knowledge. There is a phenomenon of 'compliance', or the subjects wishing to please the investigator — especially if the subjects are his/her students (a version of positive self-presentation — see 21.2.2). This has a 'self-fulfilling prophecy' effect.

The solution to this, as when seeking naturalism, is to disguise the purpose of your observation from those being measured, or distract subjects from it (9.4, 9.5). You can even go for *double blind* methods where you don't yourself administer or score the test or questionnaire but get it done by someone else, who isn't in the know. Thus both the cases and the test administrator are in the dark about the real point of the test or whatever. A related approach is where a proxy is used who simply is not *known* to the cases. We have already seen a nice illustration of the effect this sort of thing can have in Greenbaum & Quirk (1970: 53ff., see 9.8). Though the task itself had a disguise element, there were still systematic differences in testees' linguistic behaviour depending on whether they knew those administering it and on what they thought they wanted.

21.2.2 Effects of materials, task, cases, etc.

Questionnaire and test instruments may easily incorporate in their wording effects like those just described. The subjects/informants can then produce observations which accord with built in expectations rather than the facts. An example would be a census question which, perhaps consciously for policy reasons, lumps together non-official languages as 'native languages', thus influencing respondents away from this choice and towards claiming to speak the official national language (Fasold, 1984: 115). Again, where alternative responses offered with a questionnaire item are not exhaustive, and wisely end with an open option, there is a tendency for informants to pick one of the explicit choices given by the investigator. This is likely to bias results in favour of the choices the investigator picks on if the explicit options are grossly incomplete. With an item like

> What do you usually do when you meet an unknown word when reading?
>> Guess from context
>> Use a dictionary
>> Something else, please state

there is a strong tendency for most informants to pick one or other of the two explicit choices given and not think hard about the 'something else'. Since there are well documented other alternatives known — such as skipping the word entirely or guessing from word-internal clues — these should have been offered too, since their use will definitely be under-reported otherwise.

In fact many aspects of the design of tests or questionnaire materials may have unexpected non-random effects on cases. Such is where you in effect misjudge cases' capabilities, perhaps by having overlooked some psychological factors. Greenbaum (1977) found that in some of his language manipulation tests the large number of items and their similarity tended to establish a *mental set* in the testees. That is, they got a pattern fixed in their minds from the early questions which they began to apply automatically when answering the later ones even where obviously inappropriate. In other words, when measuring a whole lot of variables, as in a survey questionnaire, the order in which you do it is important. Since earlier opinion questions or manipulation test items may effect later ones in the same session, you really need to have versions available so that the administration can be done in different (random) orders for different cases. In that way a constant *order effect* error is turned into a random one, over members of a group at least.

Somewhat differently, Price, Fluck & Giles (1983) found that English spoken with a Welsh accent was judged less 'intelligent' sounding when the judgments were asked for and given in English than when in Welsh. Asking for such judgments you seem to be not *just* measuring attitudes to the accents the subjects are asked to judge, then, but also the language of the elicitation.

But most often the problem arises from miscalculating the abilities other than those targeted in some particular kind of case in some way. If you ask young children to imitate five-word sentences you may think you are testing language comprehension and production ability for the structures exemplified in those sentences, but actually be testing their memory as much if not more. To eliminate memory from consideration you would have to choose sentences to imitate so short that there could be no question of memory contributing to the result, but that might no longer allow you to test the linguistic point you wanted to.

The last example will lead to cases probably scoring less than they 'should', but the result of misestimation of abilities may have the reverse effect. Presented with a cup and a teaspoon a child may correctly respond to the request *Put the spoon in the cup* not by understanding the vocabulary and force of the preposition *in*, as imagined, but by the non-linguistic strategy of relying on real world experience of how the two objects she is presented with are often found associated. Testees may 'correctly' answer 'comprehension' questions based on a reading text just by echoing the wording in the original text without understanding.

This is a widespread problem. In almost any language measurement technique applied to people you have to assume that part of the task, which has to be there as a vehicle for what you are really interested in, is 'easy' for all cases or at any rate has a negligible effect on scores. Or, in more norm-referenced measurement, has only a constant effect that is the same for all cases. You assume that something else is the focus of measurement and gets quantified. Thus many language tests involve the testee reading instructions and questions and writing answers but do not claim to be measuring these abilities in any way. That is fine if the testees really have no problem with these aspects, and it is some other aspect of the activity that really is the variable quantified. But you can easily misjudge. What *you* think of as a test of reading competence for foreign learners may actually be more of a test of vocabulary knowledge, or of prior familiarity with the topic of the piece, if other aspects of the text are within easy grasp of all testees.

In multi-item tests, items similarly may turn out to have a *functioning content* different from the apparent one, for a particular sort of testee (Subkoviak & Baker, 1977). For instance a multiple choice item of the form Make two existing sentences from:

> He   am   singing
> They   is
>   are

(which in effect offers six alternatives to choose two from) ostensibly taps what subject verb agreement the testee uses, and perhaps what forms of the verb *be*. But, at least as much, it probably also measures some sort of non-linguistic 'puzzle solving ability', seen in how effectively different testees can run through all the combinations without missing any. It could also be argued that understanding the instruction, especially the word *existing*, is harder than the targeted task. Other such items (from Rees, 1981) are:

> Fill the gaps to make a word:
> Kilimanjaro is a m__t__n
> Choose the number for the correct point to insert *very well*:
> (1) They say (2) our headmaster (3) speaks (4) German (5).

Such items are said to be 'contaminated', and such contamination can involve all sorts of variables. For instance the Kilimanjaro example, if intended to test knowledge of the spelling of the word *mountain*, is only a straightforward test of this if testees know the (non-linguistic) fact that Kilimanjaro is a mountain. If the testees are unaware of this, it is much harder for them to work out what word they are being asked to spell in the first place. The 'stem' of the test item then presents more problems than the supposed focus. They have to activate further reasoning to see that words like *mutton*, *mitten* and *mention* are unlikely to fit, whatever *Kilimanjaro* is, so this gets measured too. This can be a particular problem for criterion-referenced tests, as, unlike norm-referenced ones, they are typically aimed at testees of a wide variety. So it is harder to be sure that the 'functioning content' is the same, as it should be, across all takers of the test.

As Bachman points out (1990: 271ff) various studies show that instruments may also unwittingly favour cases with particular cultural backgrounds, cognitive characteristics like field independence, gender, race and age. Intelligence is often also effectively quantified (Hansen & Stansfield, 1981). The age at which young children can cope with the artificial requirements of conventional tests in class room situations may be different for different social classes (Tizard & Hughes, 1984). Further, it is not always easy to decide where the borderline is between characteristics of cases that one wants to measure along with some language ability, and ones one does not. Background factual knowledge would be a case in point: there might well be disagreement as to whether it constitutes part of a proper specification of the construct 'reading ability' or not, for example (cf. 22.3).

Attempted solutions to these problems may take the form of combining data obtained by different methods that each have their own bias (i.e. observations made with *different* values of some facets of observation). For instance to assess spoken competence you can combine the evidence of children doing an oral test with that from the children talking to each other and talking to an adult (Wald cited in Milroy, 1987: 207ff.). In a reading test you eliminate the unwanted help provided by the content of a reading passage to those who happen to be familiar with it already by using several passages on quite different topics.

On the other hand it is this matter, properly recognised, that makes quite similar tasks usable to validly measure quite different things in different areas of language study. Presenting a mixture of existing and non-existing words of English, e.g. *prod*, *plid*, to cases to be judged as existing or not is an example. Presented to foreign learners, this may be a test of their knowledge, at a minimal level, of English vocabulary items, and scored right/wrong on each item. Presented to adult native speakers, it may be a test of how quickly they are able to identify the existence of different kinds of word, and scored for response time. For the former type of case, with limited knowledge of English, knowing whether the word *is* a word of English is the hard part. For the latter type, being native speakers, that is no problem, but speed may differ for different kinds of item, and this may reveal something about how words are stored and retrieved in the 'mental lexicon'.

Finally, cases off their own bat can produce constant bias in results. Often it is a matter of choosing responses that maximise 'positive self-presentation' (Christensen, 1980: 101ff.), as already seen where cases attempt to appear to speak 'correctly' for a researcher (e.g. 7.3). Sometimes this approaches dishonesty, e.g. where in work of the opinion survey type Indians report they know more Hindi than they actually do for political reasons (Fasold, 1984; cf. also Rowntree, 1977: 44ff.). Here emphasising anonymity and the point that *individuals* are not being tested can help where this is true, in R work, though anonymity is of course the opposite of what we saw might encourage more *naturalistic* language in responses! Also you can try embedding more sensitive questions in a string of more neutral ones so as not to put interviewees on the defensive, and otherwise try to disguise or distract attention from what is sought (cf. the techniques of Chap. 9).

McEntegart & Le Page (1982: 108) found that uncooperativeness of children telling stories was not, as might be expected, random. Rather, Creoles were generally more forthcoming, so their speech samples were systematically different from those of other informants. And because their narratives contained a lot of occurrences of *and* they appeared to use more nasalised vowels. But the researchers correctly realised that, because of these differences in types of discourse collected, they could not claim validly to have measured *just* the percentage of nasalised vowels used by Creole and non-Creole children in entirely comparable terms.

Various other effects of this sort are known. Persistent uncooperativeness of a speech disabled child will make it impossible to get a valid measure of their linguistic competence. In self-report work subjects/informants asked to give information about the past may describe things more favourably than they actually were, another 'halo effect'. For example 'As a child, how many of your school friends did you speak Welsh to? More than half/less than half?'. But in some instances, e.g. constructing a case history for pathological cases, such information may have to be used.

21.2.3 Checking on systematic measurement error

A common feature of the effects discussed in this section is that they stem either from the type of case, or from the particular choices of kind of measurer, kind of task, and so forth which together constitute a particular *means* of quantifying a variable. One way of removing the unwanted feature of what is quantified is often a different controlled choice for some facet. A way of formally checking on validity from these sources is therefore to undertake research systematically quantifying the 'same' variable with different combinations of types of case and values for a range of facets to see if any unwanted effect on scores/categorisations emerges by comparison of scores obtained with particular choices. For instance Hughes *et al.* (1983) had children with good and bad handwriting make copies of a set of essays written by other children. Typical markers then had to score each essay for features unconnected with handwriting in either a nicely or poorly handwritten form. The design was such that it was possible at the end to see just how much the handwriting affected scoring of the same essay.

For more naturalistic data collection this sort of research is done in effect by workers in many fields of linguistics in the normal way, not consciously as part of what I would call 'linguometric' studies — i.e. research into the language measurement activity itself, in this instance its validity. For instance in research on the determinants of oral style sociolinguists regularly gather data from the same cases systematically with different tasks, different possibilities for attention being paid to speech, different addressees, topics etc. (Milroy, 1987: 8.2). In fact there is no clear dividing line between variables that are to be seen as somehow substantive and those that are 'just' part of the means of quantification itself. It is not uncommon for data on much the same thing to be gathered and reduced to figures in more than one way in much R and T work with learners, children and so on also. It may then enter into a profile or be reconciled in some way (15.2.2), like the informal teacher assessment and SAT tests of English attainment in the UK National Curriculum. However, where the different means differ on *many* facet choices at once, as in the National Curriculum example, comparison cannot reveal clearly precisely which choices make which differences in results (see for example Shohamy, 1984).

Where professional studies of systematic measurement errors are done, they may be combined in elaborate 'generalisability' studies using the statistics of 'analysis of variance' from which figures quantifying both random and systematic errors can be teased out (cf. Bachman, 1990). Thus in this area the distinction between reliability and validity gets blurred. This is not helped by the fact that what constitutes a 'different' value on a facet as against a variant within one value is not fixed. For instance choice of male or female measurer may be a source only of random variation administering a test, but of systematic variation holding interviews. The real problem, however, is the large number of facet variables associated with any means of quantification, only a few of which can in practice be systematically varied in any study. The investigator has to use judgment to decide which ones are worth pursuing as possible sources of bias, and choose constant values for the rest.

In principle the contrast with investigations of reliability is as follows. There you keep choices supposedly constant and compare different instances. That is, you remeasure with the same cases, the same measurer or a more or less randomly chosen one of the same type, materials of the same sort if not identical, the same task on two random occasions in the same circumstances etc. Any variation in scores/categorisations that emerges then should be random variation due to inherent unreliability 'within' the cases and facet choices. In the present instance you see if systematically different results emerge with measurers of different types, different types of case, materials of a different sort (e.g. written versus spoken), a different task (e.g. open choice versus multiple choice test item, or naturalistic interview versus reading aloud), a different topic, different circumstances, different scoring method etc. If differences do emerge, you can associate them with particular values/settings or combinations of settings for the facets of observation.

This may help you see better which means comes closest to what you intend to measure, or you may decide in future to combine scores from several approaches. Or of course you can change your claim about what is being quantified to include ability related to a particular means of quantification — e.g. cloze test ability, self-report objectivity — as well as some language ability. There is also the possibility of going for a less specified means of quantification where many facet settings are left free to vary. The result will be less reliable but perhaps more valid (Bachman, 1990: 222ff.).

Something that may help decide which facet choices to investigate is elicitation of qualitative self-report data from measurers and cases immediately after using particular means of quantification (see e.g. Nevo, 1989; Cohen, 1984). For instance, subjects in interview may afterwards be able to tell you why *they* think the language elicited from them was unrepresentative. Also systematic observation of measurement in progress may be suggestive. If even competent adults hesitate on language test items intended for learners or children, this could be a sign of a significant codebreaking element. However, often *exactly* how cases reach an answer to, say, a multiple choice item remains a mystery. They may not all reach it in the same way, and asking for introspective self-report data on how they do it may be asking too much (cf. Black & Dockrell, 1984: 112). Some effects of stimuli, instructions and so forth on cases' actual behaviour may always remain indeterminable.

Error of the sort discussed here may also be detected by the standard validity checking techniques of 22.4 and 23.7. However, it will not there be possible readily to identify particular bias with particular facet choices separately from other sources of invalidity, unless particularly sophisticated statistical approaches are used, such as the *multitrait-multimethod* design (*MTMM*) (Bachman, 1990; and for an example Bachman & Palmer, 1981). In this it is possible to systematically vary both targeted language variables (traits) *and* specific values for facets of observation (or indeed several values at once, thus comparing whole distinct methods). For instance you could quantify the same cases' written and spoken ability (two traits) by elicited material scored both by a count of errors and global rating (two values of the scoring method facet). It is expected that scores for the same trait quantified by different methods will be more similar (usually in correlation terms) than those for different traits quantified by the same method. If not, this would suggest the method has an overwhelming effect (or that the traits are not actually distinct).

Further Reading

On validity generally: Bachman (1990: Chap. 7,8), Cronbach (1984), Frankfort-Nachmias & Nachmias (1992: Chap. 7), Nunnally (1978: Chap. 3), Cohen *et al.* (1988: Chap. 6).
On the statistics of validity in this and the next two chapters:
Simple examples: Scholfield (forthcoming d)
More technical: Pedhazur & Schmelkin (1991: Chap. 3, 4), The Journal *Language Testing*.

22 Specification of the Nature of a Variable and its Operationalisation as a Source of Invalidity

22.1 Problems of Specification and Operationalisation

If a means of quantification is reliable (Chap. 19, 20) and systematic measurement errors have been taken account of or dealt with (Chap. 21), it is still not guaranteed to be valid. The core requirement remains to be ensured — that overwhelmingly the largest systematic contribution to the scores/categorisations obtained *is* derived from the relevant real-life variable or 'construct' that you are trying to quantify in the cases concerned, and not something a bit different.

This depends crucially on the matter of specification of the substance of the 'targeted' variable/construct, however simple, complex or hidden it may be. This is because a good deal of how a variable is made observable or 'operationalised' (Chap. 4–18) is directly consequent on this, subject usually to some leeway in precise choice of quantification technique — the facet choices (which may have some effects on what is actually quantified as we saw 21.2). Or, from the 'quality control' angle, you cannot check if your instrument successfully quantifies the target variable without a specification of it.

The key feature of a good specification is that it characterises the substance of the target variable or 'construct' both *positively*, perhaps by defining a domain of relevant items (10.4.2) or breaking the concept into components, specific criteria (18.3), dimensions, subtypes or examples, and *negatively*, by distinguishing it from similar notions and placing it in relation to related but different constructs. Furthermore, it should fit in with theories of the relevant subareas of language study. We saw earlier how *inexplicit* definition and its interpretation could lead to unreliability (19.3.2). However, a clear, possibly 'operational', definition of a variable, yielding reliable results, must also be the *right* definition to be valid. This is a heavily subjective matter hard either to assure by design or check up on formally.

A common approach in practice is to specify and operationalise variables simply in accord with past practice. This has the benefit of comparability. Results for cases and groups can be compared with previous results — valuable both in T and R contexts. The disadvantage is that progress may be hindered. In research especially there can be a difficult choice between using a previously used definition for comparability and an improved definition following the latest expert view. There can be considerable problems in getting any general conclusions from research in the same area where different researchers all used slightly different definitions of 'the same' variable. For example the notion of 'primary language' may be defined for self-report by cases in successive census questionnaires variously as 'first language acquired developmentally', 'language most used', 'language you can communicate most proficiently in' and so forth. Hence it becomes impossible to deduce much from comparison of the recorded numbers of cases choosing particular languages (Fasold, 1984: 13ff.).

Worst of all is, as many R reports of work do, simply to gloss over saying exactly what you counted as what and why. Other researchers will be unable to repeat ('replicate') your work exactly as a check.

22.2 The Pure Linguistic Contribution to the Specification of Variables

In attempting to specify variables relevant to quantifying language (cf. Chap. 1), not surprisingly, often some purely linguistic categories are involved. This is true whether you are specifying what to count in some author's writings or a tape of talk elicited from a child, or what the linguistic dimension of some domain of items for a multiple choice test should be, or indeed what language features in essays raters are to be guided by when marking them. Notions like sentence, word, plural, morpheme, relative clause, [r] sound, and so forth abound. Furthermore, categorisation of what is correct versus an error in naturalistic data or responses to test stimuli presupposes proper definitions of what is or is not, say, a false friend, a syntactic error, or a native-like articulation of a [θ] sound. We have also seen (Chap. 18) that clear and correct definitions of linguistic variables are needed in formulating the EV of many comparative studies, especially experiments. If you are comparing memory for 'concrete' versus 'abstract' sentences or the like, your definition of these linguistic notions is an essential part of your making/manipulation of the IV.

In the sort of instances just sketched, of course, it might seem that the simple solution is to adopt the definitions of the relevant notions provided by the discipline of linguistics. These, as we have seen (18.3), are usually cast in an explicit form which lends itself to operationalisation, and, coming from the professionals, must surely be the 'right' specifications. Furthermore, linguists' definitions of things usually have the merit of being made in the context of some overall theoretical scheme or comprehensive set of rules, not fragmentarily. Phonemes, for example, are defined both in themselves, by their allophones, and by the features that distinguish them from other phonemes in the phonological system of a language. However, despite all this, in practice things are not so straightforward.

One problem is that pure linguists do not always provide a clear answer. Thus in quantifying the length of utterances either in number of words or number of morphemes there is dissension at the theoretical level over the best criteria to use to decide what *is* a separate utterance, word or morpheme even in normal adult language, let alone that of children etc. For instance, are sequences written with a hyphen one or two words, and what words are hyphenated anyway? Dictionaries disagree. Few corners of linguistics have much settled theoretical maturity and so speak with one voice. In the end one expert's definition will not be valid from another expert's point of view. The pure linguist, not concerned with quantification, can of course go on forever discussing the minutiae of what to count as a word, and debating in the framework of Chomskian or other linguistics whether modal auxiliary verbs are really a distinct class from ordinary verbs or not and so forth.

And this is not without justification since even standard normal adult language is clearly not *naturally* made up of clearcut classes of things. Language is full of 'squishy' categories, with things like 'semi-modal verbs'. And beyond standard British or American English things are less clear still. McEntegart & Le Page (1982: 109f.) comment on the problems of defining what the loci for a given sound really are in a Creole version of English as there is not obviously a clear Creole standard to refer to.

However, the fully empirical researcher or teacher wanting to count up the length of children's sentences in words or the foreign learner's mastery of modal verb meanings or ways of expressing requests is not usually interested in this dissension, unless the disagreement is itself the object of research. Rather he/she needs to cut the Gordian knot into which the definition of these items gets tied by pure linguists and get on with counting, item construction etc. A practical solution is to use fairly theoretically middle-of-the-road pure linguists' definitions of items, constructions, and so on for English (see Gimson, 1980 for sounds; Quirk *et al.*, 1985 for grammar; and Leech, 1981 for meaning).

As a rough guide, the further you move from linguistic units like sounds or letters through words and grammatical constructions towards meanings of various sorts, especially of larger units, the greater the multiplicity of potential definitions to choose between. Textual 'cohesion' is often analysed using the categories defined by Halliday & Hasan (1976). However, pragmatic classifications of bits of language in terms of the 'speech act' or 'communicative function' they convey currently offers probably the most varied and least standardised classifications. Here the labels of the categories that are relevant, and how many there should be, are as fluid as their definitions. See Faerch & Haastrup (1984: 45ff.) and Tough (1976: 80ff.), respectively, for typical examples of definitions of sets of categories of these types. It is in this area that sets of categories and their definitions are often 'found' after gathering some data. They are often a mixture of categories of different sorts, not clearly based on any theoretical foundation and may also involve conflation of what are really crossclassificatory sets of notions (18.1).

One way out in such instances is just to use a definition that has been used before in research, as already mentioned. For instance you might use Brown's 'counting rules' for measuring length of utterance in morphemes (Bloom & Lahey, 1978: 42). See also Dulay & Burt (1982: 218) for definitions of various things counted in L2 learning research and Crystal (1982) for ones in child language and language pathology. Or, of course, you can stick your neck out and follow the definition that follows *your* favourite theoretical approach. However, you do see some idiosyncratic definitions that way. Yore & Ollila (1985), for example, distinguish concrete and abstract words most unusually by defining the former as nouns and the latter as non-nouns! At the very least you need to be explicit about what definition you did decide to use.

Further complexity is added by the occasional clash of what is established in the pure linguist's world with what has become standard in some area of applied or empirical linguistics. Phrasal verbs are a good example. A teacher, following common pedagogical usage, might make up a multiple choice test of knowledge of English phrasal verbs for foreign learners using a definition which would allow both the following items as containing valid selections from the domain of English phrasal verbs:

George has bought a new car. He finally decided
>   at/on/to/for a Ford.

Mary has chosen what to wear. She finally put
>   in/over/on/round her green dress.

However, most pure linguists would accept only the second as containing a phrasal verb, categorising the first item as containing rather a prepositional verb, with clearly distinct linguistic properties. For instance, you can *put a dress on* but not *decide a Ford on*. So in one realm the first item is valid, in another not, and for the latter you would either have to rename your test, or exclude that sort of item.

There can also be issues of policy that interact with a purely linguistic solution, especially in T circles. They arise especially in respect of different varieties of language which, to the pure linguist, are intrinsically equally 'good'. Do we assume that only the adult part of speech classification is relevant when analysing child language data, or do we accept that children may have their own distinct and equally valid systems at various developmental stages (Bloom & Lahey, 1978: 33ff.)? Do we count *I ain't got none* as wrong for an immigrant to the UK learning English in a community where this is the norm, or do we require the 'Standard English' form? Many standard published tests only count the standard form as correct (cf. Romaine, 1984: Chap. 1). Where consequent action and backwash may follow (Chap. 2), these are questions with important ethical overtones — e.g. if a test fails to distinguish language disability from normal use of a non-standard dialect. Labov (1982) details a legal case in America on just such an issue — that of whether the *Wepman Auditory Discrimination Test* failed to take due account of features of US Black English and so discriminated against some children (see also Milroy, 1987: 9.4).

There can also be clashes between cases' folk-definitions and the researcher's in instances where cases have to self-report on something assumed not to need explanation. Fasold (1984) reports a study where speakers of Sindhi who knew how to write it in Gurumakhi script as well as the more usual Arabic script responded to census questionnaire items as if they knew Punjabi, simply because Gurumakhi is the normal script used for that language. For them a language is defined by its script. In such instances the 'expert's' definition is normally assumed to be inherently more valid.

22.3 The Psycho-/Socio-/Educational Contribution to the Specification of Variables

Much language quantification is of variables that cannot sensibly be specified solely in pure linguistic terms. Hence guidance in constructing valid measures must be sought in many disciplines.

Sometimes the additional element is fairly straightforward and does not involve theory in any direct way. Achievement variables are by definition specified by the syllabus of language items and skills that the cases have been taught. These have to be sampled to make achievement test items, or define what is to be watched out for in more naturalistic observation. However, even here theory is not far away since normally the syllabus would itself find justification in such a source.

Still, most specification of 'impure' linguistic, and non-linguistic, variables again directly involves theories — within which notions like communication strategy, social class, off-task activity, keyword method, aphasic, Welsh speaker, bilingual and so forth need to find specification. Many of these are 'complex' variables which can be seen as best specifiable in terms of components which would be quantified separately and the scores combined in some way, or perhaps retained as a profile (cf. 15.2.2). Many are also not very overt (see further 23.4, 23.5). Appeal has to be made typically to theories and authoritative specifications in link subdisciplines like sociolinguistics and psycholinguistics, and the disciplines linguistics links with — sociology, psychology, education, medicine, acoustic physics, etc.

The key problem is that in these areas there is often just as much dissension and uncertainty over what is the 'right' theory within which to formulate specifications of variables as in pure linguistics. Indeed since the theories in these disciplines depend on empirical research for support, there can be an element of 'catch 22'. You need established theories to provide valid specifications of key variables. Yet the research needed to support or disconfirm the theories has to be done on the assumption that the relevant variables can be validly and reliably quantified.

Often different subdisciplines of linguistics will come up with essentially different approaches to specifying a construct. Thus 'bilingual dominance' may be specified in different terms by a sociolinguist and a psycholinguist. The former will typically view it as a matter of how much of the time someone communicates in one of the languages rather than the other, with attention also to the range of different types of situation in which someone functions in each language and the status of the addressees, e.g. which language they use addressing close relatives as against acquaintances. On the other hand the psycholinguist will conceptualise dominance as a matter of organisation of the mental lexicon and grammar and which language is more readily accessible in processing. Consequently the sociolinguist typically quantifies bilingual dominance from self-report questionnaires about occasions of use of each language, while the psycholinguist may go for spew tests and the Stroop test or general tests of language proficiency.

Views may also differ not so clearly along 'party' lines. 'Readability' of written language is of interest in stylistics and all kinds of language learning work. One approach is to characterise it as an impersonal property of a piece of writing, independent of characteristics of readers. Hence it would be operationalised by quantifying from text samples a gamut of specific variables such as:

How many clauses/words per sentence on average it has.

How many modifiers with each noun, on average.

How many rare words used.

How clearly the broad organisation of the narrative/argument/etc. — 'rhetorical structure' — is marked overtly by words like *first, then, therefore*, as against being left implicit in indirect clues.

How big the print is.

How far the factual content is general or specialist knowledge.

Exactly what the complete list should be, and how to combine the separate measurements in a valid overall measure, is still a source of difficulty (15.2). For instance some might prefer to regard readability as best defined without the last two properties listed — i.e. as a purely linguistic construct. You would then try to quantify it from the other characteristics in such a way that the resulting scores did not particularly reflect the nature of the content.

Alternatively, you could take a different theoretical stance and define readability more in personal terms from the effect of text on readers. This accords better with one popular theory of reading — the 'top-down' type. This says that we do not read so much by deciphering letters and words in succession and building up the overall meaning of what we read from the 'bottom up' — more the idea underlying the text-based definition above. Rather we read with a heavy contribution from the reader — by formulating a general expectation of the meaning from the title and early part of what we read, and our own prior real world knowledge, and thereafter only reading enough specific words to revise our expectation, the rest of the text being predictable. To actually quantify it this way you would measure competent readers, probably reactively, for a list of more specific variables relating to their behaviour that should accompany more readable versus less readable texts, such as:

How fast people read the text.

How much they understood of what they read.

How much they can skip without loss of comprehension.

How well they can predict missing bits of the text.

How difficult they judge it.

Again there would be doubt over the complete list of things of this sort to test, relative weighting of specific variables on the list and so on. Should the notion of readability include 'enjoyment'? (See further Gilliland, 1972).

In situations like this there is no obvious way of deciding *a priori* which approach is more valid. Both can be operationalised reasonably reliably. It depends on your theoretical predilections and again, probably, on the local tradition in a specific area of research. The first approach would probably appeal more to a pure linguist, the second to a psycholinguist, while stylisticians and language teachers would be divided. But you must be clear about what specification you are going by, and what it includes and excludes.

A few other equally contentious constructs are:

How to define 'fluency'. Does it just relate to speech rate (so measure number of words per minute in consecutive speech), or also to hesitation phenomena (so quantify number of filled and unfilled pauses per 100 words), or what?

How to define 'communicative language ability' for applied linguists to construct proficiency tests of, or rating scales for. What exact knowledge of facts of the world, knowledge of when and where to say things, conversational strategies etc. does it entail beyond the core *linguistic* knowledge of sounds, grammar etc.? And in what form should the specification be framed? See Bachman (1990: Chap. 4, 8).

How to define 'knowledge of vocabulary' so as to measure it in L1 and L2 acquisition. Does knowing a word mean just recognising it as an English word, when seeing or hearing it? Or does it entail knowing at least one meaning? All the meanings? The precise spelling? Being able to use it in a sentence correctly? and so on.

A final important point about more 'complex' linguistic variables is that in practice, whatever specification of the target construct you choose, you don't usually try to measure *all* the specific features which it might specify, i.e. all the individual variables which in some way seem to collectively contribute to the overall variable. Very often just one or two specific variables are selected as 'indicators' of the whole. For that see 23.2. For the 'profile' alternative to complex summary measures (e.g. Crystal's *LARSP*) see 15.2.2.

22.4 Checking on Validity: Content and Construct Validation

Two of the recognised formal means of checking on validity stem from the characteristics of good specification, as described above. Insofar as a variable admits of elaboration of its nature in terms of defined domains of items and the like, a means of quantifying it can be checked against this specification for *content validity*. Where the variable has specified relationships with other variables, either ones that contribute to it or that should be positively related to it or differ from it, the means of quantification can be checked to see if it does yield scores or categorisations that have the predicted relationship with those for the other variables — *construct validity*. However, neither of these approaches can really settle the more fundamental issue of what *is* the right specification of the construct, or what theory is the right one to accord with in the first place. As we saw above, that goes beyond linguometric research into the entirety of language-related research, both theoretical and empirical.

22.4.1 Content validity

Checking for content validity, alias 'descriptive validity', entails explicit examination of the internal makeup of test or inventory items, of any exemplification used to describe the points on a rating scale and so on. Does it reflect an appropriate sample of language material/behaviour from some population specified as representing the target variable? For this to be useful you have to have as a touchstone a clear independent idea of what sort of contents *would* provide evidence of valid measurement. If this is not available from a prior domain specification you can simply check against, e.g. a definition of 'phrasal verb' for a test of knowledge of phrasal verbs, it may entail obtaining the opinion of a group of experts, or at worst using one's own on the spot introspective judgment as to whether notional content is adequately sampled (cf. 10.4.2, and note the different sort of 'item analysis' used to enhance the discrimination of norm-referenced measures).

The most obvious kind of quantification you can examine in this way is that of achievement, as whatever instrument is used should clearly test a sample of the verbs or whatever a case is supposed to have learnt according to a specified syllabus. However, even here it may be hard to be sure just by expert judgment whether targeted variables defined in terms of language skills are really being quantified, rather than just language items. In T contexts, a measure passing this check may be said to have 'curricular validity'. A variant of this is 'instructional validity', where reference is to what was actually taught, which might not match the syllabus! This says nothing about whether the syllabus or teaching was sensible or not, of course.

Also, criterion-referenced tests generally require the definition of a 'domain' of items and skills, or of the dimensions of such a domain (10.4.2), either from a syllabus or theory. Hence they are readily amenable to content validation of actual tests against the domain. And note that insofar as the domain specified extends to choice of facets of *how* the quantification is to be done, as well as what language items and skills are involved, there is an overlap here with the issues of 21.2. However, content validation will not reveal any unwanted bias from facet choices, only whether any specification with regard to them has been met or not by a means of quantification, since in the normal way no actual scores of sample cases are involved in the checking.

Furthermore, content validation applies in principle for multi-item tests and opinion inventories of all sorts, since there should always be *some* specification which the items are supposed to accord with. This applies even if the items were obtained by a practical procedure supposed to guarantee content validity. Such are making up a test from actual erroneous utterances gathered naturalistically from typical cases, or constructing an attitude inventory using statements of opinion elicited from typical cases (Thurstone's procedure 14.2.1).

Suppose we are presented with a test claiming to be of knowledge of basic English vocabulary, consisting of a series of words out of context, to have definitions supplied. From the content validation point of view, if no specification is provided with the test, we have to think first what specification of the construct of such vocabulary knowledge it is appropriate to refer to. We might decide that basic English is the thousand most frequent words and that vocabulary knowledge is the ability to use the word appropriately. We can then consider if the items in the test seem to fit this specification. Content validation must be relative to some specification of required content, however partial, but does not guarantee all experts will agree that the specification itself is correct.

As Wiliam points out (1992), you will learn more from examining the content of an instrument in the light of some responses when it has actually been used on some typical cases. Some biases like those of 21.2.2 may be more apparent. Analogously, when you count features of speech elicited in more or less natural conversation, you can check content by considering if you have obtained a reasonable sample of instances of language features the child or learner involved might be expected to produce in that situation (see again remarks on sampling in Chap. 5 and 6).

Variables that don't lend themselves to this approach include covert ones like language learning aptitude and very broad variables like proficiency in English, where there is no 'syllabus' of language material and skills you could sample, and the job of specifying the domain theoretically is immense. Nevertheless, Hart *et al.* (1987) made great efforts here when developing their test of communicative competence in French, a broad variable if ever there was one. They tried to ensure content validity by carefully basing the subtests on separate aspects of communicative competence as defined by theoreticians, and by making the tasks the testees had to perform realistic communicative ones, as near as possible to samples of real life language use. However, they realised they lost straightforward content validity to some extent in the end by relying just on a few indicator measures of particular features of the language elicited in this way combined to form an overall measure.

Checking content validity often does not yield any coefficient putting a figure on the *amount* of validity. However, sometimes the % of items in a test judged by experts to be relevant to the specified intended content may be reported, or the % of a group of experts who judged some rating scale, set of categories or whatever to be defined validly for the intended variable, and so forth (see Cohen *et al.*, 1988: 127ff.). Indeed in the development of criterion-referenced tests this may be done quite elaborately and extend to obtaining the average rating by several experts of each item or whatever for whether it has apparently been sampled from a suitably defined domain. This is a sort of 'expert item analysis' which could lead to revision of the test if you then reject items that fall below some predecided cutting score on the rating scale (cf. Chap. 10). See further Subkoviak & Baker (1977), Hambleton *et al.* (1978).

22.4.2 Construct validity

Of the various standard validity checks, construct validity is the least well-defined, and hardest to understand clearly. In practice the term is used by measurement experts and researchers to embrace a wide variety of kind of check rather than one, some of them resembling, and indeed overlapping, those discussed at 21.2.3, 22.4.1 and 23.7. For some the term *includes* all these. Often they yield actual numerical validity coefficients e.g. of the correlational sort again (see references at end of chapter). As Cronbach says, 'construct validity is established through a long-continued interplay between observation, reasoning, and imagination' (1984: 121).

It is hard to think of a circumstance in which it would *not* in some way or other be possible — and appropriate — to investigate the construct validity of any quantification technique (though some writers give the impression that it is not required, say, if content validity can be demonstrated). And though there is always some residue of a priori assumption involved, you often feel that the notion of construct validity comes closest to the ultimate validity we are interested in. Indeed often construct validation appears as the 'last ditch' method of checking validity after the other formal methods.

The key idea behind construct validation is well summarised by Jaeger (1978: 296): 'Do measures behave in accordance with theoretical predictions for the phenomena supposedly represented?' You proceed broadly as follows. You have a technique, let us say, designed to measure the variable 'communicative competence'. You first consider the theoretical discussion and specification of communicative competence to see what other variables ought to be related to it, and which not, which should be its major component variables, what kind of cases should score highly, which not, and so on. Then you do empirical investigations on appropriate groups of cases using your measure to see if these predictions are supported. If not, you conclude your measurement technique is not a valid measure of that variable. (See further Appendix 1.)

One benefit is that, if it had not been considered already, the theoretical status of the target construct and its relationship with other variables has to be considered now in order to perform this sort of check at all. A problem, of course, is that an unexpected result often might be evidence that the theoretical predictions about the variable are wrong, not that the quantification of it is invalid. Indeed in the present shaky state of most theories in all areas of linguistics and applied linguistics, it is often hard to decide (cf. 22.2, 22.3).

Thus if you read that a particular measuring technique 'has construct validity' this can just mean that it produces results supporting hypotheses formulated from the currently conventional view of the nature of the relevant aspect of language, which may be self-perpetuating, rather than truly valid. Or it may mean that it fits in with the researcher's favourite theory, which may not be your favourite theory. In language study this is essentially a meaningless remark unless you are told *what* theoretical model is being referred to, and what it predicted about the variable your measuring technique is claimed to measure.

One might ask why all this is called *construct* validation and not something like 'inter-variable validity', since its key feature is to exploit assumed relationships between usually quite different variables. We have to go to the definition of the term 'construct', a term used in much literature (especially psychometric), and frequently already in this book, to refer to the 'real' variable that is the target of one's quantification. It has been described as 'an unobservable variable that exists in the mind of the researcher ...a constructed variable that serves as a label for many highly related observables in a particular model of reality' (Jaeger, 1978: 294), the 'observables' here being operationalised variables that you actually measure. In effect a construct is the *concept* a measurer has of what he/she is really measuring, and indeed the label 'conceptual validity' is occasionally used.

However, the term 'construct' implies a bit more than just 'the actual variable underlying a measuring technique'. First, the idea is generalised — *any* measurement technique, even one seemingly very directly measuring something, can be thought of as separate from its underlying variable/construct. And secondly, the term lays emphasis very much on the theoretical model or framework into which the construct variable fits. As we have seen, this is the source of help used here to decide if a measuring technique really is quantifying the intended variable. Is the actual underlying variable/construct the target/intended one? Thus investigating the construct validity of a measuring technique is often described as analysing the meaning of scores obtained by the technique in terms of theoretical concepts — the 'theoretical meaning of a measure' (Hoge, 1985).

Further Reading

Pedhazur & Schmelkin (1991: Chap. 4 and 8).

23 Indicators as a Source of Invalidity

23.1 Quantification by 'Indicator' Measures

Special care has to be taken when quantifying by means of what I have called 'indicators' (1.3). These arise most obviously when the targeted constructs are either the broad, complex type of variable (22.3) or hidden variables which you cannot operationalise in any direct way, such as those involved in the process of understanding language. With these you may respectively choose to, or are bound to, quantify specific variables that do not completely or directly correspond to the construct, as specified.

The analogy with measuring temperature is useful. When we measure the height of a column of mercury in a thermometer to measure the temperature of a room we are not measuring the 'temperature' at the time in any total sense, clearly, but rather one of the many specific manifestations that temperature has, *viz.* making mercury expand and contract. However, this is perfectly valid since we know — from well established theories of physics — that the degree of expansion of the mercury, the indicator variable, precisely reflects the temperature around, which in reality takes the form of the amount of vibration of all the molecules of matter in the room.

Needless to say, with socio- and psycho-type variables, including linguistic ones, indicators are not in such a perfect relationship to the intended or claimed variable, so there is always an element of not measuring quite what you want to, i.e. a constant error. But there is no getting away from the fact that many of the variables you want to measure *are* very broad and/or very hidden, and you have to do your best. Indeed, though in this chapter we focus on examples of fairly gross indicators, it can be argued that almost *all* quantification in language study involves using indicators in *some* degree in that there is a widespread habit of quantifying cases' overt behaviour/performance and claiming to measure something of their hidden ability/competence (cf. 1.2.2).

Nevertheless, an indicator measure is best thought of as a means of quantification which straightforwardly measures one variable but which one is claiming also, less obviously, quantifies another, like a word that has both a literal and metonymic meaning. It should have associated with it a clear line of reasoning, preferably within some theoretical framework, justifying its 'extra' use as an indicator of the target construct. Also, of course, the means of quantification, with respect to what it directly measures, should be as free as possible of random and systematic measurement errors, and well-defined. Indicators usually only indicate *relative* scores on the target variable, since the rationale of criterion-referenced quantification pretty well entails 'direct' measurement (but see Haertel (1985) for discussion of criterion-referenced indicators). There are several scenarios where indicators are used, which I examine now under four overlapping heads.

23.2 Indicators for Complex Variables

Often where it is quite possible in principle to quantify a range of specific things which will collectively get close to measuring everything implied by the specification of a complex variable, in fact only one or two specifics are quantified.

Good examples are 'readability' indicators commonly used for both R and T purposes. Those who go for a text-based theory of readability commonly select for quantification just a few of the potential range of properties listed in 22.3. Typical is Flesch's formula (15.2.4) based just on sentence length in words and word length in syllables. They are justified by the reasoning that sentence length is a fair indicator of sentence complexity which in turn is an indicator of syntactic difficulty. Similarly word length is regarded as an indicator of word frequency (longer words are rarer on average) which is an indicator of word or lexical difficulty. But we have only to find examples of clearly difficult tests which have short words and short sentences to show that this formula is a less than totally valid indicator of readability. In fact such texts are not common, though they do occur — e.g. certain types of modern poetry.

Those who go for a reader-based approach typically use as indicator a cloze test procedure measuring the predictability of the text. The text whose readability is to be measured is given as a cloze test in several forms, each with different sets of words omitted, perhaps between them omitting *all* the words, to different sets of readers of some targeted sort. The overall readability is calculated from the readers' success in filling the gaps (for the full procedure see e.g. Oller, 1979: 350).

Obviously in such instances you have to think hard about which of a set of measures of different specific variables is likely to be the best indicator for the overall variable you are trying to get at, given your specification of it, and how far short of full validity it may fall. It is also possible to measure a sample group using a whole lot of measures that seem to be implied by its specification and use the statistical procedure of factor analysis to identify which is the best single indicator. Or it may be that more than one are optimal depending on how far it turns out that the different specific variables make a separate contribution to the overall result and do not agree closely with each other. Generally the more different indicators for a given variable that you measure and combine the score for, the more valid your measurement is likely to be, though often for ease just one indicator is used as the basis for 'generalising' to a construct variable.

Further examples of such 'shortcut' indicators:

Five levels of L1 development in very young children quantified just from measurement of mean length of 100 utterances in morphemes in elicited natural communication rather than from, say, everything in the *LARSP*, *PRISM* and *PROPH* profiles. This is supposed to be valid in the age range 1.5 to 4 years, or MLU 1.01–4.49 (Brown, 1973; Nicolosi *et al.*, 1989: 302).

Level of L2 development of a learner quantified from: a count of number of errors in a sample of writing or speech (Larsen Freeman, 1978); or from a count of the number of modifiers (adjectives and adverbs) used (*Bilingual Inventory of Natural Language*, 1976); or from the degree of grammatical correctness reflected in errors counted and weighted (Dulay *et al.*, 1982: 252ff.).

Language proficiency of an intermediate learner of English quantified from the number of words the learner can correctly identify as being English, on being presented with non-existent and real words of various frequency levels (Meara & Jones, 1988).

Richness of style of a piece of literary text quantified just by working out the type-token ratio in a sample (i.e. number of different words used per 100 running words of text — 12.2.1). (Yule, 1968)

Amount of 'description' in native speaker child oral language quantified from counting the total of adjectives plus adverbs plus prepositions plus anaphoric (i.e. referring back) pronouns, all divided by the total number of words (Nurss & Hough, 1985).

Overall oral proficiency quantified from rating data gathered in a single oral interview situation, with one topic, interlocutor, variety of language used, amount of time to prepare speech permitted etc. I.e.

these particular choices on the variables of the speaking situation are taken as a basis to generalise to all values of those variables (Skehan, 1987).

Social class of informant quantified from an ordered categorisation of the occupation of the head of the informant's family (Milroy, 1987: 2.5).

It might be asked why indicators are used in instances where more elaborate quantification *could* be used to get closer to the full range of phenomena implied by the specification of the target construct. In part it is to achieve greater reliability, even at the cost of some validity, since as the above examples show, the chosen indicators are usually very overt and unambiguously quantifiable. Often a computer can do the quantification. However, purely practical considerations like those mentioned at 4.1 also play a part. For instance, for certain T purposes, quantification by a *quick*, reliable, but not necessarily perfectly valid, indicator is what is needed. For similar reasons, standard tests sometimes have a 'short form' as well as the full one (e.g. the *BPVS*). Such purposes are initial large scale screening for disability, or placement of learners at different levels on a short language course (2.2.2). The latter was the motivation for the development of Meara's measure above.

In research, a variable used as a control variable to select potential subjects in an investigation could cost-effectively be quantified this way. An example is seen in Blanchard (1984), who wished to select Kindergarten children suitable to participate in an investigation involving word learning. He used 'ability to name letters in test words' as a crude indicator of 'being involved with learning and having completed some abstract verbal/visual experiences', which he regarded as a prerequisite to taking part in his investigation.

23.3 Indicators for More Direct Measures

Similar to the preceding are what one might call 'indicators of convenience'. Here typically a reasonably direct but perhaps labour intensive means of quantifying the target construct is available. What is actually quantified is known to be not the most suitable variable, but is nevertheless used effectively as an indicator measure for the 'right' variable.

For example, there is a temptation for busy teachers to use a standard, existing, familiar and available test even if they know it is not a test of quite what they want, rather than make up one specially (Allen & Davies, 1977: 34). So also Hart *et al.* (1987) used some norm-referenced tests where criterion-referenced ones were really wanted, where the practical problems of obtaining criterion measurements of native speakers were too great. Again, a readily available discrete point test of language competence may be used in practice where a more pragmatic test of communicative competence is really needed, a norm-referenced test on cases it is not strictly norm-referenced to, and so forth.

Perhaps the least defensible reason for sticking to a measure of something that is known to be a less than good indicator of a target variable, where more direct measures, or better indicators, are available, is blind 'measure loyalty'. This can affect both T and R practitioners, like customers' 'brand loyalty' to the soap flakes they have always bought. The fact that you are used to a particular test or whatever, and others have often used it too, is not necessarily sufficient reason to stick with it. Such conservatism is often bound up with what is sometimes called *face validity* — the extent to which some measure 'looks' to a teacher/researcher who might use it as if it convincingly measures the relevant variable, which very often is simply a function of what that person is used to.

As an example take the *Schonell Graded Word Reading Test* which uses 'ability to read aloud successfully a graded list of words in isolation' as an indicator of 'reading ability in general' for English native speaker children. As Steadman & Gipps (1984) remark, though long ago discarded on theoretical and other grounds as a satisfactory indicator of reading ability, this went on enjoying wide popularity among teachers for whom the task of reading aloud retains 'face validity' as a measure of reading, as well as being familiar, easy and cheap to administer. A suitable cloze test, which many would regard as a theoretically better motivated indicator, still may not look so much like a good reading measure to some.

Though face validity may not seem like a genuine aspect of validity as we have discussed it, it does have practical importance particularly in a T context. It has been argued that more attention needs to be paid in validity study to the ulterior uses of measuring instruments (Chap. 2) as well as how far they quantify target constructs. And for lay consumers, quantification must not only be done but be 'seen to be done' (Bachman, 1990: 285).

But this points to the fact that in the end a great *many* variables, including many mentioned in earlier chapters, are in practice not really measured directly, but by some sort of more or less distant indicators. You could argue, for example, that using the evidence of controlled manipulation test or opinion surveys to get at aspects of natural language use is simply a special case of using indicators, which vary in the extent to which they can be regarded as valid, but are often quicker to administer and more reliable than collecting speech samples. Conversely more naturalistic measuring techniques — 'a slice of the activity we are trying to assess' — may give more valid information about use (though even here 'face validity' perhaps persuades many ahead of proven validation). But they may be less reliable than standardised manipulation tests of language-like behaviour. Hence arises the use of the less naturalistic measures as indicators of the more naturalistic ones.

Other examples:

> English speakers' natural use of *needn't/don't need to* quantified from a manipulation test — turning sentences into the negative — rather than direct observation of use in topic oriented conversation (Greenbaum & Quirk, 1970).

> Frequencies of words quantified from speakers' opinion of their frequencies rather than by direct counting of their frequency in non-reactive samples of spoken and written material.

> Quality of diphthongs produced by informants as being [əi] or [ai] quantified from sociolinguist's judgment by ear rather than analysis of the first element by a sound spectrograph (which identifies the pitch levels present in the sound, and hence its quality).

23.4 Indicators of More Covert Variables

A good example of an indicator 'of necessity', where you couldn't really measure the intended variable more fully/directly anyway, is that of response time used to measure comprehension, e.g. of the truth or falsity of statements cast in the negative and affirmative. Asking people to introspect about complexity of their processes of comprehension for different sentences in the manner of pre-behaviourist psychologists would be perhaps more direct, but highly unreliable. Here clearly what you *want* to measure is the comprehension process we go through for the two types of sentence, but what we can *actually* measure reliably and validly is the time taken to state whether a given sentence is true or false, which it can be argued logically must reflect the target construct 'complexity of the comprehension process'. But this remains a matter of theoretical faith.

As usual, there can be a trade-off between using a perhaps more valid but less reliable measuring technique and a less valid but more reliable one. But remember, if a technique doesn't have a reasonably high reliability as a minimum requirement, it can't be valid either. The dilemma is summed up by Clark (1977): 'There is no point in measuring something irrelevant because it happens to be measurable. On the other hand there is no point in intuiting the inner reality of things if there is little chance that our intuitions will correspond to anyone else's'.

Yet this is a crucial matter: a lot of psycholinguistics involves 'chronometric' work. Response times, also found referred to as 'latencies', in some form or other, are used as indicators of various different DVs in a very great number of investigations. And they come with various more specific labels, such as 'pronunciation time' (= time taken before a case starts speaking a response), 'lexical decision time' (= time taken to register acceptance or rejection of a word as belonging to the language) and 'verification time' (= time taken to register truth or falsity of a statement). To a considerable extent, psycholinguistic research involves setting up contrasting sets of linguistic stimuli of all kinds of types, i.e. subtests representing values of an EV, such as words of different sorts, sentences with different structures, truth values, pragmatic implications, and so on. These have to be processed or remembered etc. in such a way that responses can then be measured by one or other of a rather *small* set of available overt indicator variables (functioning as DVs). One is response time. Another is 'percent correct response' e.g. to multiple choice tests in research on recognition memory for words, sentences, 'content' etc. (See e.g. Garnham, 1985: 44, 124 for examples).

It can be seen that the relationship between intended/target variables and indicator variables is similar to that between theories and hypotheses in research. To be researchable, rather vague and general theoretical propositions like the linguistic relativity theory that 'language influences thought' have to be turned into, or have derived from them, specific testable hypotheses (operationalisation again). Part and parcel of this is that any general and covert variables involved have to be quantified by something specific and overt. In this example 'thought' had somehow to be quantified separately from language. In one study each child's preference for sorting blocks by shape or colour was in effect used as an indicator of the child's conceptualisation of the objects. This could then be examined against the sort of classification implicit in the structure of the child's native language for a possible relationship. Of course the use of such an indicator depends on your espousing a particular view (theory) of what 'conceptualisation' is and how it is manifested. In order to test one theory, here the theory of linguistic relativity, you have to *assume* the validity of other theories related to your means of quantification, here a theory of how conceptualisation is manifested.

Other examples of overt indicators of particularly covert variables:

Position of limits of major units of psychological processing in sentence comprehension (e.g. at phrase boundaries?) quantified from subjects' perception of where clicks interspersed in stimulus sentences occurred (Fodor & Bever, 1965).

Position of limits of major units of psychological processing in sentence production quantified from position of restarts, pauses, *um*'s etc. in speech.

Importance of a vocabulary item for L2 learners to learn quantified from a count of the relative frequency of the vocabulary item in samples of native speaker writing (and speech).

Attitude to RP and Welsh accented English quantified from willingness to fill in a questionnaire when asked to in that accent during a theatre interval (Bourhis & Giles, 1976).

23.5 Indicators of Future Performance

A special case of a covert target variable is one that will only become more overt at some time after you are trying to quantify it. The indicator here should clearly be logically derived from some sort of analysis of the essential features of the future behaviour, and where relevant the specific instructional syllabus that would be followed. As Bachman points out (1990: 250ff.), this is rarely the case, as aptitude constructs are particularly difficult to specify. Furthermore, many T uses of assessment are essentially predictive, such as the prognostic, placement and selection functions (2.2.2). Yet often what is quantified as 'predictor' of the future performance relevant to these purposes is straight language proficiency.

Language learning aptitude is the stock example. This construct was operationalised in Carroll & Sapon's famous *Modern Language Aptitude Test* (1959) by the following five indicators from which a combined score is obtained:

(1) Test of rote memory for number words learnt in a made-up language.
(2) Test of recognition of spoken words which have to be identified with written forms in a sort of phonetic transcription.
(3) Test of recognition of English words in disguised spelling.
(4) Test of ability to identify in sentences a word or construction parallel in function to a word or construction in model sentences given.
(5) Test of rote memory for Kurdish vocabulary learnt up with English translation.

Other examples of such 'predictive' indicators:

A measure of English language 'sufficiency', that is of particular aspects of proficiency predicted as adequate for the communicative requirements of some particular future course or job, e.g. technical training in Saudi Arabia (Yule, 1980).

A test of 'reading readiness' of native speaker children, used to help decide when to start teaching a child to read.

An assessment in Year 8 of the UK school system to decide which pupils should take GCSE French a year early.

23.6 The Need to Maintain the Conceptual Distinction Between Indicator and Construct

Apart from being overconfident in the degree to which an indicator reflects the intended phenomenon, a common error is actually to *mistake* the indicator for the target variable. For example you start thinking about readability as if it really consisted of nothing else *but* sentence and word length. This is particularly likely to happen when the basic phenomenon or construct you are trying to measure is not susceptible to more direct measurement (23.4). If you can measure something tangible that clearly has *something* to do with the basic phenomenon, there is a great temptation to define the basic phenomenon from what you actually can measure. Indeed there has existed a school of thought that actually favoured this extreme form of 'operational definition' whereby basic concepts are *identified* with the manifestation you actually measure. But of course you must have some independent idea, if not a clear definition, of the basic concept/construct in order to judge what indicators would be relevant. It is letting the tail wag the dog to then redefine your original construct from the indicator.

One example of this is a variable that borders on the interests of language researchers — intelligence. There has been a tendency to define this from the highly reliable and operationalised intelligence tests that have been created — i.e. to define intelligence as 'whatever intelligence tests measure'. In this way you seem to avoid the need for any independent theory-based approach to specifying intelligence at all. However, many psychologists now feel that current intelligence tests don't perhaps measure everything we would normally regard as making up someone's intelligence. In short there is a 'validity gap' between the indicator and the intended target variable. Indeed some intelligence tests (e.g. Stanford-Binet) are thought to be so heavily biased towards measuring 'verbal intelligence' that they are used by some as indicators of language ability rather than intelligence!

A more centrally linguistic example is the following. C. Osgood published a book entitled *The Measurement of Meaning* (Osgood *et al.*, 1957) which proposed a technique called the 'semantic differential' for measuring the meaning of a word by getting native speakers to place it on various seven point scales. For instance subjects were asked to give *beggar* a score between 1 and 7 (inclusive) on the scales

strong	1	2	3	4	5	6	7	weak
good	1	2	3	4	5	6	7	bad

depending on how far they felt *beggar* suggested strength or weakness and so on. Now much work has been done using this measurement technique and it has certainly proved reliable: hence you might say it is certainly measuring *something*. But from the start there was discussion, certainly by linguists, as to whether what was being measured really was 'meaning' or some direct manifestation of meaning. This question of validity is hampered here by the fact that there is tremendous theoretical variation among scholars in their opinions over what the meaning of a word is. Hence it was possible to regard the measurements as valid or invalid simply on the basis of what you are prepared to call 'meaning'.

In circumstances like this, indeed, where the very conception of the thing you want to measure is in contention, and where clear objective ways of measuring or categorising *any* version of the conception are in short supply, there is a particularly strong temptation to solve the conceptual question in favour of anything that can be objectively measured. Thus in the present example the argument would run like this 'we aren't sure what meaning is and how to measure it, but Osgood's 'semantic differential' technique seems to work and has something to do with meaning: so let's cut the philosophising and define 'meaning' as 'whatever the semantic differential measures''. By this means, of course, an ill-defined notion becomes well-defined and objective, so the whole process seems admirably scientific.

However, there is an obvious danger here, encapsulated usefully in the much quoted story of the drunk and the streetlamp. It runs like this. A drunk, coming home late at night, drops his key when trying to open his front door. Some minutes later he is discovered by a friend searching some yards away under a streetlamp. On being asked why he is looking there and not by the door, the drunk replies: 'Because there's more light here'. Now for scientists, looking under the lamp is parallel to pursuing research in areas where they have managed to develop reliable measuring techniques. But there is a danger that what can be reliably measured is not exactly what you set out to measure, and that a related important object of enquiry which is harder to measure may be either just neglected in favour of the easier to measure phenomenon, or, worse, it may get defined out of existence and supplanted by the easier to measure phenomenon.

Thus in the present example many philosophers and linguists would argue that it would be wrong to say that what the semantic differential technique measures is the only aspect of meaning worth looking at (many others exist) and that the other possible view that what it measures is in fact *all* there is to meaning would be absolutely disastrous. A more widely accepted view would be that the semantic differential validly measures not what we would regard as the central meaning of a word like *beggar*, variously referred to as 'denotational meaning', 'cognitive meaning', etc., but rather the overtones or associations the word has — dependent partly on its meaning, but also determined by non-linguistic factors. That is, how we commonly visualise beggars, our emotional response to them, etc. — what is often in everyday parlance called the 'connotations' of the word. Thus the central meaning of the word is better reflected in a dictionary definition, which would probably not indicate *beggar* as having any connection with *strong* or *weak*, *good* or *bad*: e.g. 'Person who lives by asking for money, food, etc.'.

Finally, in the T realm, a particularly deleterious effect of indicator-target variable confusion can arise from the fact that those instructing pupils/patients, to improve aspects of their language competence with a view to them taking a particular test or exam, may quite naturally focus especially on work related to what the test/exam directly measures, so as to give their patients/pupils the best chance of doing well ('backwash' 2.2.4). Yet where this test is in fact only of a gross *indicator* of the competence that is supposed to be improving, this may result in apparent progress being observed, as measured by the indicator, but in reality little progress on the full range of things the indicator is supposedly an indicator of. Thus in such circumstances 'teaching to the exam' may destroy the validity of an otherwise good indicator.

The somewhat apocryphal story of nail production in the former USSR provides a salutary analogy. Reputedly at one time 'tonnage of nails produced per year' was taken as the official indicator by which productivity of factories producing nails was assessed. Since large nails weigh more, the result, of course, was overproduction of large nails and shortage of small ones as factories adapted their production so as to appear successful on the official indicator measure. Later, to cope with this, the official indicator was altered to 'number of nails produced per year'. The reader can guess the consequence.

Some measurement experts regard possible backwash and other matters related to the *effects* of quantification, and the *uses* to which means of quantification are put, especially in T circumstances, as an additional area to be examined under the heading of validity (Messick, 1988). To be fully valid in this sense, quantification must be beneficial to learners, society etc.

23.7 Checking on Validity: Criterion Validation

As we have seen, quantifying variables in indicator capacity is frequently unavoidable. Their validity can always be checked directly against the specification of the construct they are supposed to be reflecting by construct validation, as described in 22.4.2. This would typically be the only means possible with the indicators of 23.4 above.

Another formal approach that is applicable in many 'indicator' situations is known as *criterion validation*. This comes in two specific forms known as *concurrent* and *predictive* validation. Both in principle are ways of quantifying how far a measure of one variable, e.g. an indicator, quantifies the same thing as another one that is assumed to be a more valid measure of the target construct, the 'criterion' measure. That assumption could itself be checked only by using content or construct validation of the criterion measure, of course (22.4). Thus criterion validation can be seen as simply a convenient *indirect* way of checking on the same things that content and construct validation check on — *viz.* aspects of how well the measure measures in accordance with the specification of the construct.

It should be noted here that what is called the 'criterion' in this sort of discussion of validity has no connection with the term as used earlier opposed to 'norm', distinguishing absolute from relative measurement (Chap. 10). It simply applies to whatever measure, criterion or norm referenced (but in practice usually the latter), is being taken as the touchstone compared with. This has to be carefully noted when the word *criterion* occurs in both senses in the same discussion.

Criterion validity is easy to quantify in an objective and practical way and is sometimes referred to as 'pragmatic' or 'empirical' validity (for the statistics of its quantification see further references at the end of Chap. 21). This approach to validation differs in principle from other approaches in terms of the variables involved as follows. Compared with 21.2.3 the means of quantification involved in the comparison are more clearly distinct. What are compared there are 'the same' technique with a few facet choices differently made. What are compared here are often completely different means — i.e. with almost every facet choice different, but the targeted linguistic content supposedly related. Compared with construct validation (22.4.2) what is compared here is closer to being different measures of 'the same' variable, rather than measures of completely different variables.

The difference between the two approaches *within* criterion validity is simply that concurrent validation involves a criterion measurement made more or less at the *same time as* the measurement with the technique whose validity is in question, while predictive validity involves a criterion measurement considerably *later*. Depending on such things as the nature of the variable being measured, both, one or neither of these checks may be possible in a given instance.

23.7.1 Concurrent validity

Here you simply measure a representative group of cases both by the technique whose validity you are assessing and more or less at the same time by another technique assumed to be more valid. Both techniques have to have reasonably high reliability, checked beforehand. You then compare the two sets of results and, logically, the closer they are, the more the technique in question is really measuring the same thing as the 'criterion' technique, and so the greater its 'concurrent validity', and the nearer its validity coefficient will work out to +1, usually. This is therefore a check on whether one measure does really quantify the same construct as another: a claim not to be assumed correct just because someone gave the two measures similar names (the 'jingle fallacy').

This is applicable especially in the sort of instances described in 23.2 and 23.3. For instance in the readability example you could test the concurrent validity of a Flesch type indicator, which relies on word and sentence length only, by comparing the Flesch readability scores for a number of different samples of text with the scores they obtain if you do a much more elaborate measurement including many more of the individual variables that theoretically might be relevant. In this instance the full measure has clearer a priori validity than the indicator, provided you go along with text-based measurement of readability in the first place, but is much too laborious to perform normally. Meara, validating his quick vocabulary recognition indicator (23.2) against the more elaborate and direct *Eurocentres Joint Entrance Test* of proficiency for placement purposes achieved correlations of 0.807 for learners of Germanic language backgrounds, 0.549 for French speakers (Meara *et al.*, 1994).

But this illustrates clearly how concurrent validity is meaningless without the a priori assumption that one technique in the comparison definitely is valid. Without this assumption, the fact that the Flesch index had a high concurrent validity coefficient relative to the criterion measure would tell you nothing about whether it really measured readability or not. But this is often a source of difficulty. For instance direct rating or categorising of cases by experts is often taken as a criterion against which tests and other measures of the same thing are examined, though the validity of the ratings themselves is exceedingly difficult to establish.

The choice of what serves as the criterion of course has to be made by the measurer. Typically you will choose, as in the readability example, the fuller measure rather than a partial one. Or you will choose a technique that seems to measure the required variable more directly, e.g. a less reactive approach, if you are after naturalistic language behaviour. Thus Dorian, (1981), unhappy with the information from her questionnaire about language use in E. Sutherland compared with that from her participant observation, regarded the latter as the criterion. Often the standard published instrument is chosen rather than the homemade one. The only sound choice though is of the technique that has proven content or especially *construct* validity. But this choice, essential to pragmatic validity measurement, is often in the end based on nothing more solid than the measurer's judgment. Thus depending on your theoretical persuasion, you could regard a multiple choice test of reading comprehension as the criterion and the cloze test as the one whose validity is more in question, or the reverse.

Concurrent validation is also to be found used more doubtfully where there is no obvious criterion measurement involved. Suppose you work out concurrent validity coefficients by comparing a group's results on a cloze test of reading ability and a multiple choice test, *without* (as there was assumed above) any assumption that one is more valid a priori. In short you are a theoretical fence-sitter, or you simply regard all available techniques as probably poor indicators.

In that situation if you compare trials of one with another and if scores agree well, you can conclude that the different techniques are measuring the *same* variable, but you are none the wiser about whether that variable is the one you had in mind — reading/comprehension ability — and this gets like a reliability study. Though you could say each of the techniques compared had high concurrent validity, in this instance this would *not* mean necessarily high validity in the true sense of measuring the variable intended — the procedure would be viciously circular. And if the scores were different and the validity coefficients low, e.g. 0.3 only, you wouldn't know which was the more valid of the tests compared *vis-à-vis* the intended variable.

It is rather like being told, in an unfamiliar town, that the car park is near the swimming pool, the swimming pool is next to the town hall and the town hall is behind the car park. Unless the location of *one* of the three places is actually pointed out directly, or is self-evident, you are none the wiser.

23.7.2 Predictive validity

Predictive validity, sometimes called 'forecast' validity, is quantified just like concurrent validity except for the lapse of time between the measurement to be validated and the measurement of the logically related criterion. It checks on a rather limited kind of instance, where you are measuring a variable that is by nature forward-looking, or can be regarded for some purpose as being an indicator of future performance on a related variable, as illustrated in 23.5.

Clearly someone who does well in a language learning aptitude test should do well in subsequently learning a foreign language (should he/she choose to do so), otherwise the test is not a valid measure of the variable it claims to measure. Hence we can measure the validity of such a test simply by applying it to a suitable group of people whom we follow up after some time of actually learning the foreign language. If subjective means of quantification are used, e.g. rating, the criterion measurement would best be done by a person different from the one who did the predictor one. Now if it turns out that those who did well in the aptitude test do correspondingly well when measured later by some assumed valid measure of achievement in a foreign language course, and those who did badly do badly, then we can regard the aptitude test as having 'predictive validity'.

However, it is inconvenient to have to wait some time to see if a test or whatever is valid or not. And of course it is usually impossible to control conditions satisfactorily so that all those originally tested had the same opportunity to learn or succeed. Some may get a better teacher or learn by a means of instruction which a predictive aptitude measure was not geared to. Further, some cases may drop out along the way. Especially, when a placement or selection use of a predictive indicator is involved, it is often impractical or unethical for those found unsuitable by the predictor to pursue the later learning/task or whatever at all just as part of the validity checking exercise (e.g. the last example in 23.5). So a low predictive coefficient *could* arise not because the aptitude test was a bad predictor, but for a variety of other reasons.

As usual the validity of the later 'criterion' measure has to be assumed. In our example, if the aptitude test proves to have high validity established as suggested above, it still may be invalid if the tests of language achievement or proficiency that were used to check it against are invalid. We have merely passed the buck — here the burden of proof of validity — from the aptitude tests to the other test(s) used. In fact in the present instance it has been argued that the validation of *MLAT* was often by the later use of language tests of a rather limited type (discrete point). People who do well on *MLAT* later do well in these but might not do so well on more integrative tests (e.g. cloze). The rather unnaturalistic *MLAT* is thus a good predictor of success in learning via teaching leading to unnaturalistic tests of competence.

Further Reading

Pedhazur & Schmelkin (1991: Chap. 3).

Conclusion

With consideration of validity issues we come full-circle back to where we started — the real world phenomena that it is the aim of the whole quantification exercise to reduce to figures in some way. It is paradoxical perhaps that considerations of validity, which in a way are first in one's mind when trying to quantify something, get discussed last, since understanding them depends so much on being aware of all the other aspects of the quantification process.

It will have become apparent by now that quantifying language is not a straightforward activity. While I am aware that the preceding account has a number of shortcomings, I hope that I have done something to heighten awareness of the range of problems that arise and principles that are relevant, and provide a nexus of onward references for anyone interested in this neglected broad field of what I would like to call *linguometry*. Whenever language is quantified, whether by teacher, therapist or researcher, a gamut of choices have been made that define what happens and what it can mean. If the activity is pursued without due consideration being paid to these matters, then we may but be justifying the hopefully declining view that in matters of language 'those who count don't count'.

Appendix 1

Many quality checks on measurement involve examining two or more scorings or categorisations of the same cases, using similar statistical procedures. This attempts to summarise the main situations in simple terms:

Substance	Facets	Quality Control
The sets of scores are assumed to reflect:	The means of quantification of each is meant to be:	As a check you aim to quantify:
The same variable repeated in some way	Identical but for random variation within choices on facets (e.g. parallel items, different marker of same sort, same setting on a different day)	How great an effect on measurement does this sort of intra-facet choice variation have? Random measurement error (19.3.4, 20.3)
The same variable or slightly different but heavily overlapping in substance	Identical but for a few facet choices altered (e.g. different kind of marker, open choice instead of m/c items, home versus school setting)	Do different choices like these alter the measurements obtained? Systematic measurement error (21.2.3)
One variable and another overlapping in substance (duplicatory)	Quite different (e.g. native speaker rating instead of m/c test). Usually one is quicker and easier to do than the other or precedes and predicts it	Does the quick measure produce similar measurement to the other one? Criterion validity (23.7)
One variable and others which together are components of a complex variable (complementary)	Could be similar means but different substance (e.g. counts of grammar errors, spelling errors and vocab errors)	Do the components disagree with each other but agree with the whole as expected? Construct validity — internal (22.4.2)
One variable and a different but related one (e.g. oral communicative competence and written communicative competence)	Could be similar or different facet choices, as well as different substance	Do the measures agree as expected? Construct validity — convergent (22.4.2)
One variable and a different and unrelated one (e.g. communicative competence and spelling)	Could be similar or different facet choices, as well as different substance	Do the measures show no relationship, as expected. Construct validity — divergent (22.4.2)

Appendix 2

This diagram summarises the kinds of formal check on quantification that can be done, as a function of what you have to have available to perform them:

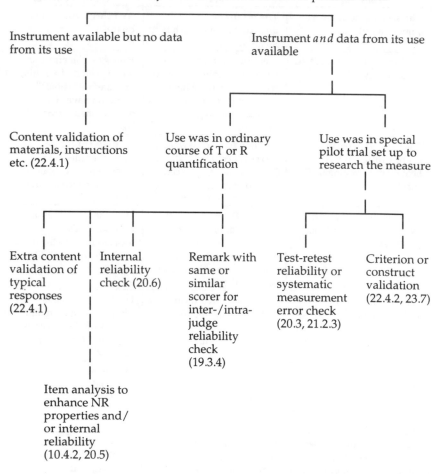

References

Agrawal, K. (1979) The short tests of linguistic skills and their calibration. *TESOL Quarterly* 13, 185–207.

Ahmed, M. (1988) Vocabulary learning strategies: A case study of Sudanese learners of English. University of Wales, Bangor: PhD Thesis.

Aitchison, J. (1987) *Words in the Mind*. Oxford: Blackwell.

Alderson, C., Krahnke, K. and Stansfield, C. (eds) (1987) *Reviews of English Language Proficiency Tests*. Washington DC: TESOL.

Alderson, J. (1987) Innovation in language testing: Can the microcomputer help? Special Report No. 1. *Language Testing Update*.

Allen, A. (1992) Development and validation of a scale to measure test-wiseness in EFL/ESL reading test takers. *Language Testing* 9.

Allen, J. and Corder, S. P. (eds) (1977) *The Edinburgh Course in Applied Linguistics Vol. 3*. Oxford: Oxford University Press.

Allen, J. and Davies, A. (eds) (1977) *The Edinburgh Course in Applied Linguistics Vol. 4*. Oxford: Oxford University Press.

Allen, P. and Carroll, S. (1987) Evaluation of classroom processes in a Canadian core French programme. *Evaluation and Research in Education* 1, 49–61.

Allwright, R. (1988) *Observation in the Language Classroom*. New York: Longman.

Anastasi, A. (1988) *Psychological Testing*. New York: Macmillan.

Anisfeld, M. (1984) *Language Development from Birth to Three*. Hillsdale, NJ: Erlbaum.

Anshen, F. (1978) *Statistics for Linguists*. Rowley, MA: Newbury House.

Arrasmith, D., Sheehan, D. and Applebaum, W. (1984) A comparison of the selected-response strategy and the constructed-response strategy for assessment of a third-grade writing task. *Journal of Educational Research* 77, 172–77.

Baars, B. (1992) A dozen competing-plans techniques for inducing predictable slips in speech and action. In B. Baars (ed.) *Experimental Slips and Human Error*. New York: Plenum press.

Bachman, L. and Palmer, A. (1981) The construct validation of the FSI Oral Interview. *Language Learning* 31, 67–86.

Bachman, L. (1990) *Fundamental Considerations in Language Testing*. Oxford: Oxford University Press.

Baetens Beardsmore, H. (1982) *Bilingualism: Basic Principles*. Clevedon: Multilingual Matters Ltd.

Bagby Atwood, E. (1986) The methods of American dialectology. In H. Allen and M. Linn (eds) *Dialect and Language Variation*. Orlando: Academic Press.

Baker, C. and Hinde, J. (1984) Language background classification. *Journal of Multilingual and Multicultural Development* 5, 43–56.

Baker, C. (1993) *Foundations of Bilingual Education and Bilingualism*. Clevedon: Multilingual Matters Ltd.

Bennett-Kastor, T. (1988) *Analyzing Children's Language*. Oxford: Blackwell.

Berry, M. (1969) *Language Disorders of Children*. New York: Appleton-Century-Crofts.

Bilingual Inventory of Natural Language (1976) Los Angeles: Checkpoint Systems.

Bilingual Syntax Measure (1975) New York: Harcourt Brace Jovanovich.

Black, H. and Dockrell, W. (1984) *Criterion-Referenced Assessment in the Classroom*. Edinburgh: The Scottish Council for Research in Education.

Blanchard, J. (1984) The effect of anthropomorphism on word learning. *Journal of Educational Research* 78, 105–10.

Bliss, J., Monk, M. and Ogborn, J. (1983) *Qualitative Data Analysis for Educational Research*. London: Croom Helm.

Bloom, L. and Lahey, M. (1978) *Language Development and Language Disorders*. New York: John Wiley and Sons.

de Bot, K., Ginsberg, R., Kramsch, C. (eds) (1991) *Foreign Language Research in Cross-Cultural Perspective*. Amsterdam: John Benjamins.

Bourhis, R. and Giles, H. (1976) The language of cooperation in Wales: A field study. *Language Sciences* 42, 13–16.

Bracken, B. (1991) *The Psychoeducational Assessment of Preschool Children* (2nd edn). Boston: Allyn and Bacon.

British Council (1987) *Survey of Overseas ESOL Professionals Following Courses in British Institutions*. London: English Language and Literature Division of the British Council.

Brody, G., Stoneman, Z. and Wheatley, P. (1984) Peer interaction in the presence and absence of observers. *Child Development* 55, 1425–28.

Brown, G. and Yule, G. (1983) *Teaching the Spoken Language*. Cambridge: Cambridge University Press.

Brown, J. (1980) Relative merits of four methods for scoring cloze tests. *The Modern Language Journal* 64, 311–17.

Brown, R. (1973) *A First Language: The Early Stages*. Cambridge, MA: Harvard University Press.

Brown, J.D. (1988) *Understanding Research in Second Language Learning*. Cambridge: Cambridge University Press.

Bruno, A. (1974) *Toward a Quantitative Methodology for Stylistic Analysis*. Berkeley: University of California Press.

Buros, O. (1978) *The Eighth Mental Measurements Yearbook*. New Jersey: The Gryphon Press.

Burroughs, G. (1971) *Design and Analysis in Educational Research*. Birmingham: Birmingham University Press.

Butler, C. (1985a) *Computers in Linguistics*. Oxford: Basil Blackwell.

— (1985b) *Statistics in Linguistics*. Oxford: Basil Blackwell.

Canale, M. and Swain, M. (1980) Theoretical bases of communicative approaches to second language teaching and testing. *Applied Linguistics* 1, 1–47.

Canter, D. (ed) (1985) *Facet Theory: Approaches to Social Research*. New York: Springer-Verlag.

Caplan, D. (1992) *Language Structure, Processing, and Disorders*. Cambridge, MA: MIT Press.

Carroll, J. and Sapon, S. (1959) *Modern Language Aptitude Test*. New York: The Psychological Corporation.

Carroll, J. (1971) Measurement properties of subjective magnitude estimates of word frequency. *Journal of Verbal Learning and Verbal Behaviour* 10.

Carter, R. (1987) *Vocabulary*. London: Allen and Unwin.

Carterette, E. (1974) *Handbook of Perception, Vol. 2*. New York: Academic Press.

Carver, R. (1974) Two dimensions of tests: Psychometric and edumetric. *American Psychologist* 29, 512–18.

Cedergren, H. and Sankoff, D. (1974) Variable rules: Performance as a statistical reflection of competence. *Language* 50, 333–55.

Chambers, E. (1964) *Statistical Calculation for Beginners*. Cambridge: Cambridge University Press.

Chambers, J. and Trudgill, P. (1980) *Dialectology*. Cambridge: Cambridge University Press.

Cheshire, J. (1982a) *Variation in an English Dialect*. Cambridge: Cambridge University Press.

— (1982b) Linguistic variation and social function. In S. Romaine (ed.) *Sociolinguistic Variation in Speech Communities*. London: Edward Arnold.

Chien, Y. and Lust, B. (1985) The concepts of topic and subject in first language acquisition of Mandarin Chinese. *Child Development* 56, 1359–75.

Chomsky, C. (1971) *The Acquisition of Syntax in Children from 5 to 10*. Cambridge, MA: MIT Press.

Christensen, L. (1980) *Experimental Methodology*. Boston: Allyn and Bacon.

Clark, H. and Clark, E. (1977) *Psychology and Language*. New York: Harcourt, Brace and Jovanovich.

Clark, R. (1977) In J. Allen and S.P. Corder (eds) *The Edinburgh Course in Applied Linguistics Vol. 4* (Chapters 4–6, p.105ff.). Oxford: Oxford University Press.

CNAA (1987) *Current Developments in School Curriculum and Examinations*.

Cohen, A. (1984) On taking language tests: What the students report. *Language Testing* 1, 70–81.

Cohen, A. and Cavalcanti, M. (1987) Giving and getting feedback on composition: A comparison of teacher and student verbal report. *Evaluation and Research in Education* 1, 63–73.

Cohen, L. (1976) *Educational Research in Classrooms and Schools*. London: Harper and Row.

Cohen, L. and Holliday, M. (1982) *Statistics for Social Scientists*. London: Harper and Row.

Cohen, L. and Manion, L. (1980) *Research Methods in Education*. London: Croom Helm.

Cohen, R., Montague, P., Nathanson, L. and Swerdlik, M. (1988) *Psychological Testing*. Mountain View, CA: Mayfield Publishing Company.

Cronbach, L. (1984) *Essentials of Psychological Testing*. New York: Harper and Row.

Crosby, F. and Nyquist, L. (1977) The female register: An empirical study of Lakoff's hypotheses. *Language in Society* 6.

Crystal, D. (1980) *Introduction to Language Pathology*. London: Edward Arnold.

Crystal, D. and Davy, D. (1969) *Investigating English Style*. London: Longman.

Crystal, D., Fletcher, P. and Garman, M. (1976) *The Grammatical Analysis of Language Disability*. London: Arnold.

Crystal, D. (1982) *Profiling Linguistic Disability*. London: Arnold.

Cunningham, C., Siegel, L., van der Spuy, Clark, M. and Bow, S. (1985) The behavioral and linguistic interactions of specifically language-delayed and normal boys with their mothers. *Child Development* 56, 1389–1403.

Cziko, G. (1981) Psychometric and edumetric approaches to language testing: Implications and applications. *Applied Linguistics* 2, 27–44.

— (1982) Improving the psychometric, criterion-referenced, and practical qualities of integrative language tests. *TESOL Quarterly* 16, 357–79.

Dagut, M. and Laufer, B. (1985) Avoidance of phrasal verbs. *Studies in Second Language Acquisition* 7, 73–9.

Dale, P. (1972) *Language Development*. Hinsdale, IL: The Dryden Press.

Davies, A. (1977) The construction of language tests (pp. 38–104). In J. Allen and A. Davies (eds) *The Edinburgh Course in Applied Linguistics Vol. 4*. Oxford: Oxford University Press.

Davidson, F., Hudson, T. and Lynch, B. (1985) Language testing: Operationalisation in classroom measurement and L2 research. In M. Celce-Muria (ed.) *Beyond Basics*. Rowley, MA: Newbury House.

Department of Education and Science (DES) and the Welsh Office (1989) *English for Ages 5 to 16*. London: HMSO.

Dittmar, N. (1976) *Sociolinguistics*. London: Arnold.

Dodson, C. (ed.) (1985) *Bilingual Education: Evaluation, Assessment and Methodology*. Cardiff: University of Wales Press.

Dorian, N. (1981) *Language Death: The Life-Cycle of a Scottish Gaelic Dialect*. Philadelphia: University of Pennsylvania Press.

— (1982) Defining the speech community to include its working margins (pp. 25–33). In S. Romaine (ed). *Sociolinguistic Variation in Speech Communities*. London: Edward Arnold.

Downes, W. (1984) *Language and Society*. London: Fontana.

Dulay, H., Burt, M. and Krashen, S. (1982) *Language Two*. Oxford: Oxford University Press.

Dunn, G. (1989) *Design and Analysis of Reliability Studies*. New York: Oxford University Press.

Dunn, l., Whetton, C. and Pintillie, D. (1982) *British Picture Vocabulary Scale*. London: NFER-Nelson.

van Els, T., Bongaerts, T., Extra, G., van Os, C. and Janssen-van Dieten, A-M. (1984)

Applied Linguistics and the Learning and Teaching of Foreign Languages. London: Edward Arnold.

Escure, G. (1982) Contrastive patterns of intragroup and intergroup interaction in the Creole continuum of Belize. *Language in Society* 11, 239–64.

Faerch, C., Haastrup, K. and Phillipson, R. (1984) *Learner Language and Language Learning*. Clevedon: Multilingual Matters Ltd.

Fasold, R. (1984) *The Sociolinguistics of Society*. Oxford: Basil Blackwell.

— (1990) *The Sociolinguistics of Language*. Oxford: Basil Blackwell.

Fischer, R. (1984) Testing written communicative competence in French. *The Modern Language Journal* 68, 13–20.

Fitzgerald, D. and Hattie, J. (1983) An evaluation of the 'Your style of learning and thinking' inventory. *British Journal of Educational Psychology* 53, 336–46.

Fletcher, P. and Garman, M. (1986) *Language Acquisition* (2nd edn). Cambridge: Cambridge University Press.

Fodor, J. and Bever, T. (1965) The psychological reality of linguistic segments. *Journal of Verbal Learning and Verbal Behavior* 4, 414–20.

Francis, W. (1983) *Dialectology*. London: Longman.

Frankfort-Nachmias, C. and Nachmias, D. (1992) *Research Methods in the Social Sciences* (4th edition). London: Edward Arnold.

Frick, T. and Semmel, M. (1978) Observational agreement and reliabilities of classroom observational measures. *Review of Educational Research* 48, 157–84.

Fromkin, V. (ed.) (1973) *Speech Errors as Linguistic Evidence*. The Hague: Mouton.

Fromkin, V. and Rodman, R. (1988) *An Introduction to Language*. New York: Holt, Rinehart and Winston.

Gardner, P. (1974) Attitude measurement: A critique of some recent research. *Educational Research* 17, 101–09.

Gardner, R. and Lambert, W. (1972) *Attitudes and Motivation in Second Language Learning*. Rowley, MA: Newbury House.

Garman, M. (1990) *Psycholinguistics*. Cambridge: Cambridge University Press.

Garnham, A. (1985) *Psycholinguistics: Central Topics*. London: Methuen.

Gibbs, G. (1989) *Certificate in Teaching in Higher Education by Open Learning Module 3 — Assessment*. Oxford: Oxford Polytechnic.

Gibson, W. (1970) Styles and statistics: A model T style machine. In D. Freeman (ed.) *Linguistics and Literary Style*. New York: Holt, Rinehart and Winston.

Gilliland, J. (1972) *Readability*. London: University of London Press.

Gimson, A. (1980) *An Introduction to the Pronunciation of English*. London: Edward Arnold.

Gipps, C. and Ewen, E. (1973) Scoring written work in English as a second language. *Educational Research* 16, 121–25.

Goodrich, H. (1977) Distractor efficiency in foreign language testing. *TESOL Quarterly* 11, 69–78.

Greenbaum, S. and Quirk, R. (1970) *Elicitation Experiments in English: Linguistic Studies in Use and Attitude*. London: Longman.

Greenbaum, S. (1977) Judgments of syntactic acceptability and frequency. *Studia Linguistica* 31, 83–105.

Greene J. (1972) *Psycholinguistics*. Harmondsworth, UK: Penguin.

Groebel, L. (1981) Reading: The student's approach as compared to their teacher's recommended method. *English Language Teaching Journal* 35, 283–87.

Haertel, E. (1985) Construct validity and criterion-referenced testing. *Review of Educational Research* 55, 23–46.

Hall, J. and Caradog Jones, D. (1950) Social grading of occupations. *The British Journal of Sociology* 1, 31–55.

Halliday, M. and Hasan, R. (1976) *Cohesion in English*. London: Longman.

Hambleton, R., Swaminathan, H., Algina, J. and Coulson, D. (1978) Criterion-referenced testing and measurement: A review of technical issues and developments. *Review of Educational Research* 48, 1–47.

Hansen, J. and Stansfield, C. (1981) The relationship between field dependent–independent cognitive styles and foreign language achievement. *Language Learning* 31, 349–67.

Hare, V. and Devine, D. (1983) Topical knowledge and topical interest predictors of listening competence. *Journal of Educational Research* 76, 157–60.

Harris, J. (1990) *Early Language Development*. London: Routledge.

Harris, R. (1984) An autobiographical longitudinal study of event memory and affect during second-language acquisition. *Journal of Multilingual and Multicultural Development* 5, 159–73.

Hart, D., Lapkin, S. and Swain, M. (1987) Communicative language tests: Perks and perils. *Evaluation and Research in Education* 1, 83–94.

Hatch, E. and Farhady, H. (1982) *Research Design and Statistics for Applied Linguistics*. Rowley, MA: Newbury House.

Heaton, J. (1975) *Writing English Language Tests*. London: Longman.

Henerson, M. (1987) *How to Measure Attitudes*. Newbury Park.

Henning, G. (1987) *A Guide to Language Testing*. Cambridge, MA: Newbury House.

Hill, G. (1982) Oral assessment: A scheme for the assessment of the oral English of trainee teachers. *World Language English* 1, 124–6.

Hill, J. (1981) Effective reading in a foreign language. *English Language Teaching Journal* 35, 270–81.

Hoge, R. (1985) The validity of direct observation measures of pupil classroom behavior. *Review of Educational Research* 55, 469–83.

Holmes, J. (1992) *An Introduction to Sociolinguistics*. Harlow: Longman.

Hopkins, D. (1985) *A teacher's Guide to Classroom Research*. Milton Keynes: Open University Press.

Hudson, R. (1980) *Sociolinguistics*. Cambridge: Cambridge University Press.

Hudson, T. (1993) Surrogate indices for item information functions in criterion-referenced language testing. *Language Testing* 10.

Hudson, T. and Lynch, B. (1984) A criterion-referenced approach to ESL achievement testing. *Language Testing* 1, 171–201.

Hughes, A. (1981) Conversational cloze as a measure of oral ability. *English Language Teaching Journal* 35, 161–68.

— (1989) *Testing for Language Teachers*. Cambridge: Cambridge University Press.

Hughes, D., Keeling, B. and Tuck, F. (1983) Effects of achievement expectations and handwriting quality on scoring essays. *Journal of Educational Measurement* 20, 65–70.

Ingram, D. (1989) *First-language Acquisition: Method, Description and Exploitation.* Cambridge: Cambridge University Press.

Ingram, E. (1974) Language testing. In J. Allen and S.P. Corder (eds) *The Edinburgh Course in Applied Linguistics Vol. 3.* Oxford: Oxford University Press.

International Computer Archive for the Humanities. Norwegian Computing Centre for the Humanities, Harald Harfagresgt 31, N-5007, Bergen.

Jaeger, R. (1978) About education indicators: Statistics on the conditions and trends in education (pp. 276–315). In L. Shulman (ed.) *Review of Research in Education 6.* Itasca, IL: F E Peacock Publishers Inc.

Johansson, S. and Hofland, K. (1989) *Frequency Analysis of English Vocabulary and Grammar.* Oxford: Oxford University Press.

Johnson, P. and Giles, H. (1982) Values, language and inter-cultural differentiation: The Welsh-English context. *Journal of Multilingual and Multicultural Devlopment* 3, 103–16.

Jones, G. (1984) L2 speaker's and the pronouns of address in Welsh. *Journal of Multilingual and Multicultural Development* 5, 131–45.

Jones, L. (1984) *The First Certificate Examination.* Cambridge: Cambridge University Press.

Jones-Sargent, V. (1983) *Tyne Bytes.* Frankfurt am Main: Peter Lang.

Karmiloff-Smith, A. (1979) *A Functional Approach to Child Language.* Cambridge: Cambridge University Press.

Keenan, J. and Brown, P. (1984) Children's reading rate and retention as a function of the number of propositions in a text. *Child Development* 55, 1556–69.

Kenny, A. (1982) *The Computation of Style.* Oxford: Pergamon Press.

Klein-Bradley, C. (1991) Ask a stupid question. In K. de Bot, R. Ginsberg, C. Kramsch, (eds) *Foreign Language Research in Cross-Cultural Perspective.* Amsterdam: John Benjamins.

Labov, W. (1972) *Sociolinguistic Patterns.* Philadelphia: Pennsylvania University Press and Oxford: Basil Blackwell.

— (1982) Objectivity and commitment in linguistic science: The case of the Black English trial in Ann Arbor. *Language in Society* 11, 165–201.

Ladefoged, P. (1982) *A Course in Phonetics* (2nd edn). New York: Harcourt Brace Jovanovich.

Langley, R. (1979) *Practical Statistics Simply Explained.* London: Pan Books.

Larsen-Freeman, D. (1978) An ESL index of development. *TESOL Quarterly* 12, 439–48.

Lee, L. and Canter, S. (1971) Developmental syntax scoring. *Journal of Speech and Hearing Disorders* 36, 315–38.

Leech, G. (1968) Theory and practice of semantic testing. *Lingua* 24.

— (1981) *Semantics: The Study of Meaning.* Harmondsworth: Penguin.

— (1986) Automatic grammatical analysis and its educational applications. In G. Leech and C. Candlin (eds) *Computers in English Language Teaching and Research.* London: Longman.

Leonard, M. (1980) Rasch promises: A layman's guide to the Rasch method of item analysis. *Educational Research* 22, 188–92.

Lesser, R. (1978) *Linguistic Investigations of Aphasia*. London: Edward Arnold.

Local, J. (1982) Modelling intonational variability in children's speech. In S. Romaine (ed.) *Sociolinguistic Variation in Speech Communities*. London: Edward Arnold.

Lovell, K. (1964) *Educational Psychology and Children*. London: University of London Press.

Lyons, J. (1977) *Semantics Vol. 1*. Cambridge: Cambridge University Press.

Macwhinney, B. and Snow C. (1985) The child language data exchange system. *Journal of Child Language* 12, 271–96.

Madsen, H. (1983) *Techniques in Testing*. Oxford: Oxford University Press.

Major, R. (1987) Measuring pronunciation accuracy using computerised techniques. *Language Testing* 4.

Matthews, M. (1990) The measurement of productive skills: Doubts concerning the assessment criteria of certain public examinations. *English Language Teaching Journal* 44.

Matsumoto, K. (1994) Introspection, verbal reports and second language learning strategy research. *The Canadian Modern Language Review* 50, 363–86.

McEntegart, D. and Le Page, R. (1982) An appraisal of the statistical techniques used in The Sociolinguistic Survey of Multilingual Communities. In S. Romaine (ed.) *Sociolinguistic Variation in Speech Communities*. London: Edward Arnold.

Meara, P. and Buxton, B. (1987) An alternative to multiple choice vocabulary tests. *Language Testing* 4, 142–54.

Meara, P. and Jones, G. (1988) Vocabulary size as a placement indicator. *British Studies in Applied Linguistics* 3. CILT.

Meara, P., Lightbown, P. and Halter, R. (1994) The effect of cognates on the applicability of YES/NO vocabulary tests. *The Canadian Modern Language Review* 50, 296–311.

Messick, S. (1988) The once and future issues of validity: Assessing the meaning and consequences of measurement. In H. Wainer and H. Braun (eds) *Test Validity*. Hillsdale, NJ: Lawrence Erlbaum.

Miller, G. (1956) The magical number seven, plus or minus two: Some limits on our capacity for processing information. *Psychological Review* 63, 81–97.

Miller, J. (1982) *Assessing Language Production in Children*. London: Edward Arnold.

Milroy, J. (1982) Probing under the tip of the iceberg: Phonological 'normalisation' and the shape of speech communities. In S. Romaine (ed.) *Sociolinguistic Variation in Speech Communities*. London: Edward Arnold.

— (1982a) Social network and linguistic focusing. In S. Romaine (ed.) *Sociolinguistic Variation in Speech Communities*. London: Edward Arnold.

— (1982b) *Language and Social Networks*. Oxford: Basil Blackwell.

— (1987) *Observing and Analysing Natural Language*. Oxford: Basil Blackwell.

Mitchelmore, M. (1981) Reporting student achievement: How many grades? *British Journal of Educational Psychology* 51, 218–27.

Mukattash, L. (1981) The evaluation and testing of English in Jordan: A critique. *English Language Teaching Journal* 35, 450–54.

Munby, J. (1978) *Communicative Syllabus Design*. Cambridge: Cambridge University Press.

Nerenz, A. and Knop, C. (1982) A time-based approach to the study of teacher effectiveness. *The Modern Language Journal* 66, 243–54.

Nevo, N. (1989) Test-taking strategies on a multiple choice test of reading comprehension. *Language Testing* 6.

NFER Nelson Publishing Company Limited, Darville House, 20 Oxford Road East, Windsor, Berkshire SL4 1DF.

Nicolosi, L., Harryman, E. and Kresheck, J. (1989) *Terminology of Communication Disorders* (3rd edn). Baltimore: Williams and Wilkins.

Nisbet, J. (1974) Adding and averaging grades. *Educational Research* 17, 95–100.

Nitko, A. (1980) Distinguishing the many varieties of criterion-referenced tests. *Review of Educational Research* 50, 461–85.

Noll, V., Scannell, D. and Craig, R. (1979) *Introduction to Educational Measurement*. USA: Houghton Mifflin Company.

Nunnally, J. (1978) *Psychometric Theory* (2nd edn). New York: McGraw-Hill Book Company.

Nurss, J. and Hough, R. (1985) Young children's oral language: The effects of task. *Journal of Educational Research* 78, 280–85.

O'Donnell, R. (1976) A critique of some indices of syntactic maturity. *Research in the Teaching of English* 10.

Ohala, J. and Jaeger, J. (eds) (1986) *Experimental Phonology*. London: Academic Press.

Oller, J. (1979) *Language Tests at School*. London: Longman.

Oltman, P., Raskin, E. and Witkin, H. (1971) *Group Embedded Figures Test*. Palo Alto, CA: Consulting Psychologists Press.

Oscarson, M. (1989) Self assessment of language proficiency: Rationale and applications. *Language Testing* 6.

— (1991) Item response theory and reduced redundancy techniques. In K. de Bot, R. Ginsberg and C. Kramsch (eds) *Foreign Language Research in Cross-Cultural Perspective*. Amsterdam: John Benjamins.

Osgood, C., Suci, G. and Tannenbaum, P. (1957) *The Measurement of Meaning*. Urbana: University of Illinois Press.

Oxford Text Archive. Oxford University Computing Service, 13 Banbury Road, Oxford.

Painter, C. (1979) *An Introduction to Instrumental Phonetics*. Baltimore: University Park Press.

Paivio, A. and Begg, I. (1981) *Psychology of Language*. Englewood Cliffs, NJ: Prentice Hall.

Partington, J. (1988) Towards a science of question setting in the GCSE. *The British Journal of Language Teaching* 26, 45–9.

Pedhazur, E. and Schmelkin, L. (1991) *Measurement, Design and Analysis*. Hillsdale, NJ: Lawrence Erlbaum Assocs.

Perkins, K. and Miller, L. (1984) Comparative analyses of English as a second language reading comprehension data: Classical test theory and latent trait measurement. *Language Testing* 1, 21–32.

Perkins, W. (1977) *Speech Pathology*. St. Louis: C.V. Mosby Company.

Petyt, K. (1980) *The Study of Dialect*. London: Andre Deutsch.

Plutchik, R. (1974) *Foundations of Experimental Research*. New York: Harper and Row.

Politzer, R. (1978) Errors of English speakers of German as perceived and evaluated by German natives. *The Modern Language Journal* 62, 253–61.

Popham, W. (1974) An approaching peril: Cloud-referenced tests. *Phi Delta Kappan* 56, 614–15.

Potts, M., Carlson, P., Cocking, R. and Copple, C. (1979) *Structure and Development in Child Language*. Ithaca, NY: Cornell University Press.

Presland, J. (1973) In search of an 'early teaching grammar'. *Educational Research* 16, 112–20.

Price, S., Fluck, M. and Giles, H. (1983) The effects of language of testing on bilingual pre-adolescents' attitudes towards Welsh and varieties of English. *Journal of Multilingual and Multicultural Development* 4, 149–61.

Prideaux, G. (1984) *Psycholinguistics: The Experimental Study of Language*. London: Croom Helm.

Pumfrey, P. (1985) *Reading Tests and Assessment Techniques*. London: Hodder and Stoughton.

Quigley, H. (1973) The pre-reading vocabulary of children leaving nursery school. *Educational Research* 16, 28–33.

Quirk, R., Greenbaum, S., Svartvik, J. and Leech, G. (1985) *A Comprehensive Grammar of the English Language*. London: Longman.

Radford, A. (1988) *Transformational Grammar*. Cambridge: Cambridge University Press.

Ramirez, A. (1984) Pupil characteristics and performance on linguistic and communicative language measures. In C. Rivera (ed.) *Communicative Competence Approaches to Language Proficiency Assessment*. Clevedon: Multilingual Matters Ltd.

Rees, A. (1981) Constructing a discrete-item grammar and vocabulary test: Some problems and proposals. *World Language English* 1 39–42.

Registrar General (1966) *Social Class*. London: General Register Office.

Registrar General (1971) *Classification of Occupations*. London: General Register Office.

Rivera, C. (ed.) (1984) *Communicative Competence Approaches to Language Proficiency Assessment*. Clevedon: Multilingual Matters Ltd.

Robson, C. (1983) *Experiment, Design and Statistics in Psychology* (2nd edn). Harmondsworth, England: Penguin.

Roid, G. and Haladyna, T. (1980) The emergence of an item-writing technology. *Review of Educational Research* 50, 293–314.

Rokeach, M. (1973) *The Nature of Human Values*. New York: Free Press.

Romaine, S. (ed.) (1982) *Sociolinguistic Variation in Speech Communities*. London: Edward Arnold.

— (1984) *The Language of Children and Adolescents*. Oxford: Basil Blackwell.

Rowntree, D. (1977) *Assessing Standards: How Shall We Know Them?* London: Harper and Row.

— (1981) *Statistics Without Tears*. Harmondsworth: Penguin Books.

Ryan, E. and Giles, H. (1982) *Attitudes towards Language Variation*. London: Edward Arnold.

Samarin, W. (1967) *Field Linguistics*. New York: Holt Rinehart and Winston.

Scholfield, P. (1991) Cluster analysis in the study of language variation: A review and an example. *Bangor Research Papers in Linguistics* 3, 55–88.

— (forthcoming a) Cutting interval scales into categories: An overview of principles relevant to language data. Bangor Research Papers in Linguistics. University of Wales Bangor, Gwynedd: Dept of Linguistics

— (forthcoming b) Statistical assessment of reliability: A guide to methods for language data with either relative or absolute interpretation. Bangor Research Papers in Linguistics. University of Wales Bangor, Gwynedd: Dept of Linguistics

— (forthcoming c) Some neglected issues of scale type of language data. Bangor Research Papers in Linguistics. University of Wales Bangor, Gwynedd: Dept of Linguistics

— (forthcoming d) Statistical assessment of validity: Examples of simple methods for language data with either relative or absolute interpretation. Bangor Research Papers in Linguistics. University of Wales Bangor, Gwynedd: Dept of Linguistics

Seliger, H. and Shohamy, E. (1989) *Second Language Research Methods*. Oxford: Oxford University Press.

Shaw, M. and Wright, J. (1967) *Scales for the Measurement of Attitudes*. New York: McGraw-Hill.

Shearer, E. (1975) A restandardisation of the Burt-Vernon and Schonell graded word reading tests. *Educational Research* 18, 67–73.

Shohamy, E. (1984) Does the testing method make a difference? The case of reading comprehension. *Language Testing* 1, 147–70.

Sikiotis, N. (1981) Reading habits and preferences of secondary-school pupils in Greece. *English Language Teaching Journal* 35, 300–6.

Simms, R. and Richgels, D. (1986) The syntactic density score revisited: Which of its components matter in the oral language of 9–15 year olds. *Language Testing* 3.

Skehan, P. (1987) Variability and language testing. In R. Ellis (ed.) *Second Language Acquisition in Context*. Englewood Cliffs, NJ: Prentice Hall.

Sommer, B. and Sommer, R. (1991) *A Practical Guide to Behavioral Research* (3rd edn). New York: Oxford University Press.

Spooncer, F. (1983) *Testing for Teaching*. London: Hodder and Stoughton.

Steadman, S. and Gipps, C. (1984) Teacher and testing: Pluses and minuses. *Educational Research* 26, 121–26.

Stern, H. (1983) *Fundamental Concepts of Language Teaching*. Oxford: Oxford University Press.

Subkoviak, M. and Baker, F. (1977) Test theory. In L. Shulman (ed.) *Review of Research in Education* 5, 275–317. Itasca, IL: F.E. Peacock Publishers Inc.

Sweetland, R. and Keyser, D. (1986) *Tests: A Comprehensive Reference for Assessment in Psychology, Education and Business*. Kansas City: Test Corporation of America.

Tarone, E. (1980) Communication strategies, foreigner talk and repair in inter-language. *Language Learning* 30.

Taylor, I. (1976) *Introduction to Psycholinguistics*. New York: Holt Rinehart and Winston.

— (1990) *Psycholinguistics: Learning and Using Language*. Englewood Cliffs, NJ: Prentice Hall.

Tesitelova, M. (1992) *Quantitative Linguistics*. Amsterdam: J. Benjamins.

Thelander, M. (1982) A qualitative approach to quantitative data of speech variation. In S. Romaine (ed.) *Sociolinguistic Variation in Speech Communities*. London: Edward Arnold.

Thompson, G.B. (1981) Individual differences attributed to self-correction in reading. *British Journal of Educational Psychology* 51, 228–9.

Tizard, B. and Hughes, M. (1984) *Young Children Learning*. London: Fontana.

Tough, J. (1976) *Listening to Children Talking: A Guide to the Appraisal of Children's Use of Language*. London: Ward Lock.

Trudgill, P. (1974) *Sociolinguistics*. Pelican.

— (1983) *On Dialect*. Oxford: Basil Blackwell.

Turner, G. (1973) *Stylistics*. Harmondsworth: Penguin.

Valette, R. (1967) *Modern Language Testing*. New York: Harcourt, Brace, Jovanovich.

Wardhaugh, R. (1986) *An Introduction to Sociolinguistics*. Oxford: Basil Blackwell.

Warren-Leubecker, A. and Bohannon, J. (1984) Intonation patterns in child-directed speech. *Child Development* 55, 1379–85.

Watson, A. (1988) Developmental spelling: A word categorising instructional experiment. *Journal of Educational Research* 82, 82–8.

Weir, C. (1988) *Communicative Language Testing*. New York: Prentice Hall.

Wells, G. (1985) *Language Development in the Pre-School Years*. Cambridge: Cambridge University Press.

Wesche, M. (1983) Communicative testing in a second language. *The Modern Language Journal* 67, 41–5.

West, R. and Davies, S. (1989) *The Longman Guide to ELT Examinations*. London: Longman.

West, R. (1991) Developments in the testing of reading. *English a World Language* 1, 60–9.

Whiteson, V. (1981) Foreign language testing: A current view. *English Language Teaching Journal* 35, 345–52.

Wiemann, J. and Backlund, P. (1980) Current theory and research in communicative competence. *Review of Educational Research* 50, 185–99.

Wigzell, R. (1992) Efficiency, cost-effectiveness and the privatisation of foreign language learning. *System* 20, 15–29.

Wiliam, D. (1992) Some technical issues in assessment: A user's guide. *British Journal of Curriculum and Assessment* 2 (3), 11–20.

Willmott, A. (1980) What *does* Rasch promise? *Educational Research* 22, 193–7.

Winford, D. (1978) Phonological hypercorrection in the process of decreolization — the case of Trinidadian English. *Journal of Linguistics* 14, 277–91.

Winograd, E., Kerr, N. and Spence, M. (1984) Voice recognition: Effects of orienting task, and a test of blind versus sighted listeners. *American Journal of Psychology* 97, 57–70.

Witkin, H., Oltman, P., Raskin, E. and Karp, S. (1971) *A Manual for the Embedded Figures Tests*. Palo Alto: Consulting Psychologists Press.

Woods, A., Fletcher, P. and Hughes, A. (1986) *Statistics in Language Studies*. Cambridge: Cambridge University Press.

Yaden, B. and Templeton, S. (eds) (1986) *Metalinguistic Awareness and Beginning Literacy*. Portsmouth, NH: Heinemann.

Yore, L. and Ollila, L. (1985) Cognitive development, sex, and abstraction in grade one word recognition. *Journal of Educational Research* 78, 242–7.

Yule, G.U. (1968) *The Statistical Study of Literary Vocabulary*. Hamden, CO: Archon Books.

Yule, G. (1980) Towards an English language 'sufficiency' test. *English Language Teaching Journal* 35, 60–2.

Index

This index is intended as a quick reference aid primarily on: (a) the multifarious terms/concepts introduced and used, and (b) the variables whose quantification is discussed. I have not attempted to index some very commonly occurring items. These include the labels related to major areas of language study such as psycholinguistics, sociolinguistics, child language, foreign language learning and language pathology as they are mentioned directly or indirectly *passim* (but on these see esp. the end of chapter references for Chapters 1–4), and related labels for types of case such as child, learner, informant, subject etc.